THERAPEUTIC NATIONS

Critical Issues in Indigenous Studies

Jeffrey P. Shepherd and Myla Vicenti Carpio
Series Editors

Advisory Board
Hokulani Aikau
Jennifer Nez Denetdale
Eva Marie Garroutte
John Maynard
Alejandra Navarro-Smith
Gladys Tzul Tzul
Keith Camacho
Margaret Elizabeth Kovach
Vicente Diaz

Therapeutic Nations

Healing in an Age of Indigenous Human Rights

DIAN MILLION

THE UNIVERSITY OF
ARIZONA PRESS
TUCSON

The University of Arizona Press
www.uapress.arizona.edu

Printed in the United States of America

Cover design by Leigh McDonald
Cover illustration: *Our Blood is Currency* by Lesley Cauldron

Publication of this book is made possible in part by the proceeds of a
permanent endowment created with the assistance of a Challenge Grant
from the National Endowment for the Humanities, a federal agency.

Library of Congress Cataloging-in-Publication Data
Million, Dian, 1950–
    Therapeutic nations : healing in an age of indigenous human rights /
Dian Million.
        pages cm. — (Critical issues in indigenous studies)
    Includes bibliographical references and index.
    ISBN 978-0-8165-3141-7 (paperback)
    1. Indigenous peoples—Canada—Government relations. 2. Indigenous
peoples—Government relations—Cross-cultural studies. 3. Indigenous
peoples—Civil rights—Canada. 4. Indigenous peoples—Civil rights—
Cross-cultural studies. 5. Indigenous peoples—Legal status, laws, etc.—
Canada. 6. Indigenous peoples—Legal status, laws, etc.—Cross-cultural
studies. 7. Truth commissions—Cross-cultural studies.
I. Title.
    E92.M57 2013
    323.1197071—dc23
                                                        2013003309

♾ This paper meets the requirements of ANSI/NISO Z39.48-1992
(Permanence of Paper).

Contents

THERAPEUTIC NATIONS

ONE

An Introduction to Healing in an Age of Indigenous Human Rights

Why sexual ab(use)   usury rights
re treaties and reserves   the book is the discourse of pain
are the rights to use us   colonial discourse   intercourse
examines the literature of damages   marketability   truth and telling[1]

If every age has its symptoms, ours appears to be the age of trauma.
Naming a wide spectrum of responses to psychic and physical events
often with little in common beyond the label, trauma has become a
portmanteau that covers a multitude of disparate injuries. Stories that
would seem to belong to different orders of experience enjoy troubling
intimacies. But whatever their origins, the effects of historical trauma
have a tenacious hold on the popular imagination.
— NANCY MILLER AND JASON TOUGAW[2]

In a 2008 news article, "Canada's Truth and Reconciliation Commission Raises Controversy," Adrian Humphreys asks her readers to contemplate how "Canada will take its historical place alongside such tarnished regimes as South Africa, Chile, El Salvador and Sierra Leone." The Truth and Reconciliation Commission of Canada (TRC) formed in response to a successful 2006 class action suit by Canadian Aboriginal peoples for their intergenerational abuse in residential schools.[3] As a result, the 2007 Indian Residential Schools Settlement Agreement provided payments to individual victims, funds for healing initiatives in Aboriginal communities, and provisions for future commemoration and memorial programs. Sixty

1

million dollars was earmarked for the TRC alone to stage a forum where residential school survivors, their families, and all those Canadians who feel the necessity will speak their truth. The goal is reconciliation between Canada and Aboriginal peoples, whose relationship was characterized in the 1996 Royal Commission on Aboriginal Peoples final report as "a fundamental contradiction at the heart of Canada."[4] The TRC can also be seen in the company of reparative initiatives emerging after a Royal Commission on Aboriginal Peoples finished its work in 1995. Canada's TRC bears some resemblance to the efforts to rewrite history made by earlier commissions in Argentina (one-time payment to victims), and Chile and Guatemala (commemoration and memorial programs).[5]

These commissions are a product of our age, an age of human rights, global violence, mass media, and neoliberalism. They appear to represent our human desires for a just peace in what appears to be an increasingly brutal world. Canada is the first western nation to use this truth-and-reconciliation process in an Indigenous context. While Australia and New Zealand can be said to have used truth-seeking processes to ameliorate relations with Maori and Aboriginal peoples, Canada is the first to adopt a TRC committed solely to finding the truth of a nation-state's abuses against an Indigenous population.[6] Canada, a country that has almost no standing national army and the desire for a worldwide reputation as a defender of human rights, seems incongruous in the company of those failed regimes that have usually hosted these commissions since the early 1970s. Priscilla Hayner wrote that the commissions may "counter what psychologist Yael Danieli calls a conspiracy of silence."[7] Claire Moon observed the truth commission as "a symbolic recognition" of something widely known but "officially denied."[8]

It's our contemporary logic that any peace after state and civic violence is rarely accomplished by silencing victims. If a victim's or a group of victims' experience has no voice, the experience returns through continuing discord. Reconciliation projects are carried out informed through this sensibility. But it's a logic that itself belongs to trauma. Trauma supposes a violence that overwhelms, wounding individual (and collective) psyche, sometimes suspending access to memory.[9] The victims of traumatic events suffer recurrent wounding if their memory/pain is not discharged. A theory of trauma is embedded in an internationally recognized economy of justice that reconciliation belongs to. I agree with Nancy Miller and Jason Tougaw in the epigraph I cite above: the ethos of this time is trauma.[10] I ask what the implications of this trauma ethos are for Indigenous peoples. In their 2009 study *The Empire of Trauma*, Didier Fassin and Richard Rechtman observe, "Trauma has become a major signifier of our age. It is our normal means of relating present suffering to past violence."[11] Canadian Aboriginal peoples, subjects of a history of colonial violence, are thickly ensconced in the intensities, logics, and languages of trauma, particularly now as they are called on to speak as subjects of "truth and reconciliation." Truth commissions operate within an economy of crisis, disclosure, and catharsis. The belief is that when victims of state violence speak their truth in the presence of oppressors, a new story will emerge, a reconciled national history. Claire Moon surmises that the reach for reconciliation lies in "the attempt to acknowledge suffering, ameliorate trauma, and simultaneously found political legitimacy."[12] For Canadian Aboriginal peoples the TRC is a forum that mayhaps is a place to speak their truth.

In the following chapters, I suggest that witnessing one's truth to power is a convoluted undertaking. "Witnessing" in the highly prescribed roles and subject positions evoked in the context of a commission established in the name of human rights is, as I argue here, better understood as a site where we might evaluate what "power" is in our times. My first observation in this vein is that the international law that enables Indigenous trauma to appeal for justice is the same sphere in which we articulate political rights as polities with rights to self-determination. I don't see these as necessarily compatible projects.

The political emergence of Indigenous peoples to collectively vex notions of nation-state sovereignty in globalization, this time of densely networked transnational capitalism with an attending neoliberalism, is a surprising birth. Moreover, indigenism is now empowered in the 2006 United Nations Declaration on the Rights of Indigenous Peoples.[13] To articulate indigenism directly questions what western nation-states believe is the political subject of their liberal order. Povinelli suggests that indigenism poses the affective limit where liberalism defines its difference: "the cunning of recognition, as opposed to the law of recognition" . . . a "dense relation between intimate sovereignty and liberal humanism" that challenges states' desires for hegemonic constitution.[14] Indigenous peoples preexist nation-states and reject nation-state authority to grant them a right to a political self-determination that they have never relinquished. However, claims to Indigenous self-determination might work for a peaceful "coexistence" rather than territorial secession, they remain a denial of the primacy of any nation-state's sovereignty. In any case such a claim causes all parties to fiercely articulate what the substance of their nations is or will be. Thus, there is an agonistic heart to the self-determination Indigenous peoples affectively work out, a site of "intimate," painful political, social, and personal conundrums with the state. Human rights law appears to empower self-determination claims and then act as a buffer between any Indigenous peoples' ontological will to be and any nation-state's self-determined right to uncompromisingly thwart that will. In the places where the Indigenous have asserted self-determination, this has resulted in fierce moves and countermoves that Roger Maaka and Augie Fleras identify as a cycle of "domination-resistance-domination."[15] Reconciliation practices first used in those instances of extreme violence I name above now move to ease tensions between state and Indigenous as they seek equitable relations. Maaka and Fleras have critically observed the tensions produced between two meanings of self-determination. One is an inherent Indigenous autonomy that honors "distinctive ways of looking at the world," that makes these distinctions part of the partnership and critically recognizes "that Indigenous peoples alone possess the right to decide . . . what is best."[16] The other is a state-determined devolution of its own forms to allow for a neoliberal self-management and self-sufficiency.

These are positions familiar to Indigenous peoples in both Canada and the United States. Informed by these different poles of self-determination, I see the TRC as a last link in a recent policy chain that begins with the establishment of the Royal Commission on Aboriginal Peoples (RCAP) in 1991. The RCAP's massive five-year, $60 million research sought to explain inherent antagonisms in nation-state–Indigenous relations after they exploded along their fault lines at Oka in the summer of 1990. As a mass media spectacle mesmerizing Canada in the summer of 1990, Oka became symbolic for myriad struggles, tensions, and violations that surfaced as Canadian Aboriginal peoples struggled to attain political presence and bring two hundred years of Canadian colonial violence into public view. The Kahnawake Mohawk defended their ancestral burial grounds after the neighboring town of Oka moved to seize them to build a golf course. Oka and the province of Quebec, failing in their own policing measures, sought help from Canada in the form of peace-keeping troops launched to quell an Indian "uprising." The violence in that policing action that involved the Canadian army effectively *and* affectively conveyed to white and Indigenous alike the wide gulf between Canada's multicultural mosaic sociopolitical imaginary and the Mohawk's self-determined necessity.

Unlike in the United States, where American Indian nations' treaty rights to self-governance were embedded early on in constitutional legal principles, Canadian Aboriginal peoples had no constitutional recognition of rights until recently. Oka occurred amid the irresolution and rancor that tabled Canada's efforts to define Indigenous self-determination in light of its patriated constitution, its effort to define its own nation from Britain throughout the 1980s and early 1990s. While Canada acknowledged Aboriginal people's treaty rights in Section 35 of its remodeled constitution in 1982, it only haltingly negotiates what Aboriginal self-government as a constitutional reality means. This was left to "unfold."

The five-year RCAP produced a comprehensive, five-volume, 3,500-page report that was then the most expensive and minute examination of Indigenous and Canadian relations ever undertaken. The report featured widespread Canadian Aboriginal participation, voice, and witnessing. The RCAP recommended far-reaching political changes at the same time that Canada's will to make such changes politically and socially appeared inert. Marlene Brant Castellano (Mohawk), who served as a codirector of RCAP's research, observed that "it will become effective to the extent that it is taken up and used by citizens who share the vision of a renewed relationship that serves the common good."[17] While Oka may have been the most-televised of the policing actions in Indigenous Canada at that time, the RCAP recommendations reiterating an urgent Indigenous demand for an end to Canada's paternalistic hold is also the first call for official reconciliation. Both of these "events" can be understood through a rapidly evolving matrix of human rights law and humanitarian practice applied to Indigenous peoples differently in different nation-states.

Since 1996 Canada has tabled, ignored, or deferred most of RCAP's ardent recommendations to enact Aboriginal self-determination. However, one Aboriginal experience that RCAP highlighted came to the fore as a defining truth of Canada's legacy: the treatment of at least three generations of children—their removal from their homes, their neglect, their starvation, and their sexual abuse. Canada confronted its colonial past fused in the reality of literally thousands of now-adult residential-school survivors' abuse cases in Canadian courts. Those cases of sexual abuse, substantiated by Canada's own judicial system, threatened to bankrupt churches and state. Aboriginal peoples and Canada called for the establishment of a Truth and Reconciliation Commission. Indigenous peoples embraced their grandparents', their parents', and their own residential school experiences as a *wound*, calling Canada out as a perpetrator of abuse. These cases coupled with ongoing national reports highlighting intense disparities in health and well-being between Indigenous and mainstream Canadians sparked a number of social and personal health initiatives that are largely known as healing. Healing highlights Canada's historical legacy of colonization as it became linked in a direct causal relationship to Indigenous people's contemporary poor health, both physical and mental, substance abuse, suicide risk, and early death, understood as a holistic, tightly intertwined effect. The colonized subject became a trauma victim.

While Canada bypassed or ignored the substantive Indigenous political empowerment called for in the RCAP report, Truth and Reconciliation reaffirms the people's systemic inequality and endemic social suffering as a pathology, a wound that is solely an outcome of past colonial policies. This is a complex move, where healing encompasses Canada's dialogue with Indigenous peoples, moving the focus from one of political self-determination to one where self-determination becomes intertwined with state-determined biopolitical programs for emotional and psychological self-care informed by trauma. In this context, well-being, physical and mental health, is articulated as a key component for human development within self-determination goals at the same time an autonomous self-determination is left vague and poorly defined. With the establishment of the TRC, Aboriginal peoples seem to become the subject of a humanitarian project. Whether this assists or appropriates the Aboriginal peoples from being subjects of their own polities negotiating for political empowerment is one of the questions I ask here.

This text, *Therapeutic Nations: Healing in an Age of Indigenous Human Rights*, addresses this Aboriginal "wounded" subjectivity as an agonistic site in the affective and moral power relations wherein Indigenous peoples articulate their self-determination within a neoliberal Canada. When Indigenous peoples speak their own contemporary conditions as subjects of historical trauma, they position this generation to reference an affective discipline of shame intrinsically woven into the moralized discourses and embodied practices attached to Indian sexuality that informed their own and generations of their extended families' physical and psychic abuse in residential schools. These racialized, sexualized, and gendered discourses configure the historical moments where Canada constitutes its legitimacy, collapsing the rich diversity of Indigenous polities into a unified subject "Indian," mobilized and managed from birth to death in the Indian Act. Bonita Lawrence says of the Indian Act that it "is much more than a body of laws that for over a century have controlled every aspect of Indian life. As a regulatory regime, the Indian Act . . . [is an] organizing . . . conceptual framework that has shaped contemporary Native life in ways that are now so familiar as to almost seem natural."[18]

More specifically, I argue that this "contemporary shaping" of Native life that Lawrence speaks of is a normative violence. I contend that this normative violence is integral to the regulatory force of the Indian Act. It is a regulatory violence that coalesces in the evisceration of Indigenous women's constitutive power to inform their own Indigenous nations. It is regulatory power that affectively positions Indigenous women as the figurative center of any Indigenous nation's inability to govern. The Indian Act's ongoing effect creates a particularly intense contradiction that is reproduced in discourse and violent practice as Indigenous peoples in Canada seek to define self-determination. Gender inequality and gender violence haunt the constitution of new polities in the articulation of any Indigenous self-determination. To take such a stand requires that we understand the increasing gender violence perpetrated against Indigenous women as more than an attack on individuals, and as a mobile but durable feature of colonial power relations.

Indigenous women are often murdered and raped, mentally and emotionally annihilated in a maelstrom of violence that includes family, a family that has expansive meaning to the question of what Indigenous self-determination is in Canada and the United States. Sometimes obscured in the fight to end violence against women is the parallel amount of tremendous violence perpetrated against Indigenous sexual minorities. To take this into account is to acknowledge that it is actually gender violence that marks the evisceration of Indigenous nations. This violence also marks a besieged site wherein Indigenous peoples attempt the "healing" and revitalization of their polities. An Indigenous gendered concept of polity contradicts any western liberal governing principle still vested in a white male heteronormative subject. This points to a site of violence well beyond Canada's singular focus on residential-school experience. And while it is a pervasive gender violence that is inherent in ongoing Indigenous–state relations, in the end it is the intergenerational experience of residential schools that is articulated among Aboriginal peoples as the wound to their most basic relations: in family between men and women, between mothers and fathers and children, extending outward in the relations that are community and, finally, nation. Articulating this violence as trauma, Indigenous peoples have come to use forms that originate internationally to locally locate themselves as the interlocutors of their own experience, to witness Canada's prior violent state policies to eliminate Indigenous subjectivity, experience, and polity.

I see a present necessity to speak Indigenous trauma within the vortex of an internationally proffered human right to self-determination and a resulting humanitarian therapeutic. It is a nexus where after World War II universal human rights offers self-determination to the prior subjects of colonization. It is in the company of a United Nations where Indigenous peoples take these proffered rights seriously as inherent rights never ceded and move to bring them into international and national law. This struggle to transform a liberal expectation of rights extended to individuals to the collective rights of peoples is now a triumph culminating in the 2007 signing of the United Nations Declaration on the Rights of Indigenous Peoples. But to enact any actually practiced Indigenous self-determination threatens any nation-state's imagined homogeneous territorial sovereignty. Initially, four leading western nation-states — the United States, Canada, New Zealand, and Australia — each with a large and active Indigenous rights movement, refused to sign this Declaration of Indigenous Rights. While we may celebrate the long, hard work that is represented in this landmark declaration, the site wherein Indigenous peoples officially become subjects of "human rights" must also be seen as a volatile place in a volatile time. Human rights and any necessary humanitarianism that protects our rights must be understood as fungible: developing, ongoing tumultuous global political alignments after World War II that morph again at the end of the cold war and again in the rise of the present "trade wars." There are moments of seeming progress. However, these are transitive moments where liberal western politics and capitalist economies moved from a disciplinary colonialism to a normative welfare-state "caring capital" that has now dissolved into our present, a well-integrated neoliberal multicultural biopolitics.

The term *healing* is often associated in a trauma economy as the afterward, as the culmination or satisfactory resolution of illness or, for the Indigenous, a promised safety and revitalization from prior colonial violence. Below I pose the need to examine these terms in what I argue is a very new sociopolitical moment. The subtitle to this text, "Healing in an Age of Indigenous Human Rights," brings into juxtaposition terms that I claim point to an integrated neoliberal economy of political, socioeconomic, and affective personal management carried out in the name of human development. Human development as a progressive field of thought and action represents a horizon of opportunity as well as a limitation to the aspirations of Indigenous peoples. In the name of human development, Canada poses many economic and social projects in Indigenous communities, usually associated with nation-state neoliberal governance. These are often posited in human potential practices intermixed with sometimes quasi-religious fervor, with languages that borrow heavily from economic, behavioral, and developmental psychology. I suggest that the many diverse projects that we understand today as Indigenous healing are informed amid the political, social environments, "moments" that accompany neoliberalism. Here, I give some context for the terms *human rights, indigenism,* and *neoliberal.*

The Inextricable Relationship: A New World Order and Indigenous Human Rights

Our Indigenous presence is valorized in the 2007 United Nations Declaration on the Rights of Indigenous Peoples. It is a celebratory moment since thousands of Native peoples worked extensively for thirty years to achieve this recognition. Their achievement is no small matter in the ongoing articulation of human rights law. Human rights and Indigenism as a collective political identity are closely aligned. The institution and evolution of global law creating an extra-state forum for grievance and respite known as human rights came into being in the last three generations. In this section I state why this space wherein Indigenous peoples seek protections can never be perceived as any neutral, objective, or safer legal space.

Indigenous identity among First Nations, Aboriginal, Alaskan Native, or American Indian peoples, or the myriad peoples evoked by this term, was not a given. Such an identity represents a growing collective political will that formed after World War II, first in the shadows of developing UN human rights discourses and then later in their full light as twenty years of Indigenous struggle and discussion slowly carved out a position. In the chaotic two decades (1955–75) following the formation of the United Nations, with its 1948 Universal Declaration of Human Rights, European colonialism imploded. There was jostling and realignment as the United States became a superpower moving to establish antiracism as a new imaginary for a world it sought to order. After the Jewish Holocaust, at the end of a world war, western nations formed a new global collectivity, the United Nations, initially made up of mostly World War II victors and their allies. Their first initiatives had far-reaching imperatives that in practice appeared to challenge all the logics that had sanctioned pre–World War II colonialism. Human rights are first a set of collective agreements that nation-states have made and entered into ostensibly to protect basic rights for individual citizens. This international order that holds the Holocaust as its memorial was born simultaneously with a reordered capitalist economic order that I discuss below.

Michael Ignatieff and Amy Gutmann, in *Human Rights as Politics and Idolatry*, depict such law as founded on a principle that each human is entitled to "equal moral consideration. Human rights is the language that systematically embodies this intuition."[19] After the carnage of a second world war, human rights law was "intended to restore agency, to give individuals the civic courage to stand up when the state ordered them to do wrong," as it had in Nazi Germany.[20] It was considered moral progress. Thus, human rights stands for a complex of constantly emerging law evolving to express a certain desire for justice. For instance, the judicial articulation of genocide in 1948 made it less moral for nations to murder their own citizens, particularly racial minorities. The Universal Declaration of Human Rights, adopted in 1948 and clarified in Article 1 of the International Covenant on Civil and Political Rights affirming self-determination as a right of all peoples, created a language that is said to have "ignited both the colonial revolutions abroad and the civil rights revolution at home."[21]

If there is a new legal structure protecting the rights of citizens, there also develops a sphere of action where those rights are ostensibly protected. The creation of a legal framework for human rights also begat an "advocacy revolution" that in turn recognized humanitarian "victims" and those who would "represent victims." In the last thirty years we have seen the "emergence of a network of non-governmental human rights organizations," (NGOs) that gained "historically unprecedented power to make their cases known to the world." Never "neutral," but potent, advocacy had effect: "Naming and shaming for human rights abuses now have real consequences."[22] Shame as it is operationalized within an international economy for effecting political pressure suggests a shift in emphasis from empowering political agency to one of victimology.

Randall Williams explicates the conflicting agendas contained in a UN imagined as "the answer to the search for an oppositional framework capable of contesting the globalized force and world devastations of contemporary capitalism" or, conversely, as "a convenient cover for the extension of capitalist-democratic uneven relations of power reinforcing imperialistic hegemonic control."[23] It is all that, a field of hegemonic maneuver and its accompanying and constitutive violence and counterstruggles to obtain relief and justice for losers. It is now a field where a dissolving welfare-state capitalism once positioned as benefactor abandons the subjects of its development to allow capital to choose its most "viable." It is a field of humanitarian struggle between life and death. Susan Koshy conveys the continuity and trajectory incited wherein "[n]eocolonial strategies of power are increasingly articulated not through the language of the civilizing mission . . . or American-sponsored discourses of anticommunism . . . but through a new universalist ethics of human rights, labor standards, environmental standards and intellectual property rights."[24]

The universal subject of a positive human rights is the citizen of a nation-state imagined within a positive sovereignty.[25] At this point much of humanity remains outside of this positive sovereignty as the stateless, or refugees, or those marginalized within states too poor or too weak to provide for or defend them. They become the subject of a new negative human rights. As Jacques Rancière surmises, "the Rights of Man turned out to be the rights of the rightless, of the populations hunted out of their homes and land and threatened by ethnic slaughter . . . as the rights of the victims, the rights of those who were unable to enact any rights or even any claim in their name, so that eventually their rights had to be upheld by others, at the cost of shattering the edifice of International Rights, in the name of a new right to 'humanitarian interference'—which ultimately boiled down to the right to invasion."[26]

Humanitarian campaigns performing within the sites of multiple forces and agendas are never neutral. After the collapse of the Soviet bloc that signaled the end of the cold war, United Nations peacekeepers were increasingly relegated to "policing" the sites of spectacular political destabilization in the name of humanitarianism. These societies' disintegration now signifies some of the worst horrors of a new century and another world order: Sarajevo, Kosovo, and Rwanda. In part, truth and reconciliation as a human rights process, like the one that Canada evoked to reconcile the Indigenous with the nation-state, is born in the aftermath of these "war[s] of all against all."[27] Didier Fassin and Mariella Pandolfi saw this as a crucial shift. It is a move from the moral justification of hegemonic states declaring "just wars" to one of where stronger states intervene in weaker states as moral humanitarian intervention without equal regard for their "sovereignty": "humanitarianism has become the justification for extralegal action."[28] Achille Mbembe clarifies that "[c]ontemporary wars belong to a new moment and can hardly be understood through earlier theories of "contractual violence" or typologies of "just" and "unjust wars."[29] These interventions increasingly conflate war and natural disaster as humanitarian crisis points to be managed by intervention, "a form of naturalization—or depoliticization—of war."[30] Fassin and Pandolfi are joined by Vanessa Pupavac in seeing policing actions where, authorized or not, strong nation-states take up "crisis management," for "emergency intervention." Pupavac notes that this is increasingly accompanied by "psycho-social intervention," with whole populations deemed traumatized.[31] The relations of world trade organizations, world banks, and transnational capital to these increasing sites of "insecurity" in once "developing," now humanely policed non–First World nations are a factor in this new milieu that isn't discussed often in the same breath.

Indigenous peoples live globally in the very midst of these conflagrations. Oil or other capitalist resources figured now in scarcity have set Indigenous communities up in heightened antagonistic relations with nation-states and transnational corporations who scramble for the profits under our lands. Human rights and humanitarianism often still encompass Indigenous hopes for justice, for equity, and for the space to present a platform to continue to struggle for these ideals. Still, these are spaces where there are multiple agendas performed, none of them totally neutral and never merely allied with the "powerless." Perpetrator and victim are marked political positions that must be unpacked in this formation. As Indigenous peoples, we are now called on to use instruments of truth-telling: international forums, reconciliation, and reparations as part of a formal trauma ethos as it gives shape to relations between the weak and the strong in our age. I ask why our Indigenous political presence, a global presence, is valorized now? What in particular is important internationally about our presence now in the midst of what I describe above? What in this milieu supports Indigenous self-determination as we might have once imagined it? These are larger questions that also inform this text.

Human rights as a field of struggle, as a field of advocacy, poses an international arena wherein Indigenous peoples have consistently engaged, now more often in moral affective contestation with the nation-states whose "sovereignty" they challenge. This is an engagement that requires successful affective argument given the turn to a moral ethos of trauma. Canada looked to this field of human rights law in the establishment of the Truth and Reconciliation Commission, where it asks for a reconciliation between a victim and a perpetrator in the same moment that any actual political power for Canadian Indigenous peoples is continuously deferred to a future self-healing from capitalism's present and ongoing violence. Canadian Indigenous peoples, particularly women, utilized the field of human rights from early on to shame and bring the Canadian government into negotiation with them in a variety of ways, not all in agreement with one another. Within the auspices of something called human rights, we enact healing projects and self-determination. I think that while *healing* has become a ubiquitous word, there is less examination of the terms of this "healing" from a wound characterized as colonization. Likewise, on what terms is "self-determination" offered in this political moment?

Indigenism: Development, Decolonization, and the Fourth World

Indigenous claims are those of particularity and place. The discussion of "who we are" is at this point internationally contested (among Indigenous peoples, between states, and across human rights and international Indigenous organizations) and at the level of a newly emergent international law underlining the status of Indigenous peoples as supra-state, as not synonymous with the states that claimed to have subsumed them. Indigenous peoples understand their knowledge as inextricable from their lived experience in their distinct places, in spiritual relationships with land and life, and from traditions that change but are millennial.

The scope of indigenism as both political identity and as lived ways of life includes myriad peoples in all the continents excepting Antarctica, whose societies predate the nation-states that came to surround them. In this work I most usually refer to indigenism not as our individual millennial ways of life, although it is exactly those ways that are at stake, those of Athabascan, or Inuit, or Maori. I speak to a current articulation that brings a multitude together in our times. As a specifically named political identity, indigenism formed in an environment created by the post–WWII liberal human rights and liberation movements that were understood as decolonization. At least since 1960 Indigenous peoples from the Americas have increasingly been able to deploy effective counterdiscourse to local and regional and, most importantly, global discourses that maintain certain rights to nation-states. The rise of indigenism is not an accident at this historical moment. It is an alternative, active, and mobile set of meanings available in the midst of present globalization, mass diasporas, and multiplicity.

An analysis of Indigenous peoples' entry into the field of human rights is bound up with the story of decolonization, the reorganized capitalist forces released at the end of the Second World War. Indigenous peoples initially saw their own condition as similar to that of the emergent Third World, the multitude of peoples who achieved nation-state status as direct rule broke down in a realignment of power between formerly colonial nations and an economically ascendant United States. Decolonization was hastened by national revolutionary movements in Algeria and in most of the former colonies in a struggle for self-determination and sovereignty. For hegemonic states, decolonization represented two simultaneous actions: colonial powers' (British, French, Dutch, etc.) recognition of the impending implosion of their direct rule in former colonies, and their commitment to a revised strategy of *development*.[32] The power dynamics aligning western nations and these myriad emerging nation-states changed with the ascendance of the Soviet Socialist Republic, and US excursions into Asia. In cold war struggles to align peoples to bipolar liberal or socialist capitalist interests, the worldwide language of *decolonization/development* blossomed.

The narrative put in place is still familiar today. Development was a process in which "underdeveloped" newly decolonized nation-states would be brought into parity with the First World, the developed western nations. Cooper and Packard characterize a "development orthodoxy" that in the beginning assumed that "foreign aid and investments on favorable terms, the transfer of knowledge of production techniques, measures to promote health and education, and economic planning would lead impoverished countries to become 'normal' market economies."[33] That theory was quickly challenged by Marxist socialist critiques of actual economic conditions that marked the new states' entry: neocolonialism, dependency, and underdevelopment, where no easy transfer of "knowledge" or "production technique" would account for embedded colonial structural imbalances. "Development" as a liberal progressive discourse did not attend to the actual experiences of different peoples who had been racialized, who had been torn asunder, who experienced land theft and impoverishment, all conditions that continued, albeit by different means. The post–world war formation of capital, reorganized and heralded by a universalism ensconced in the "Rights of Man," or human rights, was not less racist but posed and practiced racialization projects differently.[34] Decolonization created new nations but brought former colonies "into a relationship with the United States, or the then Union of Soviet Socialist Republics, and international organizations—a world of sovereign equivalency but enormous de facto inequalities" that for the first time made development "simultaneously a global issue and a concern of states."[35]

Indigenism was in full flower well before Larry Red Shirt, a Lakota, led a contingent through the front door of the Palais de Nations in Geneva in 1977. As nation-states like Canada and the United States went through civil rights revolutions in the 1960s, American and Canadian Indigenous peoples began to organize their own resistance. Indigenism bloomed as a powerful political consciousness. Indigenous peoples undertook lateral organizing across nation-state borders on the basis of shared cultural tenets and experiences. Indigenous peoples proposed indigenism as a political stance that took positions against unrestrained socialist and capitalist development.

It was purposeful and symbolic for the Haudenosaunee to lead, because they had been to the Palais de Nations before, when it housed the League of Nations. Between 1921 and 1923 the Cayuga Iroquois leader Deskaheh led a sovereignty delegation to the League of Nations.[36] Although he had supporters among these statesmen, Canadian delegates manipulated the League to reject hearing his Iroquois sovereignty argument on the grounds that Indians were Canada's domestic concern. Deskaheh made a profound impact on those who did hear him. In 1927, after Deskaheh's failed attempt to speak, Canada effectively banned Indians from organizing their fight for lands and resources promised in treaties, a restriction on Indian organizing that held until 1951. Canadian Indigenous peoples, men or women, did not attain an unrestricted right to vote until 1960.

After restrictions on organizing were repealed in a revision of the Canadian Indian Act, new efforts were quickly formed. George Manuel, a Shuswap from interior British Columbia and an influential leader in the National Indian Brotherhood, traveled extensively. Impressed by Maori efforts to rearticulate their treaty rights, Manuel and others organized the World Council of Indigenous Peoples, an organization that included groups as widely diverse as the Maori from New Zealand and the Sami, Indigenous peoples who lived in circumpolar Europe. Manuel wrote a popular and far-reaching text with Michael Posluns, *The Fourth World: An Indian Reality*, posing the "Fourth World" as an alternative to both capitalist and socialist economic development.[37] The contingent led by Larry Red Shirt and Leon Shenendoah to the 1977 International Non-governmental Organizations (NGOs) Conference on Discrimination against Indigenous Populations in the Americas opened the door to all of their subsequent triumphs and defeats. The conference, "attended by 165 delegates from North, Central and South America," was followed quickly by many Indigenous groups who gained entry recognized as NGOs. Glenn Morris states that after the American Indian Movement's International Treaty Council achieved NGO status in 1977, nine more organizations quickly joined: Four Directions Council, Grand Council of the Crees, Indigenous World Association, Indian Law Resource Center, Inuit Circumpolar Conference, National Aboriginal and Islander Legal Service, National Indian Youth Council, South American Indian Council, and Manuel's World Council of Indigenous Peoples. Canadian Aboriginal peoples were well represented and eloquent.[38]

Statements made by the first Indigenous participants in the United Nations are unabashed critiques of western colonialism and of western development in the form of multinational corporate activity. In these statements they equated "development" with the destruction of their peoples and to a holistic web of life, the Earth, and all entities. Ingrid Washinawatok recalled their warning: "Economics and technology may assist you, but they will also destroy you if you do not use the principles of equality. Profit and loss will mean nothing to your future generations."[39] It was both the continuities found in their diverse lifeways and their ideals that they posed as indigenism, as living societies that recognized a different concept of polity. Haudenosaunee Oren Lyons made the comparison between a humanist government and his own: "I do not see a delegation for the four-footed. I see no seat for the eagles. We forget and we consider ourselves superior, but we are after all a mere part of the Creation."[40]

The United Nations recognized no polity that was not anthropocentric. The discourses of decolonization presented language to claim self-determination, to reach for "sovereignty." In this collective of state nationalisms, Indigenous peoples were sometimes seen as potential allies, as "little brothers" by the decolonizing Third World nations. In this view, Indigenous nations suffered from *internal colonization*. Third World politicos believed that the internally colonized Indigenous peoples would logically follow certain principles to argue for "decolonization."[41] The United States, Canada, Australia, and New Zealand, all with large Indigenous populations, continued to see Indigenous peoples as minorities. Indigenous grievances were the "domestic affairs" of their nation-states. This began to shift as Indigenous peoples waged a persistent campaign within the United Nations for recognition as peoples with rights to self-determination. The indigene's actual political practices, not always posed as nationalism, didn't conform to any expectations. They would come to confound any westernized notion of nation, national liberation, or nation-state nationalism, liberal or socialist, as the Sandinistas unfortunately found out in Nicaragua in 1986 when the Miskito Indians positioned the Sandinistas' socialist revolutionary movement in the role of a colonizer. Decidedly against the Sandinista plan for their "development," the Miskito articulated an Indigenous anticapitalist (liberal or socialist) stance, with both capitalist and socialist forces claiming them.[42] Later, the Ejército Zapatista de Liberación Nacional mesmerized the world when it marched out of the Lacandon rain forest in Mexico on January 1, 1994, to make a prophetic protest on the first day of the enactment of NAFTA, the North American Free Trade Agreement. The Zapatista, based in the Mexican state of Chiapas, survivors of relocation and land loss for more than a century, succinctly named what the new struggles would be for Indigenous peoples in the twenty-first century: "The Movimiento Civil Zapatista is a movement that opposes social solidarity to organized crime from the power of money and government."[43] Thus, Castell observes "the Zapatista's opposition to the new global order is twofold: they fight against the exclusionary consequences of economic modernization; but they also challenge the inevitability of a new geopolitical order under which capitalism becomes universally accepted."[44]

Most certainly the Third World—a term that denoted the developmental hierarchy formed after World War II, with colonial powers as a First World, positioning the USSR as the Second—did not immediately see the potential of a Fourth World that George Manuel put forth as an Indigenous agenda. However, there would be strikingly different experiences between the South, Central, and North American Indigenous nationalisms that were evoked by any human rights configured self-determination.[45] The Zapatistas were prescient in naming and articulating the neoliberalism that is now our economic and social present.

Neoliberalism: Evoking an Indigenous Therapeutic Community

Neoliberalism overturns the order that I write of above. David Harvey sums its reach: "Neoliberalism has become a hegemonic discourse with pervasive effects on ways of thought and political-economic practices to the point where it is now part of the commonsense way we interpret, live in, and understand the world."[46] Neoliberalism reaches beyond economics to become a way of life. Neoliberalism is imbued with a powerful belief in the goodness of the market, in a claim that individual pursuits of self-interest will promote the public good. If the market knows best, then governments should give capitalism room to work; nations should deregulate those social practices (state institutions and legislative measures) that seek to control the markets. Neoliberalism overturned Keynesian principles of welfare-state capitalism organizing nation-state economies since the Great Depression.

Nancy Fraser, writing extensively on the structural and social outcomes of this shift, characterized the old order as "state-organized capitalism." In that form nation-states had "aimed at mobilizing [their] capacities to support national economic development in the name—if not always in the interest—of the national citizenry."[47] Socialists had also believed in a nationalist socialist capitalism tamed to serve the masses. For them, the nation existed "to mitigate the effects of private ownership and market allocation," to serve as a buffer between capital and society.[48] Fraser explained how neoliberalism had totally reversed state-organized capitalism to promote "privatization and deregulation; in place of public provision and social citizenship, 'trickle-down' and 'personal responsibility'; in place of the welfare and developmental states, the lean, mean 'competition state.'"[49] Harvey quotes Margaret Thatcher's belief as she imposed neoliberalism on Britain: "'there is no such thing as society, only individual men and women' and she subsequently added, their families. All forms of social solidarity were to be dissolved in favour of individualism, private property, personal responsibility and family values."[50] Politics and governance became couched as privatized, local events in the name of community.

It is in the sense that neoliberal governments seek to locate responsibility at the local level where neoliberalism does not seem anathema to Indigenous self-governance; although self-governance should not be mistaken for self-determination, neoliberalism isn't totally anathema to self-determination either. Some Indigenous governances in South America have utilized neoliberal political strategy to gain power. Bolivia would serve as a good example. Nikolas Rose posed these preferences as a move from state-centered governance to certain biopolitical practices "of ecology, of family, of personal and cultural identity and lifestyle."[51] Rose differentiated the particularity of these social relocations as "ethopower," or an "ethopolitics." Ethopolitics, Rose figured, worked "through the values, beliefs, and sentiments thought to underpin the techniques of responsible self-government and the management of one's obligations to others. In ethopolitics, life itself, in its everyday manifestations, is the object of adjudication."[52] Rose saw this move into an "ethopolitic" as a moral rationalizing in the community weighing choices, individually or as a community for conducting "life." For Rose this change is a "[p]olitics . . . returned to the society itself, but no longer in a social form: in the form of individual morality, organizational responsibility, and ethical community." In this view, life as the foundation of politics, is thrown back and mediated at the "community level."[53] It would be very wrong to present neoliberalism, then, as only a set of economic projects; it produces surprising new ways of life across multiple societies. Wanda Vrasti poses that neoliberalism extends capital to all spheres of life, to "align social and ethical life with economic criteria and expectations."[54]

Aihwa Ong, in her article "Neoliberalism as a Mobile Technology," presents "neoliberalism as a migratory set of practices," "opportunistic in diverse situations." It is a style of governance that affords "mutating configurations of possibility," assemblages that produce "indiscriminate couplings" with unlikely partners." Using sexually metaphorical language to explain how neoliberal practices make "promiscuous entanglements" with no predetermined outcome, Ong surmises the goal is to foster certain kinds of "self-enterprising subjects." She illustrates that neoliberalism is creative and adaptive in multiple circumstances with different peoples, "graduated governing, spaces and populations with differing tolerances, skills."[55] In that neoliberal ethopolitics seeks to capitalize life; to bring all life and social life into the sphere of capital; it becomes an important element in working out the conditions for Indigenous self-determination I explore throughout the following chapters.

Canada, and the United States with some differences, entered this arena of neoliberal ethopolitics just as Indigenous peoples began to define the scope of their rights to self-government. Canada responded by largely devolving, or returning responsibility for, First Nations and Aboriginal peoples' economic grievances (endemic poverty, poor housing, and joblessness) to Indigenous communities to solve, as a matter left eventually to their own self-governing economic development initiatives. Government programs for health and education were also slated to return to the community for administration, touted as moves for self-determination. Issues of multiple-generation poverty, poor health, drug dependence, and family disintegration remained. These deep intergenerational inequities and their "behaviors" hit people in the heart of where they lived, effecting and affecting them in countless ways. These "social problems" have been mostly relegated to health and healing programs that were never adequately funded, or never adequately given actual form by real transfers of power to Canadian Aboriginal governments.[56] Most recently, funds attached to residential school healing were provisional to the communities while their "trauma" was relegated to a site for the national reconciliation of the nation. Healing is discursively linked to self-determination but in practice rarely informs the political spaces where those conversations take place. Healing gets deferred to conversations about "capacity building" and "human capital," both areas that Roger Maaka and Augie Fleras deem state-determination discourses often organized around programs of self-managing rather than any Indigenous autonomy.[57]

As the neoliberal turn took place, poverty, drug addiction, alcoholism, and social dissolution became medicalized and portrayed as colonial trauma. Canada often posed this trauma as a threat to future economic and social development. Still there were many reasons for Canadian Native peoples to claim ownership for healing, many reasons for them to own and to voice trauma. By 1998 when Canada, as a first move in its reconciliation for the residential school abuse cases, released $350 million dollars in funds for a Healing Project, it was administered by an Indigenous-controlled entity, the Aboriginal Healing Fund. In total, the Healing Fund would operate for 11 years, in comparison to the 150+ years of colonial violence, a fact not lost on any of the First Nations and Indigenous peoples of Canada. The Healing programs were to be tightly organized around alcohol, drug, and sexual abuse, and incest survival. Thus, their trauma is positioned particularly indexing certain outcomes in order to also position certain cures.

The rise of an international infrastructure of human rights law with limited but moral shaming power to intervene in Canada and US domestic affairs provides a forum that illuminates intimate relations of family in Indian Country; it provides a space for articulating what colonialism actually is in Indigenous terms: a painful dismembering of families and societies. But, in tandem with utilizing an international medicalized discourse of trauma, community healing also involves myriad psy-technologies aimed at the "reconstitution" of the most basic of Indigenous human relations, those among women, men, and children; the relations in family; and in community in the name and jargon of human development. Those peoples colonized and subsumed in North America's two large nation-states live and articulate their own ideas about self-determination in the constant presence of interventions with heavy socioeconomic, psychological, and medical components. Thus, Healing as community health and revitalization is an experiment—with uneven results. Native peoples participate in programs to holistically envision their nations. They envision personal development as community development. They do so utilizing a bevy of self-practices that are indicative of the particular form of governance particular to neoliberal ethopolitics. They also imagine and act on their own Indigenous spiritual and communal practices that mitigate the medico-moral affective valences that form neoliberal subjects. This appears to be a moment of great contradiction. Indigenous peoples in North America can now point to many successes in improving their health across several domains. On closer examination, these successes aren't contradictory with a notion of biopower achieved through the productive (and reproductive) powers of populations—rather than through their repression.

But this is a cautionary rather than a celebratory tale I am weaving. In both Canada and the United States, at the same moment that we work to "heal," we are also continuously assailed by the ongoing damages that are wreaked by racism, gender violence, political powerlessness, and the continuing breakdown of our affective networks, our communities, and our families. If the state abdicates any responsible agency in addressing the cold and hard social outcomes of the market in these new neoliberal social experiments, it would matter how any family, community, or Indigenous nation is positioned to capital, to their decision to "develop." This is part of the dilemma that faces present Indigenous communities, who are far from homogeneous or agreeing on what those positions should be. But since this development is linked to a "stigmata" pointing to our historical relations with nations, it becomes relevant to explore the nature of the "wounds" that are now consistently explicated in self-determination discourse.

The Domestic Site of Our Wound: Sexuality, Abuse, and Reconciliation

Truth and reconciliation commissions offer both victim and perpetrator a forum to testify to their experiences. Canadian Indigenous peoples' call for and Canada's agreement in establishing the Truth and Reconciliation Commission to relieve tensions around the residential-school abuse cases had some precedent. Australia used a truth-seeking process to examine its history of Aboriginal child abduction, child neglect, and sexual abuses reminiscent of the later Canadian truth and reconciliation project. The Aussie conversation opened in 1996 with the establishment of a National Inquiry into Separation of Aboriginal and Torres Strait Islander Children from their Families, in response to Australian Aboriginal calls for justice before reconciliation, part of their larger goals for self-determination. The Australian Human Rights and Equal Opportunity Commission charged with carrying out the study issued their report in 1997. The report *Bringing Them Home* sparked an explosive national debate on reconciliation between a divided Australian national public and Aboriginals.[58] While many non-Aboriginal Australians moved to support the process, expressed spontaneously in a "Sorry Day," no further reconciliation occurred. The report recommended restitution and compensation. Australia's cooled ardor for reconciliation then precipitated moves that are startling to any progressive notion of Indigenous–settler reconciliation. Australia, similar to Canada, had embraced a reconciliation organized around at least symbolically taking blame for the violent affective and material outcomes of colonial racial policies. Then Australia changed governments and positions.

In 2007 they became the first of the settler colonial nation-states to rescind Aboriginal self-determination, using child welfare accusations of widespread child sexual abuse as an excuse to police sexually "deviant" Aboriginal families. In April 2007, after the release of a joint Aboriginal–Australian report entitled *Ampe Akelyernemane Meke Mekarle "Little Children Are Sacred,"* requesting aid for Aboriginal efforts to stem child abuse, Australia's prime minister John Howard declared a "national emergency," finding "child sexual assault to be widespread throughout Aboriginal communities."[59] Australia then voided reconciliation, canceling remaining Indigenous self-determination initiatives by instituting wide-reaching powers over Aboriginal families in seventy-one northern communities. This actively rescinded any self-governance over self-determined Aboriginal territories these peoples had won in earlier Indigenous rights negotiations. As many have observed, this "emergency" and humanitarian intervention eerily reiterates other international "crisis" interventions. Howard had already ended treaty negotiations, summarily abolishing the Aboriginal and Torres Strait Islander Commission in 2004. The 2007 mobilization of troops and police into the communities ended Aboriginal self-governance in practice. The intervention was draconian imposing and enforcing of immediate "supervisory" policies, that is, "privatizing of Indigenous lands, the corporatising of Indigenous governance, and the disciplining of Indigenous labour."[60] In November 2007 a new government under Kevin Rudd issued an official "apology" to Aboriginal peoples for the historic child removals, but it did not rescind the restructuring of their communities. Rudd has subsequently extended these programs. Australia appears as a contradiction to the path that Canada, New Zealand, and the United States have taken. But is it? Self-determination may continue to be valorized symbolically, but it has no necessary guarantee in practice in neoliberalism. Nation-states like Australia don't necessarily see self-determination as politic to their own multicultural practices now, while "community security" is. Will Kymlicka observed that this kind of abrogation would be much harder where Aboriginal peoples' treaty rights are constitutionally recognized, as in Canada and the United States.[61] Still, these events and the language that Canadian and Australian Aboriginal peoples speak to negotiate past and present relations within these two colonial settler states are not that different. A Canadian state establishing a human rights truth commission and a state's authoritarian abolishment of self-determination are constitutive events in the state of present Indigenous–settler state relations utilizing the parameters of a discourse enabled or in defiance of human rights.

These articulations organized around child abuse, sexual abuse, and ultimately gender violence as reparable or as causes of trauma that are reparable or as deviancies to be policed actually have increased in Indigenous self-determination and human rights discourses. Violence (specifically violence against women, rape, and sexual abuse against both sexes and children) figures prominently in the discourses that inform present conversations on past colonial damages and current self-determination. These are volatile sites with uneven outcomes. While the United States never admits to being a colonizer, it led the pack of these former settler states (United States, Canada, New Zealand, and Australia) that initially refused or attempted to block the International Declaration of Indigenous Rights. Nevertheless, in 2007 the United States became an international subject of criticism in an Amnesty International report, *Maze of Injustice*, citing matchless figures for the rape and sexual abuse of American Indian and Alaskan Native women. The United States was not alone. In 2004 Amnesty

International had first called Canada out in a report called *Stolen Sisters*.[62] Presently, violence against Indigenous women is a key index to a hollowing out of any Indigenous self-determination in Canada and the United States, as it poses a loss of integrity to women's and the Indigenous nation's body/ social body. It also follows that state projects of apology and reparations around Indigenous peoples form around gender, sex, and domesticity, because these are sites of revitalized, old but still virulent indigene–settler relations in the past and in its haunted heart now. It's not surprising that the reconciliation that indigenes are called on to trust as acts of justice do not actually stop the removal of Indigenous children from their families or stop the brutality against Indigenous women, or stop the social welfare interventions and criminalization that are endemic to Indigenous peoples and nations. Our imaginary for progressive moments is strained constantly by the ways in which the languages of victim and justice are fluidly mobilized by different political agendas. As Rauna Kuokkanen points out in her critical assessment of this neoliberal moment, it is a prolific sexual violence (rape, murder, sex trafficking, etc.) against Indigenous women and children that exemplifies early twenty-first-century experience.[63] There is a fluid discourse on sexuality and violation, and its articulation as crime, in any conversation Indigenous peoples now have with settler nationalisms in an era of human rights. In addition to its gross physical and material effect, sexual violence arouses powerful affective resonance to words such as *victim, trauma, healing* and *self-determination*. They came into juxtaposition with each other only in a very recent "past." They occur in the paradigm shift in international relations wherein trauma becomes an ethos.

What, then, is indexical about this violence and the ways in which we witness it and speak of it? Why is gendered sexual abuse so critical *now* to the discourse on our past colonization or our position within a global Indigenous politic, or to the politics of our self-determination? Of Australia, Elizabeth Povinelli marked sexuality as the site of an interruption, the limits of that nation's imagination for "other," one that confounds most of western liberalism's desire and current claims for multicultural tolerance. Imagining and constructing the sexual nature of the "other" (sex, race, nation) has generated generations of legislation and morally based policing in all settler nations, which never fully abates but morphs. The affective power of sex and reproductive discourse is ubiquitous in this biopolitical moment to mobilize nation-state populations to action, aligned to different projects in different times, certainly. Unspeakable acts of violence against Indigenous women effectively police them and their communities, but rarely the perpetrator. It is also a discourse that usually remains silent on the equally ubiquitous and brutal murder, rape, and abuse of gay, lesbian, bisexual, and transsexual Indigenous peoples, since recognizing this larger space of gender violence cannot garner the same affective force everywhere. Yet this gender violence *is* the same force articulated differently in different situations.

James Wilets observed that "violence against women and sexual minorities is predicated upon assumptions of a polar construction of gender, in which nonconformity with gender role expectations is enforced through violent and non-violent means . . . violence against both groups [is] rooted in a system of male dominance."[64] Thomas Lemke presents Foucault's insight that sexuality is positioned as "the pivot of two axes."[65] Thus, sexuality assumes a privileged position, since its effects are situated on the microlevel of the body and on the macrolevel of a population."[66] Also citing Foucault, Bruce Burgett reminds, "Sexuality is not the most intractable element in power relations, but one . . . endowed with the greatest instrumentality: useful for the greatest number of maneuvers and capable of serving . . . as a linchpin for the most varied strategies."[67] Sexuality is a relational force integral to the social discipline and self-discipline of the body, producing the social body in medico-moral discourses in different moments that have a history and a genealogy. Sexuality marks an affective nexus of moral intensities that mark our time or any time. The basic struggle for the constitutive power of political bodies is crossed by nations' and states' necessity to own women's generative powers literally and figuratively. The struggle to subsume women's powers in the production of nations and states is an old narrative I revisit in this work, but the moves of capitalism to subsume the generative powers of life are not wholly known. I offer here that First Nations and American Indian women's bodies mark this abject subject position, "inherently rapable," as Andrea Smith among others have so clearly demarcated.[68] Indigenous women hold a peculiar position within a contemporary circuit of international biopower. Our suffering is highly mediated, its representation to ourselves and to our relations locally, nationally, and internationally form, interrupt, and constrict larger discourses that *create* power in our time. Still, it is not this abject position that makes us core to this nexus of violence in our times, I think. Aboriginal women, Indigenous women, speak from their intersubjective position as part of kinship systems fragmented and manipulated to inform "reconciliation" and "healing." Women have, as my friend Elizabeth Woody wrote, "[lain] as volcanoes before men," seen as docile yet highly disruptive of normalized narratives in neoliberal or Indigenous heteropatriarchal nationalisms.[69] They do, as Sean Eudaily reminds, offer tactical resistance, "taking identities and liberties produced by the dominant form of power as tools for said power's subversion."[70] We speak to, and from, life, an ancient position of vitality that has surprising alliances in these neoliberal times. We speak from a vital imaginary for a different politic for our times, for our nations, for worlds.

Hologram

Indigenous positioning in a global therapeutic works with Indigenous women's desire to heal families, nations, and the Earth. At the same time it eludes their desire, because in the end such an ethos is often other than healing. I take seriously the women's analyses, statements, thoughts, poems, and memoirs as a Rosetta stone in reading the power relations that Indigenous peoples now inhabit in a new world order. The term *Rosetta stone* alludes to a linguistic keystone containing more than one language, the possibility of translation, if one language is known, to unlock others present that are necessary for meaning. I may use another metaphor as well: hologram. A hologram is a trick of illumination, a capturing of light that contains many facets of an image, each containing a whole picture, depending on scale recognizable or unrecognizable.

We have recognized the need to identify our own Indigenous positions as an ethical act. This means I acknowledge the space of telling I undertake from my position as an Indigenous academic writer to be no less complex than one in the community; both are bound up by a necessary politic of speech we have established. I cannot claim mine as a community voice, while I also acknowledge that I have a responsibility to more than my own interest. I look upon my work as work positioned in dialogue with Elizabeth Cook-Lynn's remark, "Without the critical analysis of reasonable scholars in every discipline, the politics of colonialism, strengthened in this century as it always has been by economic and global interests, will again deny the right of indigenous peoples to speak for themselves. It is a right no people should be denied."[71] To take this elder Dakota stateswoman's words to heart is to interrogate the position that Natives and Native scholars occupy whenever we attempt to speak and be heard, where we must continuously articulate our specificity in an academic setting where the subject of "Indians" belongs to everyone, but a responsibility *to* Indians, *to* Native peoples and nations appears to be no one's. I also take seriously Andrea Smith's call to claim American Indian studies as "an intellectual project that can have non-Native communities as its object of study."[72] Thus, I attempt to write from American Indian studies as an ethical act, and as Cook-Lynn reminds me above, "with a responsibility *to* Indians, *to* communities." But I do not write *about* Indians.

I write from the position that as Indigenous scholars we are engaged seriously in thinking the relations of power, where we make propositions while acknowledging how we are embedded in the major events and language of our times. Likewise, as an ethical act and a theoretical one, I work from my position as an Indigenous feminist and offer my Indigenous feminist critique, which has given me a commitment in seeing what we have fought for over the last forty years as a rich source of theoretical intense dreaming, insight, and ethically based action that I hope is historicized in this work. I offer this work as an Indigenous feminist critique of trauma, human rights, and self-determination in our time, a position I more fully explicate below.

I have thought about "kinships" because our lives are full of them, and generally they trace the transformations in our loyalties, work, and growth as political beings. Gloria Bird once responded to Elizabeth Cook-Lynn, answering the Dakota woman's question of whether our personal story should be the one we tell. Bird observed that each life held the intimate details of our particular encounter with the powers always present in our formation; and our lived resistance. It is the story she chose to tell. She reminded me, "Colonization is a relationship after all."[73] I have never read Bird's comment as an invitation to write a biography, but rather to claim a political space from which I am committed to explicate and disassemble the colonial "Indian." I claim the Indigenous, the spaces where we reclaim our power to pose the world differently, and one must start from home. I speak to the gifts of love I have received in all my relations, my family and the alliances I made that informed and gave me the tools I work with here. The space of writing or speaking ourselves as "Indian" is always a contested space, fraught with the politics of its continuous formation. Most always its nomenclature is confusing. In this work I write as an Athabascan woman, a daughter, a sister, and a mother, as well as a writer, a poet, and, in this work, a genealogist. I do not isolate these from one another, since I live them all simultaneously. My mother's rural village childhood and my urban one in Anchorage mark me. My childhood as a truck driver's daughter on the road in Alaska and in Oregon forms me; being part of a family that dissolved and reunited, being institutionalized as a child, being a community worker and a poet and now an academic are parts of me never separate from what I do. No simple identity explains the complex places from whence our questions and our work arise. When I began this work I felt kinship with others who are LBGT, although I do not identify as "Two-Spirit." And while I also claim kinship with others who were institutionalized as children, I also know that our personal experiences are always part of the myriad forces in play in any time. I do not necessarily separate the "ivory tower," an academic American Indian studies, from the "community," since the communities that formed me are in me.

At times I have felt pulled by the tension between the currents in my life and work. To think about this I originally used a model I took from Beatrice Hanssen's work in critical theory. In her effort to salvage important points from the cacophonous and unending disagreement between postmodernism and critical theory, Hanssen used the notion of the *agon*, the *agonist*, not to capture *antagonism*, the rough edges, but the products of their interaction, the theses that they produce together, however strenuously. Hanssen characterizes the act of "speaking" within such a discourse as "from the very start . . . structured by struggle and 'agonist.' . . . *Agon* here refers to the inherent . . . interplay between the multiple differences that inflect the structural position of speaking partners."[74] I thought at first to work in between the tension of these sites I claim my voice from. I do not seek a synthesis. I don't force anything into agreement. In writing this work I became convinced to use another metaphor, borrowing from Jeannette Armstrong's Okanogan language: *naw'qinwixw*. I have stopped thinking in terms of an internal struggle and now work relaxed into the sociality of working toward a more expansive idea of community that I see as an Indigenous feminist one articulated and emerging from struggle, where in love and honor we can hold in light open embrace difference and an expansive number of alliances with others whose goal is for generative life and not death. I think the larger thing I am doing is asking how we might hold one another in respect, and that respect is a criterion in struggle. Jeannette Armstrong poses an explanation for her word, her world in that word that I offer only in suggestion.

> I'll try and tell you how I see it, what I know about it, how I think about it, how I feel about it, how I feel it might affect me, or affect things that I know about, and that will help inform you. But I'm requesting the same things from you. I want you to tell me how you feel about it, how it affects you, the things you know about how it affects you. Then we'll have a better understanding; we'll have a chance at a better understanding of what it is we need to do. We can only do that by giving as much clarity from our diverse points of view. So, to seek the most diverse view is what *naw'qinwixw* asks for.[75]

It is the inclusiveness that this statement witnesses and that Jeannette performs in her work that strikes me as a characteristic of the way that indigenism and indigenist women's vision has grown to inform in practice the often agonistic struggle for life itself in an age of self-determination. I think it is in naw'qinwixw that Indigenous peoples of many genders, ages, and abilities perform radical acts of determination around, above, and outside of nation-states' heteronormative, homophobic, misogynist regulatory Indian policies. In my reading naw'qinwixw informs first practices, effectively performed ethical acts of interrelationship that involve all in any sustained effort to live in a place, with one another, generatively with life, rather than as that which seeks to control.

Therapeutic Nations is first informed among the voices of Canadian Indigenous women as they emerged into public discourse from the 1970s through the 1990s articulating the intimate violence in their lives. Native women in Canada spoke very early and very directly to this violence. Classic statements made by Maria Campbell, Lee Maracle, and others linked this violence to the violent outcomes of a still ongoing Canadian colonialism. In establishing a space and a genre that enabled a generation of women to speak, they also created a space to speak for those who experienced "domestic" violence perpetrated in the Canadian residential schooling. I also situate this work within a body of work by women whose diverse projects have recently come to be known as Indigenous feminisms. This growing body of work includes Lee Maracle, writing in the 1980s, and the incredible work of more recent scholars such as Lisa Kahaleole Hall. The diversity of this field has many positions, some that I admit I have yet to explore. For this work I am indebted to Sarah Deer for her critical work in deconstructing the violence inherent in liberal, racialized, heteronormative law and offering many credible Indigenous alternative justice practices available to our own polities. I also have relied heavily on Audra Simpson and Jennifer Denetdale for enormously important critiques of the raced, gendered, and militarized Indigenous nation. In this same vein it is difficult to understand colonial boundary transgressions on our bodies, lands, and psyches without the work of Mishuana Goeman. I make alliance with the work of Andrea Smith in particular for a critique of gender violence as central to our colonization. I build and cite from many women who have worked either from an Indigenous feminist position in Canada or who inform throughout the present work what I believe to be their absolutely critical argument for the transformation of any present notion of Indigenous nationalism.

Why Foucault? Why Not Foucault?

Foucault's work remains now as the most cogent critique of western hegemonic power available, of biopower. Valverde notes that Foucault's interests were in the "analyses of mechanisms and diagrams of governance"; he was not interested in "discourses" for their own sake and thus not interested in what trendsetters thought, or in internal textual constitutions of discourse, but rather in "its effects," especially when the horizon problematized social relations in new ways. He was interested in articulating the "technologies of governance" never limited to a "single institution or profession," giving him an ability to articulate principles that still inform critiques across multiple academic disciplines to this day.

I share this interest, and *Therapeutic Nations* is such an analysis, a reading of multiple texts across academic and public sites, and a genealogy inspired by Foucault that ranges across disciplines in order to see a shared horizon of thought in the social relations that mark our present experience. I build a dialogic space wherein texts and voices, Indigenous and non-Indigenous, are contemporaries in a field of discourse in their respective times. These are public voices, voices that have already been mediated by multiple forces. In earlier works, I have identified the importance of the different ways that our voices are always mediated by power. I create the space I spoke to above where my loyalties are to the Indigenous; thus, I do not see any need for declaring a sense of false neutrality. I absolutely honor Indigenous peoples' right to speak for themselves as interlocutors of their own experience. In this writing I am interested in capturing the dialogic forces in public discourse. I work within a tension where I value our Indigenous voices, mediated and entered into public discourse as they position, interrupt, and are positioned in the discourses in play at any time. I do not imagine these positions as static, nor do I have any illusions that discourse alone is where power solely "resides" or that it is the only way that we might make the changes we are able to make. I only suggest resistance in the presence of capitalized ways of life that presently speak as neoliberalism. Foucault has indispensable insights and the most powerful thesis of biopower that we have available to us. I foreground Foucault's analysis of biopower and the resulting *biopolitics* as a philosophical and political knowledge that I needed to understand. Western "rational" governance has lifted the processes of life, minute details, and biological facts and incorporated them into data by which our lives are managed and increasingly understood. These figures, images, knowledges become the proofs for the social science mob assessments of our assimilation or our ongoing degradation and deterioration within democracy, numbers to track, to manage and define our difference in multiculturalism. Thomas Lemke speaks to this deep intrusion: "Biopolitics requires a systemic knowledge of life and of 'living beings.' Systems of knowledge provide cognitive and normative maps that open up biopolitical spaces . . . [t]hey make the reality of life conceivable and calculable in such a way that it can be shaped and transformed."[76] Contemplating Lemke's words, I think, if the something we have called "colonialism," neoliberal capitalism in this moment, can be taken as such pervasive effort to make life calculable, to bring it into "management" to make it produce, in what ways do we use it, elude it, transgress it, and mobilize it?

With his focus on the discursive, Foucault failed to address the vitality and intensity of the forces that are beyond the words and discourses of any moment, the affect that is actually our lived sensory being-ness. While I utilize the discursive analysis tools offered by Foucault, I enrich these tools with the insights of theorists whose present work on *affect* may seem to work at cross purposes. It is a cross-fertilization project that I work out here chapter by chapter. I find it immensely important to put an analysis of affect and emotion, a felt theory, back into our quest to understand both classic colonialism and our present in neoliberal governance, because affect is now so profoundly implicated in these neoliberal relations that I seek to show here. There is no agreement between the "tools" to analyze the discursive and the affective. Those who are the architects of affect analyses have posed work that sometimes moves on and undoes that of the earlier concepts that we use to comprehend the forces within discourse. Here I will attempt to keep these theoretical forces in a particular relation with each other while working and understanding their differences. I respect the agon in this relationship while I practice naw'qinwixw.

Thus, in trying to imagine and feel our human desires, I find the abstraction sometimes necessary in explanation hugely sterile and lacking key parts of the strength of resistance. I prefer to look to Jordan Camp's co-articulation with New Orleans resident Sunni Patterson's account of the power of struggle. Sunni writes "And we know this place, for we have seen more times than we'd like to imagine."[77] Jordan responds by riffing with Robin D. G. Kelley to cite Sunni's performance of "poetic knowledge," where through her music and poetry she cuts through the bullshit . . . to "counter the ideological obfuscations about race and power in hegemonic political and mass mediated discourses,"[78] to express "it's ever-changing yet forever the same." Jordan, through his intuitive relation to Robin D. G. Kelley, cites the power of felt knowledge, felt theory here, as "poetic knowledge" that incites for life: "progressive social movements do not simply produce statistics and narratives of oppression; rather the best ones do what great poetry always does: transport us to another place, compel us to look at horrors and, more importantly, enable us to imagine a new society. . . .

It is that imagination, that effort to see the future in the present, that I shall call "poetry" or "poetic knowledge."[79] I would add that what good social movement, good social analysis, and good poetry have in common is the ability to incite, as in arouse, *as in feel* (as Patterson does informed by Camp informed by Kelley) to make relations.

I follow this introductory chapter with chapter 2, "Gendered Racialized Sexuality: The Formation of States," to discuss the affective gendered heterosexually normative formation of the Canadian nation-state, with its enduring influence across generations. The reconfigured power relationships between Aboriginal women and men has striking resonance in subsequent generations as we begin to express the content of nation and community self-determination. I state why the affective becomes necessary to our analyses of politics, personal and political, in this historical moment as well as others. Chapter 3, "Felt Theory," then argues the impact of Canadian First Nations women's experiential affective narrative on late 1980s social sciences, history, and literature. I argue that the personal testimonies and literatures of Maria Campbell, Lee Maracle, Ruby Slipperjack, and others were political acts in themselves in their time that exploded the measured "objective" accounts of Canadian (and US) colonial histories. I examine the characteristics of their felt knowledges as a limit and boundary where white academia designated them incomprehensible, where Indigenous intellectual production became highly mediated and contested. Then in chapter 4, "The 'Indian Problem': Anomie and Its Discontents," I create a genealogical account of the "psychological shift" that occurred from the late 1960s to the early 1980s as initially normative western social science assessments of Indian "damage," anomie, are taken up and repositioned within criminological and second-wave feminist assessments of the victim posed for justice. The "Indian problem" marks sites where an emerging world of international human rights discourses quickly reconceptualizes *anomie* into *trauma*. I offer an account of how Indigenous scholars such as Maria Yellow Horse Brave Heart and Eduardo Duran mobilize a concept of historical trauma to work for the specific experiences of Indigenous peoples. In chapter 5, "Therapeutic Nations," I pose the first of two different visions for polities, one informed by human development and one by Indigenous women as they historically and presently critique Aboriginal nationalisms. Intergenerational trauma is a diagnosis in which healing is now enacted through myriad practices of self. In chapter 6, "What Will Our Nations Be?," I contrast the human developmental vision of healing with that of Indigenous women's activism in Canada, a movement that presents a sense of community wellness that goes beyond trauma. Indigenous women offer a specific vision of polity that encompasses diverse alliances, one that is informed by practices of naw'qinwixw in political struggles for land, food, and environmental justice. In these performed affective acts, an alternate vision of polity and justice emerges that potentially performs self-determined autonomy rather than self-management.

Finally, in chapter 7, "(Un)Making the Biopolitical Citizen," I explore the concepts of biopower, biopolitics, and biosociality as ways of perceiving western nation-states' mode of governance in neoliberalism. Health and the affective attachment and desire for well-being are key to modes of governance and self-management in a biopolitical state. On the other hand, Indigenous peoples regularly perform differently imagined practices of nation and polity. Often informed reflexively within UN campaigns for justice, community healing movements, Indigenous spiritualities, and Indigenous polity, present self-determination movements are rich with alternative visions and performances that, like life itself, might exceed any neoliberalism that seeks to appropriate it. I gloss this as an Indigenous intense dreaming, because it helps me imagine the conditions under which we might produce our own truths in a so-called postmodern, postcolonial milieu where any Indigenous knowledges (narratives, stories, dreams, ceremony, dance, disciplines), framed by community practices (what is actually done), informed within historical and future tenses of the community dreamed, are continuously in play and negotiating western narrative and theoretical terrains. Given that our own subjectivity and performance is not dreamed or performed in isolation, I seek more specific insights. My concern is with the political weight and motion of the commitments that inform both western and Indigenist performances of polity and justice.[80]

TWO

Gendered Racialized Sexuality

The Formation of States

It is important to honour the missing and murdered women. It is unacceptable to marginalize these women. The Creator did not create garbage. He created beauty.

—DAVID SMOKE[1]

The Canadian TRC specifically addressed sexual abuse of Indian children in residential schools. As a separate issue, Canada and the United States also came under human rights scrutiny from Amnesty International for failing to protect Indigenous women from sexual violence. These campaigns to educate and advocate have much to teach us about how violence against Indigenous women is presented to two different nation-state publics.

In *Canada: Stolen Sisters: A Human Rights Response to Discrimination and Violence against Indigenous Women in Canada* and *Maze of Injustice: The Failure to Protect Indigenous Women from Sexual Violence in the USA*, Amnesty International (AI) cites rape, murder, and daily violence against Indigenous women at the epicenter of an endemic violence that Indigenous peoples experience in both countries.[2] AI protests actually join a tsunami of literature, narratives, and analyses produced by Native women themselves over the past four decades. However, it was Amnesty's worldwide reputation as a pioneering human rights NGO that lent a discursive weight that the women did not have alone. The reports highlight the different discourses that exist in Canada and in the United States for explaining this violence. How AI's campaigns frame the violence against Indigenous women illustrates how such violence lends its moral force to other political aims, both Indigenous and nation-state. AI's spotlight on gendered sexual violence focuses attention on the fact that Canada and the United States were both constituted in this violence. The political and social destruction of Indigenous societies was in part accomplished by discipline of children's bodies, as in the residential schooling systems, or in unchecked violence perpetrated on Aboriginal women's bodies. There is also an affective aspect of this discipline that mostly goes unmarked in histories and literatures of colonization.

In the first section of this chapter, I compare these two important Amnesty reports in the way they present gender violence against Indigenous women to their respective Indigenous and nation-state publics. I explore first how this violence is expressed in Canada as an aspect of a long, reprehensible relationship now under reconciliation, while in the United States it is posed as a major deterrent to self-determination for American Indian nations. I consider the way Sarah Deer, a leading indigenist legal scholar and activist, poses the question of self-determination and gender violence. In the second section I contextualize this violence by returning to well-discussed nineteenth- and early twentieth-century colonial projects to review how gendered raced sexual violence becomes constitutive to the nation-states. There I pose different questions about the shame that was produced by a Canadian public's discipline in what amounted to an apartheid. I then speak to how affect mobilizes present political assessments of profaned Indian women and their families. On the other hand, such an analysis brings us back again to the import of the campaigns for justice that North American Indigenous women posed to AI and the transformational potential in women's statements of respect for life.

Disappeared

Produced cooperatively with the Native Women's Association of Canada, Amnesty International's *Stolen Sisters* documents the long record of disappeared Aboriginal women, some never found after decades of inquiry.[3] It is also the account of the found and abused bodies of Aboriginal sisters, mothers, and aunts, whose deaths barely register as crimes to the Canadian justice system. AI positions the disappeared and murdered women at the epicenter of a deep-seated disrespect Canada holds for Aboriginal life made manifest. From the statistics, it would appear that it is hardly a crime to rape, kill, and "disappear" an Aboriginal woman, and perhaps even less notable if she has become "untouchable" or homeless or has entered the sex trade. *Stolen Sisters* situates this gendered violence within a long history of colonial violence against Indigenous people stemming from the formation of the

Canadian state. Through innumerable cases *Stolen Sisters* identifies and tracks the considerable Canadian indifference to Indigenous women's lives as a recognizable history. Here AI can refer to an already released Royal Commission on Aboriginal Peoples (RCAP) national investigation that admits to the systemic violence that formed these Canadian–Indigenous colonial relationships. Hence, Amnesty International and the Native Women's Association of Canada could articulate Aboriginal women's plight as a heinous and pressing issue of colonial violence that deserves particular and immediate attention. In Canada, the RCAP investigation that contextually grounds *Stolen Sisters* also grounds Canada's present commitment to internationally recognized processes for "truth and reconciliation." But *Stolen Sisters* must be seen first as the effort of Aboriginal women in Canada to bring this violence in their lives into sharper focus than is available in the Canadian discourse that RCAP established after 1996. *Stolen Sisters* validates the women's and families' voices, reclaiming the worth of those murdered, those whom Canada has judged amoral, sexualized, and discarded. It also shows the ability of Canadian Indigenous women to articulate their experiences to a growing international conversation on violence against women. The Native Women's Association and other groups of Indigenous women in Canada can reference a track record of successful prior human rights campaigns that cited Canada for sexual discrimination against Native women embedded in the Indian Act.[4] *Stolen Sisters* has a context built on this larger available knowledge.

On the other hand, the United States convened no Royal Commission, or any commission dedicated to righting colonial violence, since it never admits to colonialism. Here, Amnesty International took a different tack. *Maze of Injustice* testifies to an entire spectrum of atrocious violence against American Indian and Alaskan Native women, from rape to brutal murder, some where torture was a clear aspect. *Maze* utilizes a plethora of statistical evidence whose shortcomings the authors also make evident. The report makes clear that the violence it details may be only a fraction of what occurs, since most of this type of crime goes unreported in Indian Country. This too is a report whose existence represents American Indian women's numerous efforts to gather information and to act on their own behalf, so, as in *Stolen Sisters*, the women are the interlocutors. The importance of having Native women speak themselves is made more evident than in the earlier *Stolen Sisters*. *Maze of Injustice* features the words of Native women who were violated, along with their pictures, on numerous pages of the report. Groups of Native women who offer domestic violence support services are also prominently featured. *Maze of Injustice* is twice as long as *Stolen Sisters* and highly produced, featuring sophisticated photography and graphics. While both reports must inform and "sell" to an audience that may not know "Indian Country" and has little understanding of Indian histories, or Indian law, *Maze of Injustice* also has no Royal Commission report or visibility from prior successful human rights campaigns waged by Indian women. As with *Stolen Sisters*, *Maze of Injustice*'s argument positions the violence perpetrated against Native women to their marginalization in American society, with colonization underlying the women's devaluation in American and American Indian societies: "Indigenous peoples in the USA face deeply entrenched marginalization—the result of a long history of systemic and pervasive abuse and persecution."[5] The women's torture is linked to a long and violent colonial historical relationship, but it is also linked to Indigenous peoples' relations with the United States in the present: "Sexual violence against Indigenous women today is informed and conditioned by this legacy of widespread and egregious human rights abuses. It has been compounded by the federal government's steady erosion of tribal government authority and its chronic under-resourcing of those law enforcement agencies and service providers which should protect Indigenous women from sexual violence."[6]

Maze of Injustice is also directly positioned to address a larger campaign to strengthen and fully fund Title IX, a newly inserted tribal title in the national Violence Against Women Act (VAWA). This was a late but significant attempt to address the violence that Native women activists had made clear for years that so glaringly leapt off the page of any preliminary crime statistics report in Indian Country. The violence that *Maze of Injustice* illustrates cites the more pressing issue to American Indian nations, the lack of Indian jurisdiction in their own lands. *Maze of Injustice* presents highly affective and material evidence in support of tribal nations' ardent campaigns to return or reinvigorate local policing jurisdiction within Indian nations. While First Nations and other Indigenous peoples in Canada also work to determine their nationalisms, American Indian nations are considered as such by the United States. In addition the United States currently has an official policy of self-determination wherein policing, among other powers, is a part of American Indian nations' governance. Still, this is an irregular and limited power in practice, existing in some places and not in others. *Maze of Injustice* makes this clear. In Alaska, protection for Native women in rural villages has been thwarted by the state and the lack of territorial jurisdiction in the Alaskan Native Claims Settlement Act. Hence, *Maze of Injustice* spotlights a crucial movement, drawing its name from a reference to these mazes of conflicting jurisdictions (maze of injustice) that defy rationality. These jurisdictional nightmares have enabled some nations to operate as "sacrifice zones" that protect corporations conducting resource extraction, while they cannot protect their own citizens. Thus, American Indian reserved lands, cross-cut by these conflicting jurisdictions, sediments of previous colonial campaigns to constrain Indian sovereignty, make it difficult to get aid in an emergency. Or they are without resources or jurisdiction to prosecute violent offenders within their own lands. This "issue," an "Indian problem," has been created by the US intergenerational dismantling of lives, of lands and polity, through allotment and state and federal incursions into Indian jurisdiction. Currently, regaining or creating more jurisdiction is a key legislative initiative of tribal nations in the United States.[7] It is a campaign to end the lawless zones the United States has created in Indian treaty lands to substantiate a more meaningful self-determination, the illusive but stated current policy of the United States. American Indian nations have made violence against women an issue that threatens the nation as a whole. As Muskogee Creek legal scholar Sarah Deer points out in her essay "Sovereignty of the Soul: Exploring the Intersection of Rape Law Reform and Federal Indian Law,"

> For tribal governments, defining and adjudicating crimes such as sexual assault can be the purest exercise of sovereignty. What crime, other than murder, strikes at the hearts of its citizens more deeply than rape? Sexual violence impinges on our spiritual selves, creating emotional wounds that can feed into community trauma . . . the historical trauma of sexual abuse compounds the negative experiences of Native American women who are raped today. For sovereign tribal nations, the question is not just about protecting and responding to individual women who are sexually assaulted but also addressing the foundational wellness of the community where it occurs. . . . The strength of the anti-rape sentiment in the community will ultimately illuminate the strength and resolve of the entire community to preserve and live healthy and happy lives.[8]

Sarah Deer's argument speaks directly to the violation of the sovereignty of any Native woman's body in relation to the sovereignty of a Native nation, a trauma that occludes any community health foundational to a self-determining people. As Deer says, "What crime, other than murder, strikes at the hearts of its citizens more deeply than rape?" Within the actual embodied physical violation, there is an affective disintegration. Rape interrupts and dissolves the ontological presence of person and community, their desire to be, to go on, to endure, to have integrity. Rape strikes fear in the relations that make community. Without saying so directly, Deer invokes Indian women's important primary position as mother, directly implicated in the reproductive powers of the nation to reproduce itself, whether through child-bearing, parenting, or its spirit to endure and go on, central to its sense of well-being. In many Indigenous traditions of customary law, women figure as this embodiment of the relations that configure order to the community, the community's relationship to the earth and to life. In portraying rape as a crime against the community's "foundational wellness," it signifies that there is no law that will protect this center, not the customary, and certainly not the colonizer's. In the absence of customary order, in the colonial imposition of another order that transgresses and forbids the Indigenous nations' own jurisdiction, it is a compromise with colonial jurisdiction that must be asked for. It cannot be first a plea for the strengthening of customary law, of women's centrality to Indigenous order, because that order is not available; it has been destroyed or thwarted.

Deer clearly states the need for jurisdiction, for protection as a sovereignty issue: "It is important that we not disregard the intersection between the rape of indigenous women and the destruction of indigenous legal systems."[9] But Sarah Deer might caution that while returning jurisdiction to Native nations, to their policing, to their courts is a vital first step, it is only a first step. Making the disappeared visible as an object of colonial law is not the same as changing a society where rape is constitutive to deeper relations. "Reform" hasn't stopped anything. She reminds: "Though feminists have been successful at developing and implementing major reforms of rape law since the early 1970s, it is not clear that these efforts have necessarily improved the climate for survivors of sexual assault . . . [the challenge is] that indigenous women who are raped in the United States today face a legacy of laws that have historically encouraged the systemic rape of Native women."[10]

Deer has also written that ending violence against Indian women is more complex than increasing policing and prosecution in communities that are already overly represented in crime statistics, jails, and prisons.[11] A systemic misogyny in the system is also present in sex discrimination and heterosexual monism in the communities.[12] Rape and sexual violence have always been normative to the subjugation of colonized peoples. Colonization, as Andrea Smith reminds, is a gendered heterosexual colonization profoundly insinuated into the most intimate of relations, which is my subsequent discussion in this chapter. Even a cursory reading of literatures on colonization in Africa or Australia (or even if we reduce this reading to Canada and the United States) reveals that the rape, murder, and sexualization of Indigenous women has been constitutive to the founding of western nation-states.[13] Both Amnesty International reports indicate that this is so.

Then what makes this effort to highlight the existence of this sexual violence in our own generation or to move for its recognition and policing different?

Perhaps it is important to ask what is actually produced by this effort, what languages and social forces our movements mobilize. Or how is this violence both expressed and mobilized by power in our time? It is easy to identify some part of this immediately. Our efforts as Indigenous women are critical local actions and part of a worldwide push to bring violence against women to the forefront of human rights issues, a move now approximately forty years in the making with uneven results. Deer passionately and rightfully foregrounds rape as a primary violation of the integrity of Indigenous woman and nation.

Yet ironically, the victims of sexual crime become more entwined with policing, welfare management, and imprisonment now—because of the success of women's prior demand that sexual violence be policed. Increased surveillance, monitoring, and imprisonment without changes in respect and value for women do not produce safety, as Deer indicates. Presently there is a push from international human rights agencies charged with monitoring Indigenous human rights violations even in the United States, thus AI's appearance in this arena. Yet this move to internationalize aspects of the earlier vigorous, white, second-wave feminist agenda to change state response to sexual violence has critics at this point too. The early radical feminist work to criminalize domestic violence was most successful at creating an intensified site of state action that did not protect women so much as opened them up to further legal and therapeutic scrutiny. US and Canadian societies became more hypervigilant around sexual crime but not less misogynistic. They also became more invasive and controlling. Kristin Bumiller in *In an Abusive State* relates how once grassroots, women-centered, feminist domestic-violence networks became co-opted over time in neoliberal state turns to "workfare." As these feminist networks sought more legitimacy and funding for operations, they often advised women to take state funding. Women leaving abusive situations without other support systems were introduced to neoliberal workfare programs as these became more coercive and more policed. Women who lost legitimate means of support and turned to economic crimes such as petty theft or prostitution faced being incarcerated in increasingly punitive justice systems.[14] Across a wide spectrum of political analyses, there is agreement that western states became more invested in imbuing policing "domestic" welfare arenas with therapeutic techniques. Bumiller is critical of taking this model as an international intervention in nonwestern societies. She contends that we should understand what happened here.

Increases in women's imprisonment accompanied these post–second wave feminist social changes as they hit the new neoliberal realities, but then so did women's participation in the multinational labor markets and the newly gender-integrated militaries as they took on policing around the world. Neoliberalism as it became entrenched was imbued with progressive narratives of equality with excitement and opportunities posed in a new global economy. The new society was therapeutic and restorative as the law came to figure the victim and the perpetrator as sites for self-help, or for medicalized behavioral modifications. Policing interventions were increased in segments of the population deemed "unproductive": those on welfare, people on probation, the homeless, and the mentally ill. Welfare mothers often occupy a particularly unsafe position where any actual autonomy from social welfare is difficult to achieve, and policing for noncompliance infractions is severe. Any shift in gender relations in western societies did not immediately appear to be beneficial or change the dynamics between the Indigenous and settler states except that Indigenous women were at higher risk in and beyond their communities than any other population, as both AI reports conclude. When abused, they also became at risk for being incarcerated. Luanna Ross wrote early on how many imprisoned American Indian women were primarily sexually abused women, women who had been brutally abused in families disintegrating from systemic economic and social violence.[15] Yet something did shift, something that is, as Bumiller indicates, not well understood. The intensified discourse on gendered relations in western societies did involve Indigenous women and their societies in ways that should be considered significant. I return to this shift at the end of this chapter. Here, I want to turn to review the dense set of relations involved.

In both *Stolen Sisters* and *Maze of Injustice*, Amnesty International frames the dehumanization that is part and parcel of the systemic and felt relations that Indigenous peoples have historically experienced in both countries. In this part I want to look at the conditions and relations specific to this knot of misogynistic disregard, relations that make violence against Indigenous women normative rather than an aberration.

Gender, Race, and Sex

Canadian colonization was achieved in ways very similar to colonization in other parts of the globe. The sexual relations of this subjugation are clear even today. Larissa Behrendt observed that "white men are inextricably linked to an historical context in which they are the heirs of white racist domination of black women by which contemporary neo-colonial power relationships carry the baggage and the legacy of frontier and colonial power relations. This legacy is found in contemporary constructions, whether fictional or in the very real parameters of the dominant legal system. These stereotypes affect Aboriginal women, in very real ways, every day."[16] So it is possible to look at colonialism in Africa or South America and see something that escapes radical differences in history or society.

Colonialism meant that Canada came to legally control and socially modify all aspects of Indigenous life and that law was both racialized and gendered and heterosexual. In that way it is biopower, a power that is concerned with "life itself," a person's sex and phenotypes (the shade of skin, hair texture, cranial measurements, etc.), and relations. The Canadian Indian Act as a primary colonial act is racial; it defines who an *Indian* is. Up until 1985 the Indian Act defined an Indian as a man. The Indian Act altered gender relations in the communities, because it is the law that constructed a hierarchal patriarchy in Indian Canada. It legislates and morally polices a heterosexual norm. Canada's racism was (em)"bedded" in the "intimate" domains of domesticity, domiciles, conjugality, and "private" spaces.[17] The Canadian Indian Act that defines "Indian" was directly aimed at any self-definitive Indian customary law. This discursive "act" as law underwrote church and social programs to reorganize Indigenous familial and clan relations and thus reorganize social relationships at the level that "society" is conceived.[18] It introduces patriarchy and hierarchy into Indigenous social leadership, reforming them around colonially sanctioned male chiefs, Indian agents, and priests. It defined and banished Indian women who married outside the "identity." The creation of the "Indian" eventually reinforces age segregation. It is a law that supports removing three or more generations of Indian children from their communities, isolating and sex-segregating them in institutions where a mixture of state-induced poverty and banal stupidity creates conditions that eventually destroy large numbers of individuals, psychologically if not physically.[19]

Indigenous societies organized themselves through descent, adoption, and voluntary affiliation in both matrilineal and patrilineal societies that can be characterized by their great diversity. Gender relations among tribal people were variable, depending on the circulation of tribal knowledge and resources that were often distributed through the women's descent lines. More notable here, even beyond the richness in this variety of social organizations that existed prior to the Canadian state, are the power relations within and between these societies arranged through familial relations and gendered responsibilities. The heterosexual couple was not necessarily the focal point for marriages. Marriages were unions of family systems that placed larger responsibilities on clan and kinship bonds between these groups first, not on the relations between the two people.[20] The gender interventions inherent in colonial schooling had integrally explosive implications in terms of the elemental organization of "Indian" societies, whose spectrum in terms of being a "man" or "woman" was richly differentiated. This colonial "schooling" flattened a complex constellation of Indigenous familial, economic, and ceremonial roles into several one-dimensional stereotypes that narrated naive sexuality or wantonness and Indian women as "beasts of burden." Indian women's training could not be identical with one for white, middle-class "femininity," even if this is what was imagined as a model. White racial and gender stereotypes often led to an odd reversal for tribal women, who were rarely free to establish their own homes as "havens" of domesticity.

Ann Stoler observed that these arrangements had created whole worlds of colonial relations iterated across the globe: "White men used the protection of white women as a defense against imagined threats — 'the red peril,' 'the black peril' (in Africa), the 'yellow peril' (in Asia). They imposed — and European women actively participated in — protective models of womanhood and motherhood and prescriptions for domestic relations that constrained both the raced women and men in servitude and those who ostensibly ruled."[21] But sexuality, race, and gender always inhabit the heart of an affectively charged moral terrain.

In the Name of God: Sex and the State's Morals

Canada's proscription to reproduce middle-class sexual mores in Native children would always run against the "known" available nature of Native sexuality. Indians occupied a public imaginary that was intensely sexualized — where a depraved sexuality could be assumed as a norm relating to Indians — men, women, and children. As the RCAP report on residential schools conveys, "There is rarely any mention of sexual behaviour that is not a concern about sexual activity among the children, which led administrators to segregate them and lock them away at night to prevent contact."[22] John Milloy conveys the intensity of the moral construction around the children's sexuality. It was/is this "normed" racialized sexual imaginary that Canadians felt/knew about Indians that positioned the sexuality of priests, ministers, nuns, teachers, administrators, cooks, and lay people in an unexamined relation at the same time. Residential school staff and religious personnel would often enforce the heavy injunction against sex at the same moment that they acted in the excitement produced by the depraved and silenced position of their stigmata, their "sin," the ecstasies of forbidden sexuality inciting their desire and behavior.

Acting as the state's moral authority, the different churches entered their Christianization project in a contradictory and compromised position. The church narrated its moral force through its control over Native bodies by characterizing and policing Indigenous sexuality. Even if "sex" is forbidden to speak its name in this space, a set of relationships was produced through thick narratives framing Native sexuality and intimate familial relations, marriage, and parenting. Foucault conceptualizes acts of sexual coercion beyond individual pathology as "especially dense transfer point for relations of power between men and women, young people and old people . . . teachers and students, priests and laity" or between races.[23] Any "repression" of sexuality produces a plethora of relations. "Repression" multiplies these effects and affects that can refer back to moral norms in the disciplining and normalizing of subjects. Thus, it is an affectively understood sexual imaginary, a moral economy that is created between racialized Indigenous children, their families, and the white settler society.

This is parcel and part of the discipline of gender relations in Native conjugal and familial relations. Canada's Indian Act was an enveloping law that included the production and policing of Indian identity by recognizing certain conjugal relations over others, barring any nonmonogamous, nonheterosexual union. The category "Indian" is defined through state interference into the reproductive relations of Indigenous families and nations. Stoler, following Foucault, analyzed the colonization of "Natives" as a largely domestic affair on a very intimate level. In her historical evaluation of the Dutch West Indies, Stoler frames colonization as part of a transmutation, a fracture and reformation as the "empire" and its colonies argue the nature of the bourgeois citizen into being, as they attempt to differentiate themselves from "those they are not," between those who will be included in the colonial nation and those who should not. She found these interdependent domestic narrative productions inseparable in their actual performance: "Bourgeois sexuality and racialized sexuality . . . [are not] distinct kinds . . . but dependent constructs in a unified field." In this kind of formation, a "hygienic" middle-class domesticity is a result of its positioning against its definitions of the "raced" Native and the chaos of those who are of uncertain category and "blood." "Colonialism," Stoler says, "was not about the importation of middle-class sensibilities, but about the making of them."[24]

Stoler furnishes a thick suggestive text for understanding the residential schools. Class and race narratives were ancient projects in Europe that attempted to evaluate worth from differentiated human "qualities." Foucault suggests that the real development of *biopower* is here in the move to link certain qualities to different "kinds" of people in order to ascertain their value, their worthiness to be members of the "nation." The poor are the first to come under indictment as unworthy, and the move to link this quality of "poor" to lineages, descent lines, and races is made in Europe prior to any move into America, Asia, or Africa. Biopower defines any nation-state's interest in managing the biological potential of its "population," a form of governance that becomes by the nineteenth century the necessity to identify and then defend categories of purity and worthiness, categories that are ascertained in the most intimate of terms, "defining the racial coordinates and social discriminations of empire."[25] In common, Stoler reminds, were their "moral policies that shaped the boundaries of race. Each points to strategies of exclusion on the basis of social credentials, sensibility, and cultural knowledge. . . . These are the relations that create a domestic "sphere" in the nineteenth century; [where] "civility and racial membership were measured less by what people did in public than in their private lives—with whom they cohabited; who slept with whom, when and where; who suckled which children; how children were reared and by whom; what language was spoken to servants, friends, and family members at home."[26]

While residential schools' stated goals were to Christianize and civilize children and communities, in practice this meant preventing Indian communities and families from modeling their own domestic relations to their children. The residential schools would also implant a desire for a "morality" always couched in western terms, a desire for a "decency" that is always defined by a Christian discourse or, later, by a social-science mental hygienic one. It is also the institution that teaches Native children that their Indian bodies are by nature sexually depraved and that their entry into white society depends on their eternal vigilance against their own shamed and savage sexuality. But this ubiquitous thought, charged with so much unspoken "knowledge," neither protected children from their own guardians nor enabled their speech. It would just as commonly protect the perpetrators who acted on their own "true" knowledge of profane Native bodies and Native desire. This elaborately produced *shame* presented difficult and contradictory places to speak from for all concerned.[27]

Of the litany of abuses that occurred in the schools, sexual practices are among other practices that transgress the children's bodies and minds. If the nature of this relationship is about discipline rather than individual sexual satisfaction, then there is a case that this kind of powerful transgression against the children's autonomy and bodily integrity is a basic training in helplessness. A child who has no opportunity to experience control over his or her body cannot learn very easily how to make other boundaries that can be acted from. This is prerequisite for the experience Bev Sellars describes for the survivors of residential schools: "Many of us didn't know that we should have expected and demanded to be treated as human beings and not as animals or savages, as so many religious and government officials thought us to be . . ."[28] These individuals, residential school survivors, particularly as young women and mothers would again become central to a second disastrous intervention into Indigenous families, known in Canada as the Sixties Scoop. Their positioning as abject failed mothers and immoral women continues to inform present interventions into Native families that are so familiar today.

By the early part of the twentieth century, reflecting a shift from pastoral to professional surveillance, the Department of Indian Affairs (DIA) had created a specific category for "Immorality on the Reserves," which made it the Indian agent's role to monitor family, in particular women's sexual morality.[29] Women, particularly young women, could be sanctioned or incarcerated for acting outside the church's and the Indian agent's sense of proper behaviors. Women were often arbitrarily under sanction. Joan Sangster observed in her research on the Ontario Training School for Girls (OTSG) how young women unfortunate enough to become entangled in these early welfare state interventions into Native family were even more isolated than those children in residential schools. As racial and non-English-language minorities in otherwise white institutions, many children were left almost illiterate by the effects of their poverty, poor schooling, or substandard residential schooling. This led to grievous assessments. The OTSG used psychiatric evaluations to assess IQ, with the youth often judged retarded.[30] But the system was mostly interested in reforming women's morality, and so a middle-class domestic training/discipline was the school's primary education. Not all the staff were unaware that there were differences that made the women vulnerable: "One female psychologist tried to argue with the penal workers that they were not cognizant enough of the 'cultural differences' that caused a Native girl to periodically 'blow up in rage.'"[31]

Indigenous women did rebel, not only by raging but often through withdrawal or by running. Women who had been incarcerated as youth stood a good chance of being further penalized later either by further criminalization or by being marked as immoral very early on. Sangster shared the notation on one young woman's record: "When wardship was terminated at eighteen, Ellen had already also been in the local jail and mental hospital."[32] Many were depressed and, like others returning from residential schools, extremely at risk. The large-scale roundup of children in Canadian Indigenous communities as women were punished for the "moral failures" of their motherhood during the Sixties Scoop was normative Canadian nation-state response, reflecting mainstream social work's ideation on a profaned, sexualized Indian mother in contrast to its own "femininity," one conditioned by figures of stay-at-home mothers in pumps and pearls, idealized in television fantasies like *Leave It to Beaver*, produced again and revitalized in moral terms updated in sociological language rather than in the nineteenth-century state-religious discourses. The social welfare interventions into Indigenous community and sovereignty that are still pervasive in Indian Country form an epicenter of state violence and Indigenous moral pillory. This moral policing is affective control.

Emotional Colonialism: The Profaned Indian

Until now, I have mostly discussed ways in which bodies were disciplined in spaces like residential school or reserves through bodily and discursive discipline. I allude to the moral spaces that these were. Here, I want to introduce colonialism as a *felt*, affective relationship. Moral stigmata are produced and attached to race, gender, and sexualities as lived structures of feeling: intuited, perceived, felt, and, finally, in this circuit expressed as emotions. Lauren Berlant proposes the structure of feeling as "a residue of common experience sensed but not spoken in a social formation, except as the heterogeneous but common practices of a historical moment would emanate them."[33] This might mean there is more intense affect available than there is the social means to express. Affect has enormous valence beyond any particular emotion like shame, but because that is the residential-school survivor's primary affective report, I will start there and analyze some of its relations. I then move on to introduce how the inclusion of affect has import to the politic of our times.

It *felt* shameful to be an Indian in Canada for most of that nation's history. There is clearly a record of emotional management in residential schooling that also provides emotional training in adults that produces affective resonance again in a different time and for a different venue. An intensity of meaning grew thick around Native sexuality in Canada. Canadian colonialism is "felt" in that it is a broad spectrum of nuances, valences/practices with the power to generate emotionally charged meaning as *common knowledge*. Until the concept of *victimhood* prevailed in the 1980s, becoming "dramatically articulated in the vernacular of trauma," a discursive shift I detail in a consequent chapter, Canadian society remained highly segregated, an apartheid system.[34] After World War II this separation maintained by visceral felt discourses on race and raced sexuality, backed by actual or implied physical violence both in and between Indian and white communities began to break down. Still, it was a separation institutionalized in common state governance and policing practices. Canadian apartheid was also a pecking order enforced within racially informed status and shaming hierarchies. In *The School at Mopass: A Problem of Identity*, Richard King observed that inside early 1960s Indian residential schools, it was the least powerful—the ostracized, the immigrant, women, poor, and mostly white Canadian fringe—who had been given a day-to-day complete authority over the only people who could have been even more ostracized than themselves, the "Indians": "These individuals are incapable of recognizing any validity in another belief system. With these people controlling the school, there is no possibility of consulting with Indian adults or of treating Indians as equals in the planning of educational experiences for the children."[35] While King is racially and economically positioned to benefit from this hierarchy, it is the subaltern staff's fault, not his, that integration will be hard. King observes that the residential staff was deeply ignorant of Indians. One teacher admits to King that she had begun to notice Indians as humans for the first time that year: "We'd see them often—maybe a drunken Indian asleep in the back of a bus—and you'd think, 'Oh Indian,' like you think lamppost, or tree, or dog."[36] But in fact the speaker was not deeply *ignorant*. The Indian in the back of the bus was asleep—but that he was drunk was felt common knowledge, perhaps informed by disgust or boredom, but rarely curiosity, the invitation to inquiry. While *what* nonhuman category the Indian is in may be in question—"lamppost, or tree, or dog"—there is no question that he is drunk. That "the Indian" is an unconscious and unconscionable body is a *known*. It is a known that can erase other differences, a moral common knowledge not readily in question. *It is* the systemic knowledge; it feels *right*.

In a similar moment in the late 1960s, social anthropologist Niels Braroe illustrates this in *Indian and White: Self Image and Interaction in a Canadian Plains Community*. He also found this densely woven communal Canadian "ignorance" a finely tuned knowledge production that worked to create an almost total separation between the "races."[37] In Braroe's study, "Whitemen" are not as diverse as the adults that King analyzes in his residential school study, but they too are marginalized by their own location outside the economic privilege of white, middle-class Canada. Living under conditions not profoundly different from those of the Indian peoples

that were their neighbors, these white but poor Canadians feel/know themselves as vastly superior, creating the "Indian" as a "profane" person.[38] This
profaned figure was created steeped in stock assessments of negative Indian
behaviors, opinions backed by law and long social convention. An Indian
man observed, "They think they're so good and we're nothing."[39] There is
sexual connotation to everything not understood. Whites believe that Indians returning from a Sun Dance all have venereal disease, as if they had
attended an "extended orgy."[40] As Braroe put it, "Whites who have never
visited the reserve are sure that its residents are all indiscriminately promiscuous."[41] Sexual assessments join other kinds of moral judgments, building
a tight matrix creating the Indian as a "profane" figure, dehumanized and
not worthy of regard, that again allows these white people to assume that as
a white man Braroe shares their attitudes and feelings, despite their considerable differences. Canadian Indigenous peoples deflected these profane
assessments by turning in, assessing themselves within their own cultural
value systems, but given such inundation, it was hard. But new languages
also became available that made emotion of analytical importance. For
instance, by 1975 Howard Adams, a Métis scholar and activist, could speak
of *internalized colonization* as an analysis of Canadian Indian colonization
and could name shame as a key component.[42]

The "truth" in the web of historically resilient felt moral knowledge
served to identify and exclude Indians from all meaningful Canadian economic or social activities regardless of whether they accepted or sought this
differentiation.[43] Shame was the felt experience that residential-school survivors most often attached to the position of being "Indian." Shame is quintes-
sentially "embodied" sociality, a primary self-reflective axis, a social/body
relationship, in part a felt analysis, an assessment of your perceived status.[44]
Shame is part of "self-attention," the recognition of "what others think of
us."[45] Shame is visceral interest.[46] Jane Blocker writes of an early European
interest in colonized people's skin tones and blush. Europeans attempted
to read racialized peoples, since blush denotes the recognition of another's
gaze on you. In "Blushing in the Various Races of Man," Charles Darwin
speaks from an "objective" unidentified, unmarked white man's gaze on
"Maori, Tahitians, Latin Americans, Native Americans, and Africans."
These peoples blushed "when laughed at, humiliated, examined naked
. . ." Darwin reads this blushing as a sign of "shame and of self-awareness."[47]
Fanon immediately comes to mind in his vivid account of the position of
the colonized under that gaze. Jane Blocker tells us this is subjectivity and
attachment: "Subjectivity . . . depends firmly on the individual's capacity
to imagine himself as such, to see himself within a community of others,

to see himself as someone who sees."[48] This blush associated with shame is ambiguous, never directly ever correlative with guilt: "shame is not necessarily an emotion or affect produced by an awareness of one's own improper behavior; rather 'it attaches to and sharpens the sense of who one is, whereas guilt attaches to what one does.'"[49] Importantly, this is also where dehumanization is accomplished. Blocker quotes Giorgio Agamben: "Shame is what is produced in the absolute concomitance of subjectification and de-subjectification, self-loss and self-possession, servitude and sovereignty."[50]

"Emotion" is widely variable individual expression, with affect the larger charged sociality, traces of a vitality of being, prior to and not reducible to thought. Nick Crossley poses that this is not "a process [where] consciousness can transform since consciousness is itself transformed in the process."[51] Affect eludes, present before and beyond any singular consciousness. Affect has transformative power wherein building intensities electrify moments of potential. Affect has no "natural" projects; thus, affect might be imperceptible or incite or mobilize intensities of any possibility in any situation. Perhaps, important to the conversations in this book, in a moment when social suffering is highly medicalized, Crossley poses affective sociality as open "to manipulation or interpellation by various psychotherapeutic technologies and markets in which they operate," a development Habermas called a "colonization of the lifeworld."[52]

Affect should be of great interest in residential school theorizing. Fear and pain permeated Indigenous peoples' individual narratives of their school lives; isolation from parents, denials of food and comfort, and the violation of their bodies and sense of integrity, plus the "total" institution, all point to an intensely shared affective environment. Inside or outside the school, the residents' lives were fraught with a negotiation of their felt profaned status charging all their relations. They were beaten, they were lonely, they were frightened and in pain. Alternately, they were defiant, curious, bored, and excited, and they sometimes pulled off hope for the future, separately and together. This set up a constant exchange between the everyday discourse that reinforced their profane status, the emotional habitus this created, and the physical disciplining of their bodies. Yet ironically (or not) it is exactly there in that intensity that speech/expression is forbidden, punished, modulated, silenced covertly (social convention) or overtly (physical or psychological discipline). An education that denied any critical thinking (tools to self-reflect—speaking to another girl, for instance, much less keeping a diary) is a regular feature of residential-school survivors' accounts.

Likewise, we should then carefully consider all the proscribed venues for the production of Indigenous recall, memory, or affective subjective reports in myriad venues and across multiple media now: to courts, to truth and reconciliation commissions. Here I call attention to the dense amount of psychological technologies that are now in place in Indian Country to interpret our affect and emotion, to produce the speech/affect/memory we were formerly denied, to explain the feelings we weren't supposed to have, or to suggest how we "should" feel. What is the relationship between the "disciplining" affective technologies of the nineteenth century that "silenced" with the late twentieth-century technologies to produce productive "well" affect among the same group of peoples. All of these technologies came into place in the turn to therapeutic culture that is in part incited by western feminism's ardent stand against sexual violence. This movement incited widespread acceptance of first-person affective witnessing for justice that neoliberalism came to favor and appropriate in a "kinder, gentler society." This is a society that puts much stock in transforming and managing affect. Testimonials of Indigenous affect are now ubiquitous in both judicial and therapeutic spheres. Many questions arise for me about this shift. For one, why are the legal and political domains that any Indigenous nations negotiate now so intimately charged with the emotions of our trauma?

While the therapeutic turn appears to show great concern for our emotional well-being, less is understood about how affect charges positive moments, not just compromising ones. Affectively formed proposition, that is, dreaming (literally and figuratively) and action partake in these same intensities; the potential of Indigenous imaginaries, intense desires for holistic societies, or for societies with different political imagination informing them, have impact. There is in fact no shortage of these imaginaries, but not as much belief in affectively informed Indigenous conceptual frames. Indigenous intense dreaming, affectively mobilizing our own propositions for life, should be understood to be a potential in positing Indigenous alternatives, what is mobilized in being Indigenous.[53] To appreciate this power begins with being alive to the fact that affective mobilizations are the politics of our times and that Indigenous peoples have been active participants. I consider this an opening conversation that I will fill out as I move through my chapters.

The felt relations of living and articulating inside a dense nexus of racial and sexual proscriptive narratives must be central to our understanding of the "relations" that we are—not an interesting aside. The forces of affect, as well as emotional selves and psyches, have long been of interest. For instance, it is possible to track historical shifts in *emotional capitalism*. Eva Illouz follows the affective transformation of western societies that occurred after World War II, transformations she posits became attached

to economic agendas: "[W]hen we view emotions as principal characters in the story of capitalism and modernity, the conventional division
between an a-emotional public sphere and the private sphere saturated
with emotions begins to dissolve."[54] Illouz sees emotion as central to a
growing twentieth-century, middle-class, white ethos where "a culture of
emotionality" exists, where "never has the private self been so publicly
performed and harnessed to the discourses and values of the economic
and political sphere."[55] She sees this as our profoundly pervasive present.
She poses second-wave western feminism as integral to the shift from a supposed private domestic sphere to one where the centrality of therapeutic
narratives and practices reigns in our present social relations in capitalism.

Second-wave western feminisms turned the private/public articulation of western gendered power "inside out." If the nineteenth-century
gendered spaces of capitalism are spatially imagined as an outer public
male domain of laissez-faire capitalism in contrast with a private female
domestic home tucked in, a bastion of affective care, then feminism in
the late twentieth century reverses that. The "public" becomes the site
of self-care in media, on talk shows, in magazines, in self-help circles, to
examine feelings, confess personal anxiety, and discuss bodies and bodily
functions and care for the self. In a further reversal of prior relations while
capitalist consumerism is brilliantly on display everywhere, neoliberalism
keeps its workings, its actual "business/financial" dealings, in "private."[56]
James Nolan suggests that in the United States the society became more
present-oriented, living in a "ceremonial time," where "pathos" replaced
"logic" as the "dominant form of persuasion."[57]

Lauren Berlant questions "the notion and norm of political rationality
as the core practice of democracy in the United States." For Berlant the
national sphere of politics does not pose a "real or ideal scene of abstraction-
oriented deliberation," but rather "a scene for the orchestration of *public
feelings*—of the public's feelings, of feelings in public, of politics as a scene
of emotional contestation."[58] Berlant brings to the fore the present neoliberal politic, an era of deregulated but micromanaged capitalism, where
the affective mobilization of democratic citizens is routine. Berlant posits
a public conditioned by the growth of mass media where traumas, both
personal and social, are increasingly televised and narrated. This consumer
public's imagined fantasy of the "Indian" encounters the pictures and voices
of Canadian Indigenous and American Indian peoples in large numbers for
the first time in a transition, where "the centrality of liveness" takes place.
It is mass society's move "to the electronically mediated . . . affective experience of the world of events that come to consumers as though immediate

or made even more live and alive through the 'you are there' qualities of radio, television, video and film."[59] Indians appear live on the evening news, intermixed with commercials, defending abandoned prisons. Later, former American Indian Movement members appear in movies on the late channel. In Canada you can watch and vicariously feel the Mohawk defend their lands, their gravesites at Oka or Caledonia. Or you can switch the channel.

More often in the United States as in Canada, widely publicized and affective "human interest" stories such as that of Jeff Weise and the Red Lake tragedy, or the ubiquitous stories of the failure of our families all coalesce around moral crisis. Such minidramas accentuate the known felt common knowledge around racialized and sexualized minorities and Indigenous peoples, whose particular immoral marginalization often figures in stories of young debased Indian women who could not or should not parent. These women always figure in part the amoral or the abjectness of their families and societies. They are moral stories and any call for redress or reform done in their name is part of the larger power relations between Indigenous peoples and nation-states. These are nation-states who most often represent Indigenous peoples now as medicalized victims, as healing, rather than as societies who vie for political presence.

It is exactly this kind of affectively charged moral crisis couched as unspeakable "depravity" that incited Australians in 2007 to invade and instill the most regressive set of laws over Indigenous peoples in a western nation-state in close to a century. As one researcher noted, Indigenous Australians were returned to a ward status that had not been seen since the early part of the twentieth century.[60] As Will Sanders argues, it is not statistical or empirical evidence that continues to sustain the present Australia's conservative Aboriginal colonial legislation; it is ideology. In our present political moment I would argue that "ideologies" are irrational systems of thought that remain reliant on affectively mobilized "common knowledges," in this case, again around "immoral" and dangerous Indigenous sexuality. The social conditions in Northern Australian Aboriginal communities were already a site of conflicting political dreams for self-determination and state control. The state utilized crisis and "emergency" intervention as political affective work to quickly capitalize on changing political climates in Australia.

Back to the Beginning

In *Stolen Sisters* and *Maze of Injustice*, the Amnesty International reports with which I began this discussion, violence against Indigenous women continues to hold center stage to call out for the need for better policing, more jurisdiction, more funding. Often their voices are embedded within the dense networks of affectively mobilized campaign literatures for or against their communities. In part, their role is to inform, to be the face needed to "educate" a national public that is sensitized to responding to "social need" in this fashion. In Canada, and less so in the United States, human rights campaigns seek to affectively and empirically educate "publics" on what feels to them like repetitive crisis rather than the regular, ongoing outcomes of "colonial" relations. *Stolen Sisters* is a good illustration of the necessity to transform relations that are too often normalized in Indigenous women's lives as moral crisis. In the face of massive Canadian indifference to the ongoing murder and disappearance of Indigenous women, *Stolen Sisters* gathers Indigenous peoples' dehumanized murdered and disappeared mothers, aunts, sisters, and grandmothers, some of whom were sex workers, to restore their sacredness to the families who lost them. They are more than statistics. The stolen sisters and mothers are not a representation of but are constitutive to the dehumanized position that Indigenous peoples in Canada still occupy in order that *others* be the subjects of the rights they bear as the legitimate citizens of their nation-state. Indigenous peoples positioned *morally* outside those rights must appeal to human rights in order to be within a law or a polity that sees them, that promises to take their human worth into its deep concern.

The Sisters in Spirit campaign that was the impetus for AI's *Stolen Sisters* originated with the families of the disappeared and with the Native Women's Association of Canada (NWAC). Sisters in Spirit, under the auspices of the NWAC, developed internationally recognized research foregrounding violence against Canadian Indigenous women as a human rights issue. In March 2011 the Canadian government moved to deny NWAC the right to use the name *Stolen Sisters* at the same time it reduced monies that funded their unique database. The conservative Stephen Harper government cited the establishment of a new "police support center," not scheduled to open until 2013. While the government promised to increase funding to community-based projects addressing violence against Aboriginal women, and to educating their existing victims services in cultural sensitivity, the loss would be great. This is a predictable move to recolonize grassroots activism against gendered sexual violence by moving it into the folds of "legitimate" policing. While the government spoke of new funds that could be made available to NWAC, the conditions of those funds excluded their use of the name Sisters in Spirit and barred engagement in policy or research. What would be lost is an Indigenous women's campaign positioned independently that can critique the nation-state's interest and performance, not only in achieving justice for murdered women but for improving safety now and in the future. In Canada, unlike in the United States, NWAC might argue for women's central role in their nations' self-determination, but as primary advocates of women's human rights they are often seen as antithetical to their own nationalisms. Many individual Aboriginal band councils find the association's ongoing opposition to women's exclusion from band membership a threat to their sovereignty. Thus, a curtain drops, severing the relationship between the violence that destroys women and the same violence at work in the ongoing destruction of Native people's nations.

In the United States, American Indian women and their nations worked to position a similar AI report, *Maze of Injustice*, to support women's safety articulated as a self-determination issue. This is where Sarah Deer asks, "What crime, other than murder, strikes at the hearts of its citizens more deeply than rape? Sexual violence impinges on our spiritual selves, creating emotional wounds that can feed into community trauma."[61] Judged by national reaction, it is a crime greater than the methamphetamines a majority of tribal police bureaus identified as the "greatest threat" to their nations in 2006.[62] Elizabeth Kronk (Sault Ste. Marie Chippewa), a legal professor at the University of Montana, documented the rapid rise of family violence and social disintegration in the wake of meth. What both Kronk and Deer emphasize is the tribal nations' lack of jurisdiction. What both issues also have in common is that, like the violation of women's bodies and minds, the drug cartel's penetration into Native nations is a crime primarily perpetrated by non-Indians on Indians. They *are* issues of sovereignty. Sarah Deer's question resonates clearly: "What indeed strikes more fear into our hearts or permeates our nations or communities with fear?" Perhaps women's pain has more valence to elicit political response. Yet the amount of networking women did in grassroots forums, and with public and governmental agencies prior to Amnesty's intervention cannot be ignored. However, the response to fear after 9/11 usually takes the form of heightened security. The United States and Native nations responded by defining more clearly a Bureau of Indian Affairs and Federal Bureau of Investigation (and Homeland Security) policing responsibility to Indian domestic crime victims. This was coupled to hopes for a modicum of jurisdiction returned to Native nations that would include their working in a more integrated fashion with the aforementioned state–federal security policing agencies. In 2010 President Barack Obama signed into law the Tribal Law and Order Act (TLOA). As he signed this act citing violence perpetrated against American Indian women at levels three and a half times the national average, Obama characterized these assaults as "an assault on our national conscience that we can no longer ignore."[63] The TLOA has yet to be fully funded. If a funded TLOA does achieve an expansion of security measures within Native nations, it does not make it clear that any safety for women is achieved. The provisions in VAWA to strengthen American Indian nations' jurisdiction over non-Indians in an attempt to protect women has been included and bumped from several pieces of legislation moving glacially through the House and Senate. The arch need for Indigenous women as a primary victim in either Canada or the United States is a necessary conflation in law, because it is to law in both of these nation-states that Indigenous peoples are forced to go—to trust once more that law is a realm where we might stop the violence that is in fact a violence integral to this law. We imagine we must present our victim, the sacrificed victim of these nation-states' great profanity, in the hope of having order restored. We still believe that law is neutral, or that the production of the victim in law will be emancipation; we have great faith somehow that the law is redemptive, that locally or globally that law is the utopian site of redemption and restoration.

Campaigns to achieve justice or dignity, and now restitution, rely heavily on the mobilization of the peoples' affective personal and communal narrative. The struggle to revise the common knowledge of the colonial residential-school experience was such a mobilization. Indigenous women have articulated the pain and violence of colonization. But this voicing is not the final or even the most powerful of the ideas that Indigenous women have put into play in this moment. While Indigenous women open the doors to speak of the ways that men, women, and children are harmed within the relations I describe in this chapter, they are also ardent and eloquent in posing alternative Indigenous polities. Indigenous women's struggles to be interlocutors of their own experience did not happen in a vacuum, nor did their speaking to a therapeutic. In the next two chapters, "Felt Theory" and "The 'Indian Problem,'" I detail exactly how their voices, stories, languages, and concepts informed the national and international discourses on self-determination that became available to Indigenous peoples after 1960, discourses that they took part in developing. It is also an account of how those deemed profane struggle to speak, and of the strengths and weaknesses in an Indigenous adaptation of a new language, a language for action that we now call historical trauma.

THREE

Felt Theory

An ideology is made of what it does not mention; it exists because there are things which must not be spoken of.

— PIERRE MACHERY [1]

In this chapter I make a case for remembering and understanding the impact of Canadian First Nations and Métis women's first-person and experiential narratives on white, mostly male, mainstream scholarship. I argue that these narratives were political acts in themselves that in their time exploded the measured "objective" accounts of Canadian (and US) colonial histories. First Nations women in Canada changed the actual conditions for what *could be* said about the poverty and discrimination that were their daily fare. I discuss the conditions under which these women spoke at all—of sex discrimination in their lives and communities, of what it took to challenge their own families, particularly the men. It is these women's acknowledgment of their actual experiences that illuminated a space for both men and women to speak one of colonialism's nastiest "domestic" secrets. First Nation men's and women's personal testimony in the early 1990s put Canada in an international spotlight for genocidal child abuse spanning a century. Their personal testimonies shamed Canadians' simple belief in the benign nature of their child education–assimilation policies. But their stories hadn't magically appeared. They were at the heart of the struggle. Earlier First Nations and Métis women's affective personal narrative explored the racialized, gendered, and sexual nature of their colonization. In doing so, they transformed the debilitating force of an old *shame* into a powerful experience to speak from in their generation. I explore here their sixth sense about the moral affective heart of capitalism and colonialism as an analysis.

In this chapter, I build on the implications of the dense web of affective discourses, stories, and narratives of profanity and carnality that I defined previously. If in the last chapter I pose Indigenous women's centrality to those narratives, in this chapter I show how integral their voices were in reframing them, attaching them to new concepts forming within human rights and white feminist mobilizations of victims' rights for social change. While this may be so, Indigenous women did not articulate victimhood readily. Yet this "bearing witness" occurred at a moment when international rights movements solicited such personal voices. I look at the particular witness that Indigenous voice empowers and the political terms of this speaking.

By exploring the early work of Maria Campbell, Lee Maracle, Beatrice Culleton, Ruby Slipperjack, and Jeannette Armstrong, I suggest ways that Indian and Métis women participated in creating new language for communities to address the real multilayered facets of their histories and concerns by insisting on the inclusion of our lived experience, rich with emotional knowledges, of what pain and grief and hope meant or mean now in our pasts and futures. Again I underline the importance of felt experience as community knowledge, knowledge that interactively informs our positions as Indigenous scholars, particularly as Indigenous women scholars. Our felt scholarship continues to be segregated as a "feminine" experience or as polemic, or, at worst, not as knowledge at all.

I also argue that academia repeatedly produces gatekeepers to our entry into important social discourses because we seek to present our histories as affective, *felt*, intuited as well as thought. How is it that our voices, our oral traditions and our literary and historical voices, are suppressed by western knowledge that denies its own affective attachments to certain histories? What are the arguments that have been used to reduce what we say to the margins of public and academic discourse in the United States and Canada? Our voices are still positioned in a particular way, definitely reminiscent of the past silences we know so well, contingent to our present. Indigenous women have spoken and written powerfully from experiences that they have lived or have chosen to relive through the stories they choose to tell. Our voices rock the boat, and perhaps the world. Our voices are dangerous. Knowing this, we must also seek to know how our Indigenous voices are mobilized in the global meshworks that are the larger spheres that inform us and in which we take action. All of this becomes important in our ability to speak to ourselves, to inform ourselves and our generations, to counter and intervene in a constantly morphing colonial system.

Violence Is the Game and Sex Abuse Is Its Name

If abuses that Canadian priests, teachers, and caretakers committed against First Nations children remained "private" in earlier years, it was because they were part of a familiar custodial sphere figuratively and physically separated far from the so-called public domain. Residential school life and its stories were once positioned within *domestic* space—quiet, obedient, gendered, passive, and morally policed. Then, Canadian views on what constituted a "social" problem were drastically challenged by the mid-1980s. A primarily Euro-Canadian and American feminist movement successfully reordered the political significance of familial "privacy." Acts that had been nominally "private," such as wife beating, child sexual abuse, and conjugal rape, were named, politicized, and criminalized, becoming charged public issues. Still, these seemingly successful feminist campaigns in the United States and Canada did not immediately empower First Nations women, nor did they reorder their lives. Women's civil rights became an important topic in Canada, beginning with the Royal Commission on the Status of Women in 1970, where Indian women had testified on the blatantly sexist Indian Act. During the years that followed, white Canadian women's rights groups were slow to recognize the double indemnity of race and sexual discrimination—much less the necessity for solidarity with sovereignty and self-determination positions.

Indian women saw mainstream women's domestic issues politicized by this newly constituted discourse on gender and sexual abuse. Their own conditions remained buried deep in the colonial apparatus that bound colonizer and colonized. If Native women were to speak, they would need to create their own space. On their part, First Nations women in Canada often distanced themselves from white feminism, choosing strategies and language that located them within the heart of their own experiences. They ran a tightrope act between their need to organize on intimate issues and the necessity to argue for self-determination in their communities. These sovereignty movements led by Native men often mirrored dominant patriarchal values. There had been no conversation that represented a Native view of the "private sphere" or the "domestic" community conditions that were a daily part of women's and children's survival. Women's testimonies revealed an incredible chaos that had followed western interventions into Native lives. These intimate stories became empowered through an unlikely collaborator.

A range of therapeutic interventions had grown in the Indian communities during the 1970s. Alcoholics Anonymous, along with community health discussions on alcohol abuse and incest in rural areas, offered individuals new possibilities and language to narrate life experience. Many of the social and therapeutic interventions that had enabled white rape victims to politicize their experience were amenable to Native communities, who had always richly storied their experience. Personal narrative and personal testimony empowered individual experience, and "bearing witness" was a powerful tool. The growth of this emancipation narration comes into being in a complex political moment. Certainly, in the beginning it was a celebratory moment. Women and men who chose to speak their experience often revealed social distress that has been equated with individual pathology. The mainstream white society read Native stories through thick pathology narratives. Yet it is these same stories that collectively witnessed the social violence that was and is colonialism's heart. Individually or collectively, these stories were hard to "tell." They were neither emotionally easy nor communally acceptable. Women (and men) who organized against family violence and politically sanctioned sex discrimination in their communities balanced the necessity to change things with constraints to "silence" their pain and experience. To "tell" called for a reevaluation of reservation and reserve beliefs about what was appropriate to say about your own family, your community.

An intimate realignment of Indian social relationships through the Indian Act was at the core of what colonization meant in practice. The strongly gendered training in residential schools coupled with the 1876 Indian Act radically reorganized indigenous familial relations to conform to a uniform patriarchal order. Those societies that were matrilineal, or those where both mother's and father's lines had determined identity, property, and responsibility, were brought into a firm hierarchy, with Indian men positioned in a descending order of authority, and with white male Indian agents and male priests at the top. Priests often told men and women whom to marry. Old lineages were disenfranchised as Indian women and their children in interracial Indian/white marriages were banned from membership in their own communities and sometimes from their own families. Outmarriage among the men meant that their white spouses became tribal members. The Indian Act left community resources such as housing and aid to women and children in the hands of men who could marry white women and make them into instant Indians. After 1970 this provision to disenfranchise Native women for interracial marriages, as the s.12 (1) (b) marriage clause of the Indian Act, became a rallying point.

To speak about conditions for Indian women and children, Canadians began to discuss issues that were thought to be politically unspeakable.

Indian women's own activist voices were central to these discussions. Key to this articulation were grassroots organizations like the Tobique Women's Action Group, which cited changed gender relations in the bands as dangerous to their lives and any sense of community.[2] The Tobique Women's group was a dynamic band of multigenerational women from a small New Brunswick reserve; some of the women had lost Indian status by marriages to whites. They had first organized around their right to have homes in their birth communities and to regain their band status. Their initial efforts were taken to improve local living conditions for women and their children. They recognized how lopsided power relations were in their communities. Originally, they did not intend to wage a major national (and then international) campaign and win it, but they did. Despite their lack of resources (some were on welfare) and their inexperience with white Canadian local and national politics, they learned to organize. After they successfully accomplished what they had set out to do, they returned home and became involved in their communities in an attempt to live the changes. Their 1987 *Enough Is Enough* personally narrates their daily actions to rearticulate power with those men who were their own fathers, uncles, brothers, and cousins. As Sandra Lovelace Sappier recalled, "The really painful stuff was right here at home."[3]

Often during the fifteen-year effort to amend the Canadian Indian Act's blatant sexual discrimination, Indian men, both local band leaders and national political organizations, moved to thwart the women's claims. This struggle between national male political leaders' sovereignty positions and First Nations women's positions on community conditions and gender abuse continued to escalate. But in an unprecedented move, Native women had changed the tenor of these discussions. Indian women had not been allowed to vote in band elections until 1951, when the same amendments that gave them a vote made the consequences for their outmarriage much harsher. Any respite was a long time coming. The first case against sex discrimination in the Indian Act was A. G. *Canada v. Lavell* [1973] S.C.R. 282, more commonly known as Lavell-Bedard, which failed in the Supreme Court when the justices set aside race and sex discrimination issues, ruling that the Indian Act had precedence over the newly enacted Canadian Charter of Rights. The National Indian Brotherhood and the band councils took a strong stance against Indian women's rights on the grounds that it interfered with basic sovereignty issues. In doing so, whether consciously or not, Indian men reinforced colonialism's strongest defense, silence. At times the conformity between Indian and white men was overt, which Kathleen Jamieson, a Canadian legal historian, described as a "'gentlemen's agreement' . . . a powerful blanket of silence . . . temporarily imposed on discussion of the status of Indian women. It became taboo and unwise in certain circles even to mention the topic."[4]

Indian women made their issues public by waging a vigorous national and international campaign that resulted in a successful case (Lovelace) before the United Nations Human Rights Commission in 1981—embarrassing the Canadian government in the process. There, Canada was found in violation of Article 27 of the International Covenant on Civil and Political Rights. Canada promised to amend the Indian Act by mid-1981, which it then ignored for four more years. Bill C-531, the amendment that abolished the Indian Act's most deliberate sex discrimination, was not passed until 1985. C-531 has never fully alleviated the issues of band membership that the women sought. Still, in these discussions on sex discrimination, the women successfully linked community stress to the change in gender roles and responsibilities. These discussions also revealed the high rates of discrimination and until then unnamed gender violence in their communities. In doing this, they portrayed for the first time just exactly how much deeper colonization went than any standing law or even the Indian Act itself. While the white feminist movement opened Pandora's box when it successfully politicized the "private," showing it to be a wholly political space, providing discursive models for "telling," Canada and the United States resisted the truth in the emotional content of this affective knowledge: colonialism as it is *felt* by those whose experience it is. Ending the silence in the communities was a significant political action. This would not be fully appreciated until the residential-school narratives explosively shook Canada by the late 1980s and early 1990s as these same communities began to narrate the larger systemic attack that had been perpetrated on both their minds and bodies. In between were years where women developed and honed a profound literature of experience.

Bearing Witness

Preceding and joining the community voices such as the Tobique women's were individual women who published personal narratives, first as autobiography and later as fiction. What they were willing to tell and what the Canadian public was willing to hear would become a contentious issue. In 1973 Métis activist Maria Campbell published *Halfbreed*, her partly fictionalized, partly autobiographical exposure of personal and community poverty articulated to colonialism as systemic abuse.[5] She also chronicles her growth from someone who lives pain to someone who learns to act from a political consciousness, who produced a vital critical voice for the times. Describing her text, originally an unedited two-thousand-page "letter to herself," Maria Campbell's story, unlike any political or academic tome of this time, contained plain language colored by every unabashed emotion that she was able to get printed.[6] Campbell's book established a certain testimonial voice, crossing certain boundaries that had kept individual accounts "sanitary." Maria Campbell's account of Métis disenfranchisement precedes Howard Adams's 1975 text *Prison of Grass*.[7] Adams, also Métis, speaks of *internalized colonization* as shame, the pain of self-hatred from being absorbed into a racist society.[8] While history and personal story are attributes of both Adams's and Campbell's texts, and Howard Adams's personal narrative conveys his anger, in the end he chooses to remain within an academic analysis. Campbell's text *Halfbreed* uses a personalized language; it is a plainspoken narrative that appeals as a history that can be *felt* as well as intellectualized. *Halfbreed* successfully took down the barriers between the personal and the political.

Lee Maracle also risked one of these early testimonials, in the autobiographical *Indian Rebel: Struggles of a Canadian Native Woman*.[9] Like Maria Campbell, Lee Maracle detailed her emotional journey from a brutal poverty in childhood, through bouts with self-destruction, to her changed self-awareness and growing political consciousness linked to the emerging Indian movement. The original was a text narrated by Maracle under the pseudonym Bobbi Lee as an "as-told-to" monograph written and edited by two young socialists in a Vancouver activist group she worked with at the time. This narrative was not initially identified as her voice until she herself reclaimed her text later in 1990 as *Bobbi Lee: Indian Rebel*.[10] While published, *Indian Rebel* was not widely distributed, and Maracle's voice was partially silenced by the yawning voids that existed as minefields for any Native narrative. Campbell's account, widely distributed, opened a door. Janice Acoose wrote, "Maria Campbell encouraged many Indigenous people to begin writing."[11]

After *Halfbreed* and *Bobbi Lee*, Canadian Native women created fictional characters informed by their lives. Beatrice Culleton's *In Search of April Raintree* appeared in 1983, followed by Ruby Slipperjack's *Honour the Sun* (1987), and then quickly by Jeannette Armstrong's *Slash* (1988). As a tour de force, these three novels established particular powerful statements on Native experience while establishing models for an emerging First Nations literature. Literary critic and teacher Helen Hoy, writing self-reflexively on this period in *How Should I Read These?: Native Women*

Writers in Canada, admits an almost visceral reaction to Native women writers' stories.[12] Beatrice Culleton's *In Search of April Raintree* gives the first full account of the lived racialized duality of Métis experience, tracing the felt consequences through the lives of two sisters, one phenotypically Native and one who, "white" in appearance, valorizes being white.[13] It is a story of family disintegration and the state's abuse of children. In Culleton's novel, almost everyone is acting on different registers of "truth." Sister lies to sister under the illusion that her lie is an act of "protection," while at the same time the state believes and rewards only those who lie well, such as self-serving foster parents. The crux of the tragedy in this novel is the suicide of the younger sister, Cheryl, who is unable to live with the "truth" that emerges from her reconciliation with her destroyed father, a truth she is ill prepared to deal with because she believes the necessary "white" lies her sister tells. The narrator of the story, April, the elder sister, for a long time lives a lie, trying to remake herself into a person and a role that could never be her reality, that in actuality was from the beginning laden with falsehoods and self-deceptions. There is no one truth available to these sisters anywhere—in history books, from the mouths of the system's surrogates, or even within their beleaguered family. But what becomes most striking in this novel is how these many "truths" can be in play for these lives. Each sister's perception of the other's intentions is lost in the lies, silences, and misconceptions that inform and necessitate chains of equally blinded actions. April is gang-raped by three men who mistake her for Cheryl. April seeks justice, and in telling her truth, another is revealed: Cheryl's prostitution, which undermines everything April wants to believe about her sister while supporting all her own deeply misguided fears about the nature of "Indian-ness." Cheryl, "revealed," begins the slide that ends in her suicide after she meets the father whom she holds as her last illusion of a childhood that never existed. In the end, no matter what, at no time in their lives do these ill-used Métis children who become troubled women have their own truths honored. They are repeatedly punished for speaking their own truth, either directly or as a consequence of other "truths" in play that they cannot anticipate. April on the witness stand testifying to her abuse—while being judged for *her* "truthfulness"—is a profound metaphor for the conditions of Native discursive autonomy.

Culleton's April and Cheryl, as occupants of the colonial spaces "Indian" and "women," are already *known*. They inhabit an old Canadian common-sense knowledge of Indian women's immoral "nature." They are Indian woman versus the white patriarchal state, a state that first destroyed and then substituted itself for their family, which can then sit in paternal judgment of their "morals." They occupy the Canadian state's and the perpetrators' shared social knowledge/imagination of their *deviance*. Thus, the burden of "truth" on April is the same as it is on Cheryl, on Indian women, to prove they are not already guilty of being what the state believes them to be. In fact, in order to get justice in Canada or any other western state Culleton's novel illustrates another truth. Indigenous people who must tell their alternative truth go against the same state that is the protector of the civil truth that abuses them in thought and deed. We also begin to see the system, in this case, the court's attempt to produce an affective truth from these women that they themselves do not fully know. It is a complexity that they feel/know, not easily framed.

Ruby Slipperjack's story does something very different. *Honour the Sun* illustrates a child's passage into womanhood in a rural Ojibwe community using small brushstrokes of daily life, the chores and pleasures related to finding, making, and eating food; the banter of children; and the some-times alarming, violent, and gross actions of adolescents and adults, mostly men, to create a world.[14] She never directly points these actions to any "outside" or other "truth." It is a "show" rather than a "tell," because any "telling" has very different context, both for Slipperjack and for the Ojibwe community of people whose lives she stories. From about ten years of age to the age of sixteen, Owl comes to some adult awareness of what seems to be the underlying order of the place where she lives. Women attempt nurturing in this story; they attempt to take care of themselves and children, but they are often assaulted, sometimes with devastating surprise, in the middle of night by drunken men. Some adults, including women, drink and some do not, and Owl has the benefit of being with a sober woman for much of her childhood. On the edge of her own maturity, symbolized by the onset of her menstruation, her own mother begins the trek into drunkenness. Bewildered, Owl has to face the increasing sexual taunts and physical harassment of the village boys, now men, without her mother's protection. As she spends more time away at residential school, she reflects on the changes in her own life and the lives of her friends, some of whom have the village elders' patterns down even at a young age.

The great difficulty in this story for critics Helen Hoy and, later, Hart-mut Lutz is Ruby Slipperjack's "silence." They want to produce this silence into meaning. Slipperjack never "tells" us her community is in the midst of *something* someone *not them* might read as chaos. Hers is a canvas patiently painted with portrayals without explanations. You are there. You become aware of your own framing, but Slipperjack does not tell you what to think, what to feel. Helen Hoy makes a suggestion that Slipperjack's portrait has another order or pays attention to other orders that are there that outsiders cannot necessarily discern. Slipperjack speaks to the nature of her "telling" in her interview with Hartmut Lutz, who asks her directly about any "political" statement she might be making:

"Well, it says, 'this is how I feel,' 'this is what I am feeling,' 'this is what is happening around me' and 'this is how I am reacting,' 'this is how I am dealing with the situation.' That is where it stops. I cannot tell you why this and this and that happens, you figure that out yourself. Who am I to tell you something? It is there for you to see. . . . "[15]

She is not interested in how he may frame what he "sees," since it is not her concern. Slipperjack resists any framing of meaning for her personal or the community's felt relations. Her concern is that Lutz keep in mind the way a child perceives. Slipperjack works to "remind you . . . of that person you once were." She does not pose a childlike perception, but rather the perception of a person who experiences without immediate academic framing. This immediately transgresses the way western knowledge works in the necessity to isolate and define. Ruby Slipperjack shows what she knows, and what she knows is what it *feels* like to be an Ojibwe child caught in circumstances that they (her community) and she do not analyze or position to the seemingly obvious "truths" that western academics might think they readily "see."

Jeannette Armstrong's *Slash* suggests a place of mediation between women's and men's voices, speaking to the need for such a synthesis in energies.[16] Armstrong's Thomas Kelasket tells a story that has resonance with all the voices I have discussed here. Armstrong, like Maria Campbell and Lee Maracle, portrays the way poverty and racism warp and weave personal decisions. White Canadian contempt and the seeming powerlessness of elders lure Thomas into a downward spiral of drugs and jail. Thomas is like many of his generation, drawn into the Indian Movement looking for answers. It's a path known well by the mid-1980s, where experience with the American Indian Movement and the Red Power movement in Canada a decade before had informed many politically but had not nourished them spiritually. Armstrong locates spiritual nourishment, regeneration, in Kelasket's coming home to his community. Armstrong is unique in portraying that Kelasket's continuing struggle to political consciousness alone had not been enough. Kelasket had needed to *feel, not only his own pain, but his family and community's*. He needed to quell numbing rage and feel emotions that he once believed available only to women. In doing so, he might mend his fragmentation. He attends a sweat lodge, a communal act for sharing feelings and receiving emotional knowledge: "I came out of there a new person.

It was like suddenly waking up, like what those people say about being born again . . . I realized I would be able to make it then because there was something worthwhile to live for."[17] He is transformed by his experience and moves to relate. He returns home and holds ceremonies to heal his ill father: "It was me that took all hurt from him into my own body. When I held him I felt it seep into my arms. I felt it spread throughout my body and center on my chest. I found it hurt to breathe and I felt like letting go and crying in great heaving sobs like a child. But I knew I couldn't do that. I knew I had to take his hurt from him so he could get the healing he needed."[18]

In a story structured beautifully as four goings and four returns home, each returning represents another phase of learning that completes the circle of the journey that Campbell and Maracle and the others begin. Armstrong portrays a return from the personal and social disintegration that is colonialism, through knowledge and *practice* of their own culture, their family, and their people's history. Thomas Kelasket affirms his own history as a *felt knowledge that he must live in accordance with*. His felt knowledge locates his worth at home in the relations that form them as families and peoples. The struggle to feel seems paramount to the regeneration of their selves and their communities, since the meaning and worth of his journeys are deferred, or returned to the community. It is the affective experiences that these Indigenous women authors' stories pose that disturbs the white Canadian reader and critic.

Emma LaRocque, in "Here Are Our Voices—Who Will Hear?," wrote that the Canadian literary establishment had reacted in particular to any anger shown in this new Native literature—a voice that literary scholars called "polemic."[19] Native authors who wrote of their feeling of their lived experiences were branded "bitter" and "biased."[20] An incredulous Canadian public would ask, "How could all this oppression happen? How could police, priests, and teachers be so awful?"[21] LaRocque explained the more cogent element of this exchange, their anger: "Our anger, legitimate as it was and is, was exaggerated as 'militant' and used as an excuse not to hear us. There was little comprehension of an articulate anger reflecting an awakening and a call to liberation, not a psychological problem to be defused in a therapist's room."[22] LaRocque suggested that Canadians seemed unable to equate their protest to or draw any parallels with the Third World decolonization movements (Fanon et al.) or black protests that had been widely celebrated in the United States. She recalls that the Canadian market had wanted only a more "soft-sell" Native literature, and then even that seemed to get negative translation. It was all "too angry." She defends their anger, quoting Alanis Obomsawin, the noted Abenaki filmmaker: "[W]e have a lot to offer society. But we have to look at the bad stuff, and what has happened to us, and why . . . [w]e cannot do this without going through the past, and watching ourselves and analyzing ourselves, because we are carrying a pain that is 400 years old. We're carrying the pain of our fathers, our mothers, our grandfathers, our grandmothers—it's part of this land."[23] LaRocque then remarks that "[m]uch of this 400-year-old pain has been expressed in the war of words against us. And to that, we are pressed to explain, to debunk, and to dismantle. To the war of ways against us, we are moved to retrieve, redefine, and reconcile our scattered pieces. To the voices of despair among us and in us, we are challenged to dream new visions to bring hope for the future."[24]

Gloria Bird (Spokane), a poet, essayist, and coeditor of *Reinventing the Enemy's Language*, speaks in this vein again. In her introduction to *Writing the Circle*, she reflects: "As I look back to the parallels between my life and the lives of other native women writers, I notice that issues of silence (or shame, as Joy Harjo tells me) afflict us in the subterranean levels of our being . . . [p]ossibly it is most damaging that we are not allowed to express our anger."[25] She continues that "while the realities of our lives are more complicated than simply transcending pain and that pain is not the only measure of our existence, we cannot deny its impact on our experience. It is a place of beginning, as writing for catharsis is; and it is a place of ending the cycles of abuse, or any of the damaging cycles that are quickly becoming primary concerns in Indian communities."[26]

Métis/Indian/Native women were thinking and problematizing nuances of truth and telling, silence, silencing, and their lived truth practices in the 1980s in unprecedented numbers. These works denote the affectively charged experiential that became available to individuals, families, and sometimes communities but that did not always "translate" into any direct political statement. However, it is exactly this felt knowledge that fuels the real discursive shift around the histories and stories of residential schooling. One of the most important features of these stories is their existence as alternative truths, as alternate historical views. Native women told truths that challenged Canadian settler truths. Jeannette Armstrong stated this unequivocally in her essay "The Disempowerment of First North American Native Peoples and Empowerment through Their Writing," where she asserts "the telling of what really happened until *everyone* including our own peoples understands that this condition did not happen through choice."[27] The affective experience/knowledge that informed these literatures also mobilized women writing in the social sciences and history, where it is "legitimacy" that would be challenged.

In the next part of this chapter, I show how academic disciplines serve as gatekeepers that challenge alternative forms of knowing. Because the affective knowledge of our experience informs alternative productions of truth, it is challenged ferociously. History is a site where founding narratives of nations are contested and legitimated. History as a discipline became challenged by changes in theories of knowledge as well as political orders outside of any one nation as those "without history" were called to witness. Indigenous women's voices became important to founding moments of these new orders.

History and Victims

Canadian historian Scott Trevithick's 1998 "Native Residential Schooling in Canada: A Review of the Literature" reflects on but barely understands the transition that Native authors made beginning in the late 1970s.[28] The University of Toronto historian noticed, "Overnight it seems, since the early part of this decade, Native residential schools have occupied a position of . . . prominence in public and media discourse."[29] Trevithick conjectures that the residential-school historians circa 1970–80 had typically stayed focused on finding and rationalizing the government's motivation for Aboriginal residential education, one that valorized the theory that the schools had been about "assimilation through Christianization and education" rather than any lengthy and costly military subjugation.[30]

Between 1980 and 1990 the histories became punctuated with narratives written from the actual experiences of the children (now adults) who had attended the schools. He attributes this shift to recover and include their narratives to a "general growth in sensitivity towards and awareness of the deleterious effects of the schools on Natives."[31] He surmised that his discipline's scholarship had just grown better. History as a discipline had taken on a certain "eclecticism and sensitivity that reflected a creative historical methodology" that had revealed the insidious violence that residential schooling actually was.[32] Historians had become interested in more nuanced accounts of students' and parents' interventions in their experiences aided by the new attention to Indian narrative. Strangely (or perhaps not), when Trevithick shifts his analysis to Native memoir he begins to judge "temper." There was a clear "before and after" between moderately "positive accounts" and "negativity," especially in the narratives of former students. The few before were different from the many that came "after." Trevithick notes that the early Indian student memoirs were not especially critical of their experience—with the exception of Basil Johnston's *Indian School Days*, which he critiques for "sarcasm" and "latent anger."[33] He observes that the earlier accounts (pre-1980s in particular) do not testify to abuse, or they blame themselves or fellow students for it. To illustrate, Trevithick compared Louise Moine's 1975 *My Life in a Residential School* and Isabel Knockwood's 1992 *Out of the Depths*.[34] In Moine's account of a fellow student's whipping, she remarks that while the punishment was sad, the child had "deserved to be punished."[35] In contrast, Trevithick thought that Isabelle Knockwood's memoir called any corporal punishment "sheer brutality."[36]

Why this difference? He writes that "interpretations changed over time, largely *due to environmental factors* . . . Native cultures began to be revitalized, authors came to think differently about their experiences, though the experiences themselves may not have been all that dissimilar" [my emphasis].[37] Trevithick also decided to take a much more critical stand on another trend he saw, the "infiltration . . . of scholarly works by moral indignation." He began to expound at length on the rise of moral sentiment that seemed to be infecting these otherwise "ostensibly disinterested academic studies."[38] Trevithick says, "Whether morality should have a place in academic literature is a question over which there is little agreement, at least within the field of history. However, when such moral indignation results in a compromise in the professionalism of the study, it is surely regrettable."[39] What made Trevithick nervous, while he remained clueless, was his felt sense that new battle lines were being drawn in a struggle for self-definition and for "history" itself. He understood this as a struggle between agency and victimization.

In "Using the Past: History and Native American Studies," in *Studying Native America*, Richard White writes that "the response of historians to rivals is imperial. Historians recognize alternative ways of using the past in order to historicize them, domesticate them and make them part of history itself."[40] White articulates the importance in historicizing: "To describe a people as being outside history . . . is to naturalize them, to render them powerless. They are not only victims of the modern world—a world that defines itself as historical and always in the act of becoming—*but they are reduced to victims who are both incapable of understanding the narratives of their own subjugation (which are historical) and who are liable to be erased from those narratives themselves. They do not matter*" [my emphasis].[41] The world is historical, but the narratives that sustain his episteme are being challenged by emergent alternative histories. White moves to defend his history as his bastion.

White, an ethnohistorian with an intelligence and sensibility that has made him a respected force in an emerging American Indian studies, trained many current scholars in the field. As such he has had a stake in what such a field represents. Perhaps this is why White's most ardent angst was saved for writers in American Indian studies he identified as working from postcolonial or anticolonialist positions, such as M. Annette Jaimes. He presents these "postcolonialists" first in terms of their emotions as a "far more angrier and complicated attack" on Indian historiography.[42] In his critique of the developing American Indian studies literatures, he found certain kinds of "history" untenable. Although he reviews other kinds of historicizing and historiographers that are problematic to him, he responds to *anger* more intensely. While other alternative epistemological positions puzzle him or do not intellectually stand up to his rigor, these particular scholars are characterized as *angry*. They are angrier even though in his essay no one else is actually characterized as "angry." But, his problem with their emotional state aside for the moment, his larger issue is that their writing is reductive: "Postcolonial and anticolonialist scholarship praises Native American resistance, but its own concern is with atrocity and victimization. It retains the Native Americans' status as pure victim and with it the inevitable corollary: the historical status of whites as simple and malevolent aggressors."[43] Scholars in Native American studies who write thusly are *political*. White is not hesitant on this point: "Given the real horrors inflicted on Native American peoples by Europeans, Americans, and Canadians, and the political usefulness of the status of victim in late twentieth-century America, it would be surprising if a history of Native Americans as victims had failed to continue to thrive within Native American studies and Native American history."[44] Richard White, the historian, must reiterate the point that those who write the histories of subjugated peoples should not "use" the past to intervene in the *now*, because if "historical knowledge is made *simply* tactical, then the past becomes valued *only* as a tool in present struggles. The past loses its integrity. The past as past, as a different country with different concerns and rules, a place where we might actually learn something different from what we already know, vanishes. Such tactical uses of the past discredit those who use them within the academy."[45]

White does not entertain that the "past" is always already positioned as the field of our contested now. If writing "victim" has become so important politically in late twentieth-century North America that it is not surprising that such a narrative position exists (as White states above), why evoke its (the discourse of victims) seeming power and not address what the significance of the experience of *victim* had become, the import of victim, its knowledge and historical formation? Why does he elude any mention of events that often made it an international necessity to articulate such a "victim"? He moves instead to police the multiply narrated, interdisciplinary site of Native American studies. Gail Guthrie Valaskakis once called Native American studies "a topic not a methodolog[y]."[46] Scholars in American Indian studies and Indigenous studies have made identifying Indigenous methodology and theory a priority. That methodology and theory will emerge as a product of intellectual work in American Indian studies and Indigenous studies. History cannot colonize American Indian studies' political production just because it does not satisfy its methodology or its theoretical philosophy. If Native American studies, First Nations studies, or Indigenous studies stake out certain territory in academia, what makes it correct that history can colonize such a site without criticism? These academic sites were wrought in many places as sites of radical critique. Why question why such an academic endeavor with such a history produces literatures that arise from different scholars' differently located methodologies and critiques?

And if we go along with his concern for history, White argues for a cloistered history that can be separate from the consequences of knowledge. If what the discipline of history produces is knowledge, then it cannot, by the terms of its own formation, be apolitical, since knowledge is power in western societies, and power is always political. There is no history that is not contested or argued into being history, so in alluding to the substance of an argument he does not share with us, he only leaves us stranded at the edge of a tantalizing question that does have deep consequence for our times — it became a necessity for the "victims" of history to rearticulate the terms of history.[47] And how did the terms of this argumentation come about? White's real task in this essay seems to be to tell us what history is and why certain Native narratives are not it; or why certain works in Native American studies are not *it*, and even more destructively, which Native writers legitimately write *it* or not. Thus, he avoids responding, for instance, to Angela Cavender Wilson, *a historian*, who critiques historians and a "history" that ignores oral narrative as legitimate information in historical writing.[48]

It was in this spirit that White's most ardent critique became focused on M. Annette Jaimes, a radical educator and a political activist. Jaimes has written numerous critiques on the policing that has gone on in terms of the development of American Indian studies as a discipline. She has been against a model of multidisciplinarity in the field, because it does not attempt any holistic approach, with holism as a value that she attributes to an "Indian" intellectualism. That is, an American Indian studies scholar should be adept across a variety of fields to gain perspective on his or her study, with final loyalty toward Indian or indigenous knowledge models. White in this essay attempts to defrock Jaimes by associating her with the American Indian Movement. He of course also dismisses her scholarship as pure "victimology." Thus, the above criticisms that I already note are in the main aimed at Jaimes.

What exactly seems to be the trigger for White's necessity to undermine both Jaimes's scholarship and her political affiliation? Jaimes's writing that White so soundly dismisses is the introduction to a text that she edited in 1992 called *The State of Native America*.[49] That anthology contained many articles that provided analyses of colonialism in the United States from a distinct position: *indigenism*. In her introduction she states that the United States and Canada have by their long and unrelenting attacks on Indian sovereignty, health, and welfare attempted a *genocide*. It is the word *genocide* that Richard White reacts to with revulsion. It is a word that arouses in both White and most western, male, white historians a flat denial. White is picky. Perhaps some instances of history such as the decimation of the California Indians could be considered genocide, but it is in very poor form to evoke it as an American or a Canadian policy.

Genocide is a very particular word in western experience. It has immediate affective content. White immediately gives *agency* as the reason indigenes cannot claim genocide. We were always co-actors in our own history. But really, why can indigenes not claim genocide? Perhaps the concept of genocide as it developed from the murder of the European Jews was what Claude Denis called a "limit-experience," a particularly ecstatic experience for the western democracies, an experience that divides time, signals a shift in the ethos.[50] The West claims the Jewish genocide as a moment from which other moments may be counted in a paradigm shift. Before this particular mass murder, there was no imaginary for genocide, no matter how many millions of American or African inhabitants died as a result of civilizing and enslavement campaigns. There was no genocide before the German state mass-murdered Jews, and no law addressing genocide. It is for this reason that historians such as White can become rigid around the mention of genocide. The conquering of the Americas is refused as primary genocide because Europeans had no compunction about killing humans *that were not then* considered human (savages and barbarians). This particular demarcation between the "innocent" killing fields of yore and what is considered beyond western moral imagination is now centered in a very recent "past." This limit, this difference, is now forever enshrined in the World War II Jewish experience; the events revealed as a victorious western alliance pushed into what they believed to be a fellow civilized country and confronted a barbarism and savagery that deflated any lingering notions of an innate western rationality. It is the moment when the European imagination halted and failed, confronted as it was perhaps with the outcomes of its particular logics. There is *before* and *after* the Jewish Holocaust, and according to history the poor Natives lay on the wrong side of this event in western imagination. There was only one *Jewish Holocaust*, but "genocide" is a feature with massive precedent in the Americas and is a practice that continues unabated.[51]

I believe we must understand the paradigm for justice that this event defined. The great desire for justice stemming from this same limit moment is now enshrined in the form of a human rights agenda that affects how states treat "minority" populations. In addition to condemning any state's right to murder its citizens without international comment, the Jewish Holocaust established the post-WWII moral ground for relations between those with great power and those who are subject to its effects/affects, between colonizer and colonized. It doesn't matter if this human rights infrastructure is largely ineffective; it is now the only show in town. Indigenism both challenges and uses this paradigm. Indigenism presents a founding illogic in western liberal desires for justice for colonial acts.

These states (United States and Canada) that now think of themselves as the most powerful argument for human rights were each founded in the very exclusion that created the "minorities" they are charged to protect, except that the reduction and inclusion of the Indigenous to minority status does not protect Indigenous peoples; it normalizes them, bringing them back into its order to erase their larger claims. Indigenous claims always point to the nation-state's authority in colonialism and genocide. Indigenism breaks with the liberal state's analysis of who and what is a minority, because the project of "human rights" that recognizes indigenism enables a demand for more than civil rights. Indigenism makes claims for sovereignty for autochthonous peoples. Western nation-states that spent most of their formative years trying to extinguish such peoples in futile but cutthroat assimilation programs do not have an answer—only programs for catharsis, where the peoples are reduced to "victims" and nations move to heal their founding violence. Western nations founded thus are now forever impaled on the double horns of a philosophical conundrum embedded in their legitimacy, or the violence of their exclusions.

Further, indigenism must live in the halls of a paradigm where we must "bear witness" to our pasts to bring forth our new day. Thus, any founding moments of indigenism—of self-determination rather than self-management—must understand the economy of violence, catharsis, and healing in the order that forms after World War II. It is a paradigm informed within the limit experience of the Jewish Holocaust, now a universal imaginary, an "archetype" that crosses endlessly in a chiasmus of meaning between psychology and history, between the personal and the collective.[52] We live in a world where we must take for granted that "[t]rauma . . . is not only an unfortunate by-product of modernity, but a central feature of it."[53] Because we have emerged to ask for recognition as nations in this time, we along with all who go there are immersed in the universal language that this order imagines itself in. Canadian society and Indigenous nations pose a healing within the terms of trauma, but not as a static fixed position. Thus, if the terms of oppression of Indigenous peoples are historical, in part acts formed in discursive "narratives of subjugation," which I agree they are, then the question of agency and victimization will most certainly remain elusive in the conversation as White posed it. Such narratives and concepts are not being addressed for *what* they are. What are these narratives of subjugation that White evokes and does not identify?

Narratives of subjugation are discernible in the rationale for residential school TRC. The discourse around the residential schools is a conceptual site where Canada's historical narratives about "Indians" organized to be articulated into the present. It is not by chance that this argumentation about sexuality, abuse, and domestic violence emerges now, since these are a matrix of relations that defined Canadian colonialism for most of its existence. The ethical contestation forming that argument is inter-generational.[54] The intimacy of the "domestic" location that is Canadian colonization in Indian lives renders any conversation about "it" subjective and emotionally engaged. All the constructions of sexuality that narrate gendered colonial space remain charged if repositioned. This ethical contestation resonated within Native communities, informing them emotionally and physically, discursively and politically, where "what" happened and its emotional resonance cannot now be cloistered within a past that stays neatly segregated.

Witness to Genocide

First Nations, American Indian, Alaskan Native, and Indigenous women wrote powerful and empowering stories of their lives throughout the 1980s. They performed political work on national platforms and worked to establish programs at home. Native women formed their own writers groups and schools. Jeannette Armstrong, a member of the Penticton Band, a writer and activist, began working with the En'owkin Centre, a cultural arts center established by the Okanagan Nation in conjunction with their Okanagan College and the University of Victoria. As part of their mandate to produce community-based histories and curriculums, Armstrong and others working with En'owkin founded Theytus Books in 1980. Theytus was extremely influential as a venue for women and First Nations peoples' voices from the 1980s and remains the oldest First Nations–owned and operated press in Canada. Later, Armstrong worked to establish the En'owkin School of International Writing. First Nations women were ready to speak, and it was the time to do so. Many presses, such as the Women's Press of Toronto, sprang up, ones who published with alternative or feminist goals to produce marginalized women's voices. While history as a discipline remained resistant to the affective evidence their language posed, history passed into the hands of people on the street who could now produce their own. "Bearing witness," originally a term related to survivors of the Jewish Holocaust, began to pass to all of those who would seek justice in a time where people rose around the world to relate their memories and witness to crimes against them.

Canadian Indigenous women would first begin to witness to their felt colonial experience in these new forums to protest their exclusion from their own nations, then in a recognition negotiation with the state. They challenged both the Canadian state's sexist Indian Act and their nations' exclusion of women who had lost Indian status through that act. Indigenous women in Canada posed their exclusion as a human rights abuse, thus reaching out internationally. It was definitely the time to do so. Worldwide Indigenous women's voices witnessed state violence, colonial violence. Theirs was personal and political power found in finding and making relations, a "radical relationality."[55] The Tobique women who found one another, who witnessed to Canada what their exclusion meant, also witnessed to themselves what they could do to protect their children and to change what appeared to be unchangeable. When Sandra Lovelace Sappier spoke to the Human Rights Commission of Canada in 1981, she posed an even deeper conundrum for Indigenous nations about the nature of "nation." The Tobique women's voices joined a growing multitude.

Kay Schaffer and Sidonie Smith observe in *Human Rights and Narrated Lives: The Ethics of Recognition* that the "post–Cold War decade of the 1990s . . . labeled the decade of human rights . . . has also been described as the decade of life narratives."[56] Venturing further, they state, "Indeed, over the last twenty years, life narratives have become one of the most potent vehicles for advancing human rights claims."[57] They reflect on a global phenomenon of narrated lives and the ethics of global recognition in a human rights sphere. They bring to the fore the positioning of testimonial voices as primary advocates for justice and for a more humane world. Schaffer and Smith also carefully articulate "the affective, emotional and cognitive dimensions that activate or fail to activate ethical imperatives."[58] Schaffer and Smith point to the production, circulation, and reception of myriad such stories that now enter the global field of politics, the Indigenous among them. They remark, "All stories emerge in complex and uneven relationships of power."[59] Schaffer and Smith ably show the many levels of mediation that any person's story negotiates into the highly political site of its production in a human rights field, or into any public discourse. Each story or group of stories is produced depending on vast differences in context and historical timing, is "heard" or silenced: "They enter and travel through global circuits of exchange that affect the import of the stories: through official UN mechanisms for recognition and redress; through national inquiries and international tribunals; through talk-shows, news, broadcasts, the web, rights brochures, and the like; through publication channels dependent on the popularity of narratives of victimization; through personal appearances in activist or state organized venues; and through other peoples stories."[60] Stories form bridges that other people might cross, to feel their way into another experience. That is the promise of witness. These feelings, these affects, are part of their power of transformation in politically charged arenas, as "embodied pain, shame, distress, anguish, humiliation, anger, rage, fear, terror, can promote healing and solidarity . . . and provide avenues for empathy across circuits of difference."[61] If the Declaration of Human Rights in 1948 opened a door, then the UN human rights circuit is imagined and practiced as a global forum, as the audience and arbitrator of violations against such rights as they are continuously developed, with the individual imagined as the legatee. This sphere is moral and affective and traumatic. Schaffer and Smith point to links between increasing violence and diaspora after the end of the cold war and the increasing power that the emerging Holocaust literature had in framing trauma as an ethos. They point out, "Unprecedented global unrest has called forth and called for repeated acts of remembering, through which people reclaim identities at home, in transit, and in new communities and nations."[62] It is a historical moment that in addition to being a narrative turn, is a psychic turn. It engages a particular frame for telling life experiences in twenty-first-century state violence: "a psychoanalytic understanding of trauma and the healing process."[63] It is understood that the danger in such a frame disbursed at local levels is that it can foreclose on other kinds of storytelling, other tropes, other kinds of knowledge that the community can and wishes to produce. As Indigenous peoples, we are actively engaged in a political ethos that engages our remembering and telling our histories, our experiences with systems. This appears to be the bottom line in this moment where social justice is embedded in an economy of human rights where the testimony of our lived experiences becomes currency.

In retrospect, this chapter shows the conditions of "speaking," particular to those conditions that Canadian Indigenous women negotiated in making the colonial conditions of their lives known, a speaking that was finally involved in larger processes for a justice that became increasingly posited in belief in processes outside nation-states. They negotiated first in their own families, with men, often their own fathers and brothers, to regain the place to speak. They negotiated both social and political barriers to their voices, emerging powerfully, speaking and writing and founding presses, all acts that were influential in changing Canada's idea of itself. These are women who still speak from their hearts, both at home and internationally in circuits of power that presently mediate and produce the conditions for justice.

In the next chapter I explore the genealogy of trauma in Canada wherein First Nations and Indigenous peoples mobilize *historical trauma* to empower a past, to heal a present, to empower a future.

FOUR

The "Indian Problem"

Anomie and Its Discontents

What finally broke the seal on the residential school system . . . making
public the story of neglect and physical and cultural abuse, was, ironically,
the deepest secret of all—the pervasive sexual abuse of the children.

—THE REPORT OF THE ROYAL COMMISSION
ON ABORIGINAL PEOPLES [1]

In a 2008 commentary on research surrounding mental health in Indian
Country, Audra Simpson asks, in tandem with W. E. B. Du Bois, "How
does it feel to be a Problem?"[2] Her commentary astutely assesses how those
once denied any subjectivity come to the fore in a neoliberal moment
as an intense site of interest focused on their "condition." In this chapter I construct a genealogy of anomie, victimology, and trauma to show
the power and compromise in the affective discursive space First Nations
peoples appropriated to articulate the damages wrought by colonization. To
reiterate a point made earlier, trauma was not a given. They utilized other
sources of meaning that did not lend themselves necessarily to any medicalized analyses. The move to use trauma theory by First Nations women
and peoples illustrated an active mobilization for justice attached to ardent
national discourses on domestic violence and finally a burgeoning worldwide movement for the reparation of historical trauma. It is also attached to
their hope, their desire for restored relations in family, in community, and
in nation. In the beginning of this chapter, I review different western sociological views of the "Indian problem," first as anthropologically informed
sociology shifts informed by western feminist victimology activism to the
psychologically informed discourse on trauma. I then move to show how
Indigenous peoples came into and mobilized these concepts, a mobilization that empowers residential school cases into an international forum. I
end by showing how this forum becomes about health rather than justice.

"We Were Not Normal"

In June 1991 Chief Bev Sellars of the Xats'ull Cmetem' First Nations (Soda Creek Band) addressed participants at a historic First National Conference on Residential Schools in Vancouver, British Columbia. Welcoming the participants and her fellow residential-school survivors, she spoke from her heart on what their childhood experiences denied them as adults. But, as a chief and a leader, she also spoke of the opportunity to turn their tragedy around, to empower a future that only they would have the power to imagine. She knew personally what the cost had been to them: "We were not normal children at these schools, we were more like robots, always taking orders, never involved in decision-making of any kind. We were never asked what we thought or even encouraged to think for ourselves. We learned soon after arriving at the schools not to express ourselves. We got into trouble when we spoke our minds, expressed feelings, or dared to question anything."[3] Chief Sellars made the connection for the residential school conference between their common Indian "educational" experience and their larger social reality in contemporary Canada: "We have been forced to deal with the residential school issues and we now know that all the suicides, the alcoholism, the very low self-esteem of our people, the sexual abuse, the loss of our language and culture, the family breakdown, the dependency on others, the loss of pride, the loss of parental skills, and all the other social problems that have plagued our people can be traced directly back to the schools."[4]

In the survivors' testimonies, the harm they suffered had centered not only on their physical abuse, but on the manipulative management of their emotions, which made their later articulation tortured and laborious, since they had usually never verbalized them as children. They didn't always have a language for their experiences. They had been punished for speaking their own language and were ill taught in the dominant English. The schooling had made or had attempted to create automatons. Their independent thinking, critical thinking, was forbidden. Later, they coped without an ability to name or explain their complex feelings, particularly their experience with sexual assaults. Mostly, the kind of confession that this called for didn't exist in their communities' cultural practice; moreover, they didn't have the authority to speak or to be believed. The children frequently became ineffective adults or parents, because they had been removed from parenting models and could not cope with the force of their own feelings or others'. Many drank themselves to death. Twenty-one of the first men who testified to their sexual abuse subsequently committed suicide.[5] But Bev Sellars concluded that their abuse did not have to be their destiny. They could do something now. It was true that some residential-school victims had already ended their lives, and their chance to change their lives. But those who had made the choice to live could work for change. The answer was to strengthen Native family bonds and to revive the traditions. To revive the peoples would take a sustained effort, but it was their choice as Indigenous nations. The solution to their problems would have to come from within their own communities. The church and the state should be made accountable, but in the end, they, the First Nations peoples, would have to be responsible for one another and for any life they could have beyond bare existence. Sellars concluded, "It's time we started living again, and not just surviving, as so many of us did for so long," to "begin the task of rebuilding our nations."[6] Canadian Indigenous peoples might act together for once to determine for themselves another kind of future.

Situated securely in a Canadian experience educated by the Mohawk standoff at Oka in 1990, and the Royal Commission investigation that resulted, Chief Sellars could articulate their past experience to the impact their powerful testimonial evidence had had in Canada. She could link their common pain to account for the painful realities in their communities. She would make a call for action, knowing that their testimonies had hit an affective public nerve. Unfortunately, each personal revelation had cost residential survivors a great deal, some their lives. The personal and social costs to the former school residents were staggering, immeasurable.

On the other hand, Sellars recognized the imperative move it had been for them to publicly tell *then*, exactly when they did. Bev Sellars was correct. Nothing else, no other act, no other political movement so thoroughly interrogated the outcome of Canada's historical Indian policy, or its future, as well as the residential school cases had. Canada had documented it. Chief Sellars, building on the momentum of that powerful narrative moment, asked that they translate its impact into concrete actions at the community level. At the heart of this act lay their most personal and intimate relationships, ones that had often been distorted or destroyed, devalued or lost. This was what was meant by "identity crisis." In Indigenous familial kinships dense intensities of relationship exist where the individual attaches. Indigenous identity is formed and located within these larger familial (not always blood) relations.

It's necessary to step back for a minute and consider that the First Nations peoples at the point Sellars spoke had point and counterpoint relations with a Canadian national discourse on child sexual abuse. The experiences that they suffered had been increasingly politicized. Child abuse and above all sexual abuse became centered in moral debates and in an expanded Canadian state jurisdiction over the bodies of women and children, and the body of the nation. The abuse that First Nations peoples suffered was recognized *as abuse* more readily at the time they began to tell and there *was* a language for it. It was also more punishable.

But, as peoples not necessarily victims, they wanted more. While there was no absolute or universal agreement among the peoples or Native leaders on cause and effect, Bev Sellars and many others made childhood abuse directly responsible for their ongoing social and physical suffering in Canada. Canadian First Nations peoples would claim *victimhood* based on Canada's failure to manage the church schools, and on Indian policy that amounted to state terror over a span of generations. They didn't do this individually, but communally, as peoples that went against the Canadian state's usual ability to redress individual "wrongs." The Canadian First Nations first linked this demand for justice to their larger demand for a greater degree of autonomy, self-determination, and sovereignty. However, the "arenas" they entered to articulate this case for communal redress for residential school abuse were contentious and volatile because *the* power relations between those deemed powerful and those who were not could never be otherwise. Their experiences would become mobilized within an international system for mediation, between "victims" and "perpetrators." So, to ask for justice for past wrongs the First Nations Peoples would have to fully assume this *victimhood* at the same time they sought political power and autonomy, spheres that speak the very opposite languages. Thus, Aboriginal individuals and nations who joined together to pursue Canada entered a complex arena with multiple and conflicting discourses and a huge chronicle of local and international practices.

How such a framework of explanations came into practice is the subject of this chapter. The complex of pain and dissolution that Bev Sellars identifies in the communities has a history in Canada. It was not new to speak of "the Indian problem," the euphemism for Canadian colonialism's systemic violence, but the language that is now used to express it, the therapeutic language of trauma, is a recent development. This "language" that Indigenous people in Canada chose to speak their experience in has a genealogy.

Anomie

In a post–World War II environment, Canada became self-conscious about "their" racialized and marginalized subjects. The "Indian" became a subject of intensely conflicted public and private emotions in Canada: disgust, love, hate, confusion, anger—all played a part. Canadians were not solely driven by a sense of altruism when they became worried about "their Indian problem" in the 1950s and 1960s. Aboriginal peoples lived segregated and controlled under a tight colonial Indian Act bureaucracy, impoverished and suffering from a variety of social ills attributed to "anomie," commonly referred to as the "Indian Problem." The "Indian problem" became a political detriment in a world where a new emphasis on responsibility toward minority and marginalized peoples emerged. International decolonization movements inspired reinvigorated Aboriginal thought and activism. A persistent and accumulative Aboriginal resistance undermined public confidence in residential schools. Indian education became a focal point for social change, for imagining new relations between the state and Native peoples. In 1965 Alberta regional school superintendent G. K. Gooderham speculated on prospects for the task Canadians saw ahead. He spoke of educational integration as part of something larger that could neither be controlled nor staved off.

> We have every reason to be deeply concerned about the problem of integration; we have no right to fail in its solution. . . . If we are to make a prognosis about Indian education, we must endeavor to estimate what Canadians will allow. Why has there been so much more interest and concern about Indian people? It is not the latest fad, nor is it a sudden growth in or spread of altruism. World race problems have forced Canadians to examine the situation at home . . . [a]ll coloured people have spoken more emphatically, and the white race must mend its ways or prepare for trouble . . . we cannot afford to have the world look into Canada to find one group crowded into ghettos, ostracized from society, limited, in many instances, in their citizenship and legal rights.[7]

Gooderham's worry about social unrest and his nation's international reputation perhaps denotes a new human rights awareness. He doesn't include Native participation in the social change that would be necessary; it was a change that would be fueled and tempered by "what they will allow," the degree to which white Canadians like himself might imagine the relationship differently. By the 1960s white Canadian educators knew that solving their "Indian problem" would mean something more than just physically mixing Indian and white bodies in provincial schoolrooms. Canadian Aboriginal peoples were virtually segregated from other Canadians, not just by their physical location on reserves in rural areas but by a deep-seated social distancing that was neither hidden nor apologetic. Ample rationalization for this social distance could be found in texts across disciplines and in "common sense." This comfortable "knowledge" denoting the nature of the "Indian" enabled Diamond Jenness, a renowned Canadian anthropologist, to republish with modest revision his 1963 sixth edition of *The Indians of Canada*. Changed little from its 1932 edition, *The Indians of Canada* informs readers that Indians were "[h]elplessly . . . tossed at the mercy of the tide, unable to gain a secure foothold."[8] In Jenness's evaluation, Indian history was synonymous with nature, and nature had run its course for Natives, who were not inventive, socially productive, or adaptive. Their anticipated demise was always around the corner and had no human agent. The Indians had drowned. Jenness's metaphor likens Euro-Canadian civilization to a deluge, another force of nature that cannot be resisted. Canadian sociologists presented the seemingly depraved contemporary Indian condition as anomie, French sociologist Emile Durkheim's term for individual disintegration in a moral vacuum, a context of the decline in social cohesion in rapidly industrializing societies. Anomie came to pervade and structure broader social thought regarding the Indian. In educational reform texts such as Richard King's 1967 *The School at Mopass* and Henry Zentner's 1973 sociological essay "Reservation Social Structure and Anomie: A Case Study," Canadian Indians are characterized by a damaged identity characterized as anomic. Sociologist Zentner observed Canadian Indians and Indians living in the United States as "essentially similar." In his example, an anonymous "Reservation Society" manifests "characteristically high rates of child neglect, alcoholism, minor crime, truancy, illegitimacy, divorce, marital and occupational maladjustments, accidents, and other forms of dependency, when compared with ecologically similar Non-Indian communities. . . . On these as well as other grounds the society in purview exhibits an advanced state of anomie."[9] Zentner offered no definition of anomie, apparently because it was a concept with such wide acceptance. The concept stood in as shorthand for ways in which the social suffering of "Reservation Societies" made them deviant from the larger North American social norm. Aboriginal communities were "Pre-Neolithic Ethic" societies, whose cultural differences handicapped individuals' performance in modern industrial nations.

Richard King has a belief in social change, and its focus, as in other academic reform texts of its time, is on *integration*: "[i]f Indians are to acquire truly functional roles as members of Canadian society . . . [t]he artificial, arbitrary imposition of a separate legalized status to Indians must end."[10] He decides that Canadians must come to accept Natives in decision making about their own lives and the communities they live in, yet he balks at the considerable barriers to this ever happening, barriers that are social as well as legal. They remain too "different." He suggests, "Community therapy would be required." But then he admits that any easy solution at this juncture would be utopian.[11]

Anomie is a concept that allowed Canadians an analysis of Indian malady without attributing it specifically to their Indian policy, the Indians' loss of land and the destruction of traditional economies, or their residential schooling. Their anomie is a natural outcome, their racial inability or cultural inability to adapt to encroaching white society. Both King and Zentner give accounts of anomie in Indian communities that are consistent with Durkheim's anomie, "a state of social disorganization brought on by the lack of, or insufficiency of social and moral rules," or anomic suicide, "the [s]elf-destructive behavior arising from a social setting that lacks sufficient sociomoral rules to constrain actors by integrating them into the collective whole."[12] Indian societies were in chaos; integration into the dominant society would be difficult. Indians were perceived as individuals unable to go forward or back. Thus, the goal of integration into a "collective whole" (western society) in these texts confronts many seemingly insurmountable barriers. Aboriginal societies were thought to be at worst nonexistent and at best maladaptive, as they no longer produced healthy individuals. Anomie rationalized a chicken–egg conundrum.

The concept of anomie underwent a slight shift in Canada and the United States in the 1970s. While Swiss psychiatrist Wolfgang Jilek used the concept of *anomic depression* to characterize certain emotional symptoms he believed he observed among the Coast Salish in the late 1960s, he also saw worth in Salish-produced spiritual solutions.[13] In his version of anomie, Jilek used Merton's "cultural chaos or anomie" to refer to a "disassociation between culturally defined aspirations and socially structured means."[14] There was a gap between what they could aspire to and what the system would allow. This allowed for an external determinant. This assessment made sense in a new interpretive frame unclear to Jilek: the rising positioning of culture as a therapeutic tool at the same time anomie makes the shift into social science conversations on *deviance*, and criminology's on *victimhood*. Increasingly, Western medical anthropologists (such as Jilek), sociologists, and therapists framed the revitalization of Canadian Aboriginal cultures as therapeutic but not necessarily political.

Aboriginal political and social revitalization increased as Canada moved from the late 1970s to the 1980s. They joined other Indigenous peoples worldwide in defining a new political arena at the level of the United Nations, creating indigenism as a movement and a language for their increased activity. Within indigenism Aboriginal peoples in Canada saw their own cultures as holistic resources that could potentially alleviate and reverse colonial disintegration. In response to Third World colonial discourses, Indian peoples as First Nations began to steadily move this conversation into an international arena.

Harold Cardinal's 1969 response to the white paper *Unjust Society* became a best seller in Canada.[15] Harold Cardinal's text forms a triad with George Manuel and Michael Posluns's *The Fourth World: An Indian Reality* and Howard Adams's *Prison of Grass*, giving us insight into Native analysis countering the Canadian "integration" positions. National activists and male Indian leaders like Harold Cardinal produced a cogent map of future Indian initiatives that are recognizable today with only minor alteration.[16] Its major areas are familiar: aboriginal rights founded within secure land bases, Indian-directed education, and economic development. Education was inseparable from economic development in these early arguments. Everyone knew it meant more. Cardinal, himself a former residential school student and a college graduate, wrote on Indian education: "This involves a shift in power. As far as the political structure of our society will allow, the Indian people must have total control over the education of their children."[17] Cardinal proposed that in reality *integration* and *assimilation* meant the same thing—while the Indian reality was different. The realized outcomes of Indian residential schooling had been disastrous. The residential schooling system had "alienated the child from his own family; they alienated him from his own way of life without in any way preparing him for a different society."[18] This alienated person, then, had no place, "since the Indian was supposed to live in isolation from the rest of society."[19] "Alienated," the Indian could not speak, could not act, inhabiting *no place*. Here, Cardinal's analysis partially articulates *anomie*.

Adams's and Manuel and Posluns's texts appeared almost simultaneously and represent a prophetic fork in a discursive and analytical road for the First Nations. Howard Adams, a Métis scholar, studied for his PhD in the history of education at Berkeley at the height of the Third World and Black Liberation movements. He published *Prison of Grass* within a year of Manuel and Posluns's *The Fourth World*. Adams's analysis is firmly situated in a Third World socialist nationalist rhetorical argument. He calls for a liberation movement that must first be grounded in a stage of local libratory education to raise a revolutionary consciousness; that is, "liberation can take place only within a true socialist society . . . [o]nly when the native people have been politically awakened to a new socialist society will the struggle expand to a full revolutionary movement."[20] Adams's strength is that, following Fanon's insight, he does not shy away from a racial and psychological analysis of colonialism, the holding of "white ideals" at subconscious levels. He is comparative: "In all colonies, segregation induces shame for the native's degraded position."[21] The federal categories that create status, and nonstatus, and the omission of data on the Métis confuse any true picture of their conditions. There were no jobs and the lack of industrial development and employment in their own communities were for Adams obvious evidence of their colonized state. He proposed a Red nationalism but from his Métis position never fully addressed the Indian's primary issue: land rights. A prevailing opinion among treaty Indians and those who sought treaties was that secured land rights must come before any other solution to any "anomie," economic or otherwise.

A significant shift occurred when Indians, Inuit and Métis, successfully moved their conversation to the global forums on human rights in the United Nations. George Manuel and Michael Posluns's 1974 *The Fourth World* linked the grievances of Shuswap peoples to those of Maori, Aboriginal Australians, and American Indians in both hemispheres.[22] Manuel surmised there were many "Indians" in this newly connecting world. Manuel's genius was that he saw similarities in tribal people's cultural, political, and social formations. Manuel and Posluns offer indigenism as a positive cultural and intellectual tactic that opposes culture as deficit. It is an expansive vision that seeks peaceful coexistence with Canadian communities. Like Adams, Manuel was in conversation with the Third World movements. He speaks of colonialism but soundly differentiates indigenism from socialism in a demand for separate but equal institutions based on cultural nationalism: "Our celebration honors the emergence of the Fourth World: the utilization of technology and its life-enhancing potential written within the framework of the values of the peoples of the Aboriginal World . . . an integration of free communities and the free exchange of people between those communities . . . [a vision of distinct] but equal communities."[23]

It is not that Manuel disagrees so much with Cardinal and Adams on what is wrong. It is important to note that he uses the language of colonialism, as an analysis of the Aboriginal condition, but he does not propose a socialist solution. He proposes that the answer is local and global. He situates his answers within the ethical and cultural matrix that he sees as Indigenous cultures. It is a complex argument to hold and is clearly different from Cardinal's, since Manuel does not admit to cultural fragmentation or anomie but maintains that core ethics and Indian beliefs in communities would be intact enough to sustain rebuilding on, separately, with secured land and internationally recognized rights. The demand for recognition of land tenure was an unwavering Indian demand from the point of Canada's confederation on, but its evolution to a *rights*-based argument is crucial. Clearly moving on, he still positions this "future" to the remaining integration discourse in play: "Unilateral dependence can never be ended by a forced integration. *Real integration* can only be achieved through a voluntary partnership . . . the long march to the Fourth World is through home rule."[24]

The decolonization movements in Cuba and South America spoke a Marxist-inspired nationalism that inspired Black Nationalism in the United States, as well as some Métis nationalists such as Howard Adams in Canada. In practice, in the communities Indians often found Marxist analysis at odds with spiritual belief.[25] The self-determination that Canadian Native nations collectively sought and the treaty rights that US Indians fought to enforce after World War II spoke firmly to and from liberalism, a liberalism that was ironically individualistic. The axis between these two analytical positions, colonial socialist analysis and liberal "rights" analysis, had many ill-fitting narratives that have never been completely acknowledged or explored. Manuel and Posluns's *Fourth World* linked Indigenous self-determination and recognition efforts within the heart of what was liberal humanism on an international level.[26] At that moment, the new Third World nations held the power to move a number of progressive measures to assure labor and economic rights in the United Nations.[27] Perhaps the right to determination that was offered there seemed more appropriate to their circumstances. Gerald Taiaiake Alfred assesses that any complete secession or struggle as an option beyond defense was hardly viable.[28] Howard Adams posited that those who rose to leadership in the national Native organizations were moderates whose frame was the liberal politics they operated in. Will Kymlicka posits that Canada moved to incorporate more moderate voices among those who spoke for self-determination in order to quell more radical ones.[29] In any case, it was primarily a male political game from reserve to the United Nations.[30]

Anomie, Shame, and Victimhood

In 1987 Canadian criminologist Curt Griffiths and his colleagues J. Collin Yerbury and Linda Weafer assessed that the Indian was a victim of neo-colonialism. In "Canadian Natives: Victims of Socio-Structural Deprivation?," Griffiths proffered the view that Indians suffered from an intense deprivation of social status and self-esteem, that their "poverty" was in direct proportion to their lack of access to "strategic resources" (education, employment, housing, and general welfare) in an ongoing condition of virtually total dominance. Canada's Indian Act represented a paternalistic, overarching, almost medieval caste structure, bureaucratic and incapable of imagining Indian self-governance.[31] Griffiths saw reason to extend the concept of victim to Indians. They could be compared with "certain groups within society that are more prone to accidents and crime as consequences of their structural position."[32] His structural analysis puts Griffiths's and his colleagues' analysis at a theoretical crossroads then transforming the fields of criminology and law. The transition was in most ways a radical cutoff from prior ways of seeing criminals. "Victim" was a conceptual shift from anomie. Unlike earlier anomic accounts, victimology named a perpetrator, and in the above analysis of Indian victims of sociostructural deprivation, Indians were seen as victims of Canada's neocolonialism. The damage was to their selves, to their self-esteem and worth. This analysis was made possible by the deep inroads social justice advocates had made throughout the 1970s into many domains, including law.[33]

Victimology's early more conservative theorists analyzed a victim's participation in his or her own misfortune. An ardent feminist modification to victimology produced a site demanding justice for those caught up in uneven power relations, exploitation, or oppression. Victims bore witness for justice and sometimes for compensation. Radical feminist activists well into the 1980s were highly successful in extending the concept to the victims of acts that were not usually thought of as crimes, that is, incest, spousal abuse, spousal rape, and child abuse, effectively creating a new crime category, domestic abuse. These were abuses occurring in "private," at home, within marriage, the experiences of mostly women and children in domestic or custodial domains. In earlier generations domestic behaviors "behind closed doors" were thought of as sins, though not always crimes. Successful grassroots campaigns led by women resulted in new laws in both Canada and the United States that criminalized sex abuse and incest, offering the injured some hope of compensation.[34] After the 1984 Bagley Report revealed widespread child abuse across Canada, the nation revised its criminal code in 1988 to reflect the heightened awareness in both nations. With the passage of new sexual abuse codes, a deeply silenced epidemic in Indian communities became audible: incest.[35]

In 1988 Christine A. Courtois, a clinical psychologist now well known for treating the posttraumatic effects of incest/child sexual abuse and other types of complex trauma, wrote *Healing the Incest Wound*.[36] Tony Martens, Brenda Daily, and Maggie Hodgson's *The Spirit Weeps: Characteristics and Dynamics of Incest and Child Sexual Abuse with a Native Perspective* appeared in the same year, elucidating heretofore unspeakable experiences in Canadian Aboriginal communities. As leaders in the Aboriginal alcohol recovery movement, Martens, Daily, and Hodgson offered specific insight into an Aboriginal experience that was more often the subject in newly empowered Indigenous justice systems and therapeutic programs.[37] In these environments, experiences that had been unspeakable could be named as sexual abuse and be heard. Aboriginal peoples began to name their family atrocities using language connected to social justice movements. This was a language that was heavily informed by the new field of criminology studies, victimology, which I speak of above. Aboriginal victims demanded redress. From this beginning the Indigenous communities would move to redefine this language to reflect their own social values.[38] At the same time, Indigenous communities experienced an influx of self-help therapeutic groups, such as Alcoholics Anonymous. There was some difference between psychology and the self-help in peer support groups that became a common experience in Aboriginal communities at that time. One difference was the absence of a psychiatrist's formal demand to attend to a diagnosis, or a psychiatrically trained method of eliciting certain dialogues in service of a diagnosis. Valverde poses that many support groups, for instance the "consciousness-raising" groups that feminists were once famous for, were engaged in acts of *parrhesia*, a self-talk that was not confessional. Parrhesia allows for external attachment to larger social-political meanings rather than self-disclosure as narrative leading to diagnosis in a psychological truth.[39]

It is in this setting that the discourse on incest and sexual abuse became known and spoken. But the victims of sexual abuse could just as often be seen as psychological subjects implicated in the emerging idea of trauma.[40] In 1981 Courtois, along with Judith Sprei, "decided that the most accurate diagnosis for incest response was post-traumatic stress disorder (PTSD)," a move that was "controversial," considering that the PTSD diagnosis at that time was closely associated with veterans of the Vietnam War.[41] Christine Courtois situated her work as part of an emerging field built on the "unprecedented societal acknowledgment" in the 1980s of "all forms of child sexual abuse, including incest"; she attributed the change to the rise of the women's movement, and to a growing recognition of the family as a site of power and violence.[42] In agreement, psychologist Judith Herman's introduction to her work on sexual abuse survivors as trauma victims declared, "This book owes its existence to the women's liberation movement."[43] Bonnie Burstow later pointed to the critical moment this feminist intervention was in the victimology field: "With the emergence of feminist therapy, trauma became a central framework through which professional helpers view violence against women, with one consequence being a shift to trauma theory."[44]

Burstow critiques this move. Her primary concerns are that the "political is not fully integrated," and that psychiatry is not fully critiqued as an institutional technology. She notes the huge move to reform the *DSM-III*, the official diagnosis script, to include a PTSD that reflected social violence (rape, racial violence, etc.) but also saw a very proscriptive and often coercive use of psychiatry: "What we have here is a proposal that experts, not victims, name victims' experiences and that victims be talked into complying despite their reluctance. In other words, we have a coercive application of a psychiatric text and the pathologizing of clients who do not want the text to be applied to them."[45] The psychiatric diagnosis of trauma often engulfed individuals in rescripting their own accounts of themselves. The dangers in this were twofold. First, Burstow thought that the normalization inherent in the diagnosis was elitist. Second, she thought that there were inherent assumptions about the worldview held by historically victimized peoples, women, and racialized peoples: "The world is essentially benign and safe, and so general trust is appropriate, and people who have been traumatized have a less realistic picture of the world than others. . . . The first assumption smacks of elitism. For women, Blacks, natives, Arabs, and I would add, psychiatric survivors, the world is not a safe and benign place, and so mistrust is appropriate."[46] Given the history between Indigenous peoples and the settler states, no safe place had been obtainable. Mistrust *should be* a feature of appropriate mental health in Indian Country. Burstow saw how Indigenous peoples had joined with Holocaust survivors, and other survivors of state violence, to articulate trauma to their own use, but she remained critical, believing that they relied too much on psychiatric diagnosis rather than breaking with it to forge their own analyses of damages and appropriate remedy. Tufts University political scientist Robert Elias's 1986 *Politics of Victimization: Victims, Victimology, and Human Rights* argued that the time had come when victimology had outgrown its close alliance with the field of criminology into a much more expansive field, to cover victims of political oppression.[47]

Trauma, Historical Trauma, and Healing

Trauma has a huge literature genealogically related to European philosophy through Freud's melancholia. In the logic of melancholia, there is longing and irresolution in loss. The subject of melancholia is haunted and does not heal, never passes into mourning to let go of the lost object.[48] Trauma, medically, is a shock that sometimes makes affective response unavailable or unconscious to the subject; thus, trauma produces repressed memories of the experience that need to be expressed or released for there to be resolution.[49] Psychological research with and by Jewish Holocaust survivors entered publication in the 1980s, transforming ideas about memory, victims, and redress at an international level. In the United States, where trauma had been articulated originally through the study of PTSD in Vietnam War veterans, the discussion evolved from accounts concerning trauma in returning soldiers into a growing international discourse on healing nations traumatized by national civil discord and violence.[50]

Laurence Kirmeyer, Caroline Tait, and Cori Simpson portray the nationally televised events at Oka as a Canadian national trauma. Canadians saw Mohawk communities attempt to defend their traditional burial grounds when the town of Oka, Quebec, seized them to expand a golf course. After a standoff with local police, the Canadian military was brought in, in a manner reminiscent of the 1973 US standoff with the Lakota in Wounded Knee, South Dakota. In "The Mental Health of Aboriginal Peoples in Canada: Transformations of Identity and Community," Kirmeyer, Tait, and Simpson note that with Oka, "Canadians witnessed overt acts of racism and violence against Aboriginal people and had to confront a complacent self-image as a nation of tolerance."[51] They watched "the mob aggression of townspeople against women, children, and Elders from Kanawake during the Oka crisis."[52] While it may seem problematic to transfer a notion of trauma that is useful at the individual level into a concept describing an event at the level of national and international public consciousness—Canada's loss of a "complacent self-image"—from the point of view of many Aboriginal people, trauma has a logic beyond any purely psychological one that can be mobilized and adapted. For them, trauma is a logic whose time has come, and it is especially relevant to understanding the "[c]ultural trauma [that] occurs when members of a collective feel they have been subjected to a horrendous event that leaves indelible marks on their group consciousness."[53]

Trauma, and the idea of *historical trauma* as it became articulated by a wide range of Indigenous scholars, became a powerful, useful conceptual matrix in Indian Country related specifically to Indigenous experience. Lakota psychologist Maria Yellow Horse Brave Heart entered the field in 1988 with a paper, "Healing the Dysfunctional Indian Family," she coauthored with Lemyra DeBruyn and presented at the National Indian Health Board Conference. Drawing on the growing body of trauma literature produced by Holocaust scholars and survivors, *historical trauma* is a term widely disseminated by Brave Heart and used to capture the enduring nature of Indigenous injury across many generations. Nearly the first to make the link between Holocaust literatures and Indigenous experience, Brave Heart transformed the social-work field. In their groundbreaking article "The American Indian Holocaust: Healing Historical Unresolved Grief," Brave Heart and her colleague Lemyra DeBruyn spoke of "a legacy of chronic trauma and unresolved grief across generations."[54] Historical trauma stems from the genocidal conquest of the Americas attempted and achieved, an experience Brave Heart and DeBruyn compare to the Jewish Holocaust. Brave Heart and DeBruyn placed historical experiences such as boarding schools, relocations, and other more recent and contemporary state practices in this ongoing mistreatment that leaves no time for personal or community grief.

Eduardo Duran, a Jungian psychologist whose practice also includes liberation psychology, identity, and individuation studies with self-esteem work, was an early Indigenous promoter of historical wounding as an explanation. Duran also transformed his own practice, incorporating Indigenous healing and shamanic practices into his work that he grounded in Native American communities mostly in the United States. Highly respected in the healing movement, he is widely published and cited.[55] Duran is committed to the idea that community-generated healing practices are superior to western-based psychological theory. His *Transforming the Soul Wound: A Theoretical/Clinical Approach to American Indian Psychology* appeared in 1990. The 1995 *Native American Postcolonial Psychology*, coauthored with his wife, Bonnie Duran, was a best seller in Indian Country. It melds his earlier thesis on colonization and the Indigenous soul wound with trauma theory. Duran's location in liberation psychology enabled him to draw on Paulo Friere and other thinkers in Liberation theology whose spiritual and intellectual encounters with colonization in poor and oppressed and primarily Indigenous communities in the Southern Hemisphere were powerful statement and practice. In taking up a position as a liberation psychologist, Duran offers a critique of mainstream psychology, a difference that is especially important, and which I take up again in my final chapter.[56] Of Duran, Burstow observed, "Native theorists such as Duran and Duran . . . and Holocaust theorists such as Danieli point out that it is not only individuals who are traumatized. Whole communities can be traumatized. In making this claim, community theorists are not simply meaning that all people within the community are traumatized but that the community as an integral whole is traumatized."[57] Prior causal explanations such as anomie and victimization as it was initially understood depended heavily on the individual experience in chaos or violence. Danieli had shown through the Holocaust experience that whole communities could experience disjunction. Indigenous peoples, and in this case Canadian Aboriginal peoples, could quickly identify.

In 1990 one of the coauthors of *The Spirit Weeps*, Maggie Hodgson, wrote *Impact of Residential Schools and Other Root Causes of Poor Mental Health (Suicide, Family Violence, Alcohol and Drug Abuse)* for Edmonton's Nechi Institute on Alcohol and Drug Treatment.[58] The founder and executive director of the institute, an adult addictions counselor training and research center, Dr. Hodgson gave a legitimating First Nations causal frame for the forthcoming testimonies both in and out of court that emerged after Oka and the Royal Commission. Trauma became linked with the outcome of colonization in a solidified narrative for justice.

There are myriad reasons that First Nations peoples readily took up trauma as a discourse. For one, it is a powerful thesis for explaining the relations between present pain, circulating within many disparate behaviors and cycles of tragedy. It is a thesis connected to a promise for justice, since it locates blame for the historical acts of colonization to present conditions in Indigenous lives. For another, it was attached to practices of self-disclosure in the communities, allowing individuals, often for the first time, to articulate key issues in their lives and in Native communities. As Emma LaRocque in "Here Are Our Voices—Who Will Hear?" said, it was not that they had been silent; it was not that they hadn't spoken. They were not heard. But "heard" here is a complexity. Canadian mainstream "deafness" extended across many domains, in the media, in academic disciplines, such as history, and most devastatingly in their personal lives. Their statements were widely known but had no weight as any publicly accepted truth.

Tony Martens said in the introduction to the 1988 *The Spirit Weeps*, "The most universal cultural taboo about incest and child sexual abuse is not primarily that these acts do not occur; rather it is against discussing such matters."[59] The heavier proscription was on the discursive, rather than on the physical act; it was not that these acts did not "occur," but rather that they were "unspeakable." Martens' generalizing on the "universality" of the taboo on incest, sexual practices that existed as deviance, but whose experience is not spoken in this excerpt, did not immediately name the power relations between the groups involved. His Native coauthor Brenda Daily wrote, "The historical experience of Native people makes them very reluctant to reveal sexual abuse problems to outsiders."[60] This reluctance is reflected in the rationale for an educator's silence. In 1990 the director of education in the British Columbia region told the RCAP: "The sad thing is we did not know it was occurring. Students were too reticent to come forward. And it now appears that school staff likely did not know, and if they did, the morality of the day dictated that they, too, remain silent. DIAND [Department of Indian Affairs and Northern Development, now Aboriginal Affairs and Northern Development] staff have no record or recollection of reports—either verbal or written."[61]

Individuals were restrained by what could be said, what could be publicly expressed. Bev Sellars attributed their silencing to a "lack of belief": "When we did get the courage to tell our stories, people thought we were lying, or even if we were telling the truth that it must have been our fault these things happened."[62] As children and adults they had no simple access to conduits of power for "truth-telling." Their narratives were "unbelievable" because they were not then in correspondence with the narratives of white academics and bureaucrats on what their own experience *was supposed to be*; thus, their own accounts lacked legitimacy in a discursive "ring of truth" to be able to interrupt other prevailing or dominant "truth." And maybe they were unbelievable because any speech about being violated would be an emotional telling, couched in the language of shame or pain in the fragmentation of violence and memory. These and other emotive kinds of expression would never have been readily validated by academics steeped in beliefs about "objectivity." In another discursive moment their narratives would have offended prevailing public moral codes, or they might have been spun to illustrate the then-available truths on Indigenous deviance. Yet this positioning of Indigenous speech remains key, since we are always speaking and attaching to different available meanings in our lives, individually and collectively.

In the struggle to authorize trauma's discursive truth, Native voices authorize trauma, putting it into motion in their affective testimony. These Native voices become "public" only after their intensity is framed within languages authorized in social programs, ones that were designed to elicit self-examination, psychological evaluation, and testimony for legal domains on *victimization*. They become empowered by trauma's discourse at the same time they become its subjects. In the following section I look at two well-known documents of this narrative in a First Nations context: *Breaking the Silence*, the Assembly of First Nations' 1994 statement, and Rosalyn Ing's introductory use of intergenerational trauma.

Mobilizing Trauma

Breaking the Silence: An Interpretive Study of Residential School Impact and Healing as Illustrated by the Stories of First Nations Individuals was released by the Assembly of First Nations in 1994 as the crest of the residential-school abuse testimonies swept into the Canadian media from the RCAP proceedings.[63] Rosalyn Ing's decisive "The Effects of Residential Schools on Native Child-Rearing Practices," which tracks the way that residential-school survivors' institutionalization affected families, was first published in an article in the *Canadian Journal of Native Education* in 1991, and then as her dissertation "Dealing with Shame and Unresolved Trauma: Residential School and Its Impact on the 2nd and 3rd Generation Adults," in 2000.[64]

Both of these texts show exemplary uses of the trauma concepts as they were then used by national Aboriginal organizations and were understood and often interpreted in community use. *Breaking the Silence* also illustrates how Aboriginal people interpreted trauma and moved it within Indigenous discourses and logics on healing. It is also a statement of healing from fragmentation to imagine a holism to include political power.

Rosalyn Ing, a member of the Opaskwayak Cree Nation, is an influential First Nations educator. In her doctoral thesis for the University of British Columbia's Department of Educational Studies, she returned to the work she had initiated in 1991. In "Dealing with Shame and Unresolved Trauma," Ing does a qualitative research project with ten individuals, all First Nations college students or graduates, whose parents were also graduates. Her intent was to clearly show the trauma pattern among First Nations persons who could not otherwise be considered "pathological." She chose individuals "whose accomplishments include the ability to pursue and complete a university degree."[65] A college-educated Indian, she includes herself in such a category of those whom Canada had often set out as examples of success in its schooling programs.

She narrates the considerable history of Canadian assimilation programs and racialization. Significantly, she compares Indian experience with that of those who had immigrated, those who had also suffered either racialization or acceptance. Ing details who there had been an assimilation program for immigrants too, and that some had been considered "Non-Assimilable."[66] In contrast, Indians had been considered "assimilable" but in actuality were barred by race. The government had attempted to strip them of culture for entry into a society that would refuse them under any circumstances, because the *difference* that had actually mattered in the end appeared to be race, not culture.

Like *Breaking the Silence*, Ing's work claims a qualitative methodology to construct a "complex, holistic picture." The individual experiences of her research subjects could not be considered separate from the complexity of "government policies, the social conditions of the time, diseases, starvation of the affected population, the grief and loss associated with these catastrophes, the racism in society, the need for settlement of a dominant population, and legislation of the Indian Act and treaties."[67] But most of all she claimed such a method because qualitative research meticulously honors the first-person statement, the voices and interpretations of informants.

For Ing, qualitative research meant patiently working through the emotions of her interviewees and her own: "They were dignified in their anguish. I wept with them."[68] The feelings brought forward by testimony are much stronger than Rosalyn Ing's words can convey, since the affective resonance attached to their experiences is shared and visceral, belonging to survivors. First Nations researchers rejected the idea that there was any "objective" space that they could occupy and thus recorded the affective as part of the analysis. The pain of the individuals affected had been shared face to face with her and joined with her own reaction to her own pain in turn. This has been and can be the effective transfer point between the witness, the telling, and the research instrument, the telling for social change. It is a point of great density that always loses much to the abstraction of analytical language, when affect beyond language—people's eyes, sighing, tears, smiles, and grimaces—is not present.

All of the people she interviewed were either proactive or actually "activist" in healing endeavors. They established safety for themselves and their families and were active in making family and community a priority. Still, they suffered. Some of the effects that reverberated between generations were "parenting problems, need for healing, denying family," fear of speaking, and "suppressing emotion." Some of the emotions that were reported as being intergenerational were fear of reprisal, terror, pain, empathy, anger, outrage, and feeling cheated, as well as pride that they or a parent finally spoke.[69] While these individuals spoke a quiet, sturdy narrative language, they often framed their healing or the lack thereof among their families with words such as "unresolved trauma." The trauma jargon sometimes served to phrase the irresolvable anguish that might otherwise be inexpressible.[70] The schools and the assimilation projects had created difficult circumstances that took years for families to overcome, to rebuild relations and to become family. *Healing as a concept* gave these individuals and their families not only a language but an actual set of practices that could effect positive change. Thus, *trauma* and *healing* should be acknowledged as part of a language adopted, articulated, and practiced among peoples determined to act on their historical situation.

Rosalyn Ing perceived that the way these individuals came to "consciousness" was not because their residential-school experience was known in any mainstream curricula; their knowledge had not yet formed any common knowledge in Canadian society or history. The individuals had been educated by their own and other families' witnessing, perhaps reading books like those Beatrice Culleton and Ruby Slipperjack wrote, residential school reunions, literature courses, and personal search. Ing's research suggests that the rising mass of literature, autobiographies, films, caucuses, conferences, and research by First Nations peoples transformed and consolidated their own position, which enabled its widespread effectiveness as a position that Canada had to take seriously. One can see the Royal Commission on Aboriginal Peoples as a response to the increasing intensity of First Nations interlocution as well as adding to this indigenous discursive force.

Although Rosalyn Ing does not invoke it, her findings join a much larger stream of anguished witnessing on the outcomes of state violence. Yael Danieli, a member of the Group Project for Holocaust Survivors and Their Children edited *International Handbook of Multigenerational Legacies of Trauma* in 1998, with thirty-eight entries.[71] These writings include studies with the Jewish Holocaust survivors and their generations, prisoners of war, the Hiroshima bombing survivors, political torture survivors, the families of the torturers, survivors of the Turkish genocide and the Cambodian killing fields, Australian, Canadian, and American indigenous peoples, African Americans, South Africans, domestic violence survivors, and survivors of breast cancer, among others.[72]

By 1994 the emergence of unprecedented amounts of Aboriginal witness in sexual abuse trials and residential school memoirs prompted the Assembly of First Nations, an organization of First Nations government leaders, to take action. Offering an analysis of the experience that could be readily read, understood, and made available to Aboriginal citizens was the AFN's primary mission. *Breaking the Silence: An Interpretive Study of Residential School Impact and Healing as Illustrated by the Stories of First Nations Individuals* was mostly the work of two Alberta psychologists, Wilma Spearchief, a member of the Blood Nation, and Louise Million.[73] The AFN research team drew from a growing literature written by Aboriginals, including Rosilyn Ing's "The Effects of Residential Schools on Native Child-Rearing Practices," and texts authorized by the community, as in the case of Celia Haig-Brown's 1988 *Resistance and Renewal: Surviving the Indian Residential School.*[74]

Breaking the Silence made explicit that the story of residential schooling was a story of Aboriginal peoples, and that their own interpretive frame would be the frame from which they would tell the story: "Truth is built and rebuilt over time through the stories we tell, individually and together in community, about our experience of a particular event such as residential schools."[75] The researchers describe their presentation as tribal, quoting Paula Gunn Allen: "Traditional tribal narratives possess a circular structure, incorporating event within event, piling meaning upon meaning, until the accretion results in a story."[76]

Thus, the report begins with the history of assimilation, segregation, and integration. This is followed by the testimony of individuals, introduced as wounded, who tell their childhood stories of being lost, lonely, and silenced, and of trying to find ways to cope. Million and Spearchief presented these testimonies as finely layered, enhanced with details describing the emotional, mental, physical, and spiritual dimensions of the survivors' experiences. It is only after these individuals speak that the researchers introduce trauma in its own chapter. The definitions of trauma cite two studies: Christine Courtois's one on incest (1988) and Judith Herman's *Trauma and Recovery* (1992), both mentioned earlier as seminal texts in the radical feminist incursions into victimology that defined domestic abuse. Million and Spearchief link particular parts of Aboriginal testimonies to trauma but are careful to say that not every residential-school student became traumatized.

Breaking the Silence is also a detailed plan for a movement to heal fragmentation in a spectrum that goes from individual to nations, and through a trajectory that echoes the familiar sequence of trauma, repression, and resolution. However, the report calls for an Aboriginal sense of healing that is communal and defined locally. There can be no discrete "individual" per se, although respect for persons and differences is high on the list of social conditions integral to healing. Thus, *Breaking the Silence* recommends that "healing" be the careful rebuilding of Indigenous psyches, families, and communities, all of which are distinct but interdependent. Safety, respect, and responsibility rely on cooperation among individuals to create safety, to actively respect oneself and others, and to embrace cooperative responsibility. That cooperative responsibility in turn depends on a respect for actual differences, as there is no one "right" way to attain healing. In this way there will be reconciliation rather than argument between those who believe in Western therapeutic methods for healing and those who practice Indigenous spiritualities (or for those who mix the two, for that matter). Cooperation is urged between the abuse survivors and those individuals and families in the communities who feel positive about their residential schooling. The sphere of cooperation is also to be extended to allies, individuals, and agencies, churches, and non-Indian communities that support their efforts at healing.[77] According to *Breaking the Silence*, individuals come to consciousness about their pain, their past, or their residential-school experience in no linear way, but in fits and starts. Parts of the individual criteria for healing in this text echo familiar texts for substance abuse therapy, that is, "hitting bottom," "taking one step at a time." Other witnesses speak with the trauma concepts as they are widely understood now—the triggering of traumatic memory and the working through of released emotions and anger. If the working through is done correctly, as *Breaking the Silence* suggests, a deeper level of self-examination becomes possible, and the reframing of experiences has the potential to radically change one's worldview. Learning one's own people's history is included as a key step in resolving trauma for individuals, a step that involves coming to understand the position one's people occupied in the larger context of an abusive nation-state.

Breaking the Silence thus suggests a model for healing in Aboriginal communities that is holistic, meaning that it has to represent the whole community and necessarily goes beyond the individual. Healing cannot omit the larger community of Canada—which is called on to take responsibility for its own actions. The editors point out that part of assuring safety, a first criterion for healing, is out of the hands of Aboriginals themselves, since Aboriginal peoples may never be assured safety from Canada's economic and social interventions. *Breaking the Silence* is remarkable in the scope of its vision as it utilizes the logic of trauma as well as trauma as a diagnosis. It participates in a now extremely familiar discursive economy that other Indigenous peoples have made specific to their enduring oppression. What was empowering this move? Probably lots of factors, but one is important here. It welds Indigenous social dystopia to a discourse on health.

Healing in a New Global Economy

Trauma, or its diagnosis as posttraumatic stress disorder (PTSD), became the preferred international humanitarian analysis that underpinned rights struggles and sites of contestation wherein the most disadvantaged peoples on earth negotiated their ability to resurge, to reconstitute, and to prosper, to develop on their own terms. These hopes became posed as rights to health in a human rights ethos. As Joshua Breslau argues "the expansion of PTSD into the global arena has been possible because of the fit between this diagnosis and the agendas existing within global institutions. . . . PTSD expands the discourse of humanitarian crises by providing a means for discussion and comparison of psychological dimensions of suffering that carry the full legitimacy of scientific knowledge."[78] He goes on to explain trauma's present power as an explanation: "The discourse of trauma in the international arena deals fundamentally with the legitimacy of suffering on the global stage . . . it is deeply political in every case; the diagnosis of PTSD connects not only individual biographies with psychiatric symptoms, but whole societies with powerful narratives of cultural advancement, political legitimacy, and social justice."[79] Breslau posits trauma as a preferred language wherein international human rights humanitarian campaigns and the international community in the form of individual nation-states negotiate and weigh the collateral damages of development, war, mass relocations, and the outcomes of increasing disparities in income. It also reflects a prior shift from sovereign Keynesian welfare state politics to the move to neoliberal economies where the state must negotiate with the larger economy of a world "community" with humanitarian values that may have the power to intervene or to shame state action. So, after a long half century, trauma is established as the ubiquitous explanation and site for action, capable of making sense of the multiple social, psychological, and material outcomes of colonialism. It witnesses many astounding transformations in the western legal positioning of victims, while it valorizes and brings from the heart of colonization one particular experience that is identified and analyzed as the crime that most enables restitution.

The shift to this language of trauma and this analysis of harm occurred readily as Western nation-states through entities such as the World Bank urged austerity on poor nations and unbridled development in the rise of neoliberalism. There is a rising concern for the health of "developing" peoples at the level of the international community. This conversation reflects both the tensions of increased global development and the activity of burgeoning humanitarian movements to counteract neoliberal effects in western nations too—losses of key safety nets such as health benefits and losses in social welfare programs. Health becomes articulated as a basic human right. Byron J. Good includes a growing concern for mental health in his analysis of a 1995 World Mental Health report. Good points out that stresses on humans undergoing "development" were increasing globally but reminds us that the effects were already known: "such processes are of course not new, nor are they limited to so called developing countries. Forced relocation and resettlement was an explicit policy of the American government in dealing with the aboriginal peoples of North America . . . the enormously high rates of depression, suicide, alcohol addiction, demoralisation, and ill health which continue today on many American Indian reservations in the US and Canada is a stark reminder that we know all too well how severe are the mental health effects . . . and that these effects are likely to persist for many generations."[80] From this, it isn't posed that development stop in these already decimated nations or globally. Development must become humane; it should include goals for health and development.

Generally, Canada and the United States joined the world community in conceptualizing health as a much broader set of social determinants that included development. The UN World Health Organization (WHO) began a global campaign. Canada responded in 1986 with a joint agency report on a new, expansive conceptualization of health. Canada's proposal built directly on the *Declaration of Primary Health Care at Alma-Ata, the World Health Organization's Targets for Health for All* document. The declaration put into place expanded parameters for the meaning of health, to include conditions in which health could flourish: peace, shelter, education, food, income, a stable ecosystem, sustainable resources, and social justice and equity. Canada saw the heart of this as a "process of empowerment of com-munities—their ownership of their own endeavors and destinies"; thus, "community development draws on existing human and material resources *in the community* to enhance self-help and social support, and to develop flexible systems for strengthening public participation in and direction of health matters" [my emphasis].[81]

As Canada moved to adopt more neoliberal governance, this was expressed in terms of devolving responsibilities for health and welfare ser-vices and programs upon regional governments and communities. This was not accompanied by an increase in funding for the many new health or welfare initiatives that communities undertook in the name of the healing. Funding remained stagnant or declined.[82] What did increase overall was the number of self-help, psychology-based health interventions in com-munities, accompanied by an increased number of healing technologies, techniques, and processes that became institutionalized in Canada's larger health politic. The medicalization of personal and community issues per-ceived as social and economic issues in prior generations warrants a deeper conversation that I begin to undertake here. Politically, there was the "long term" plan that originated in the wake of Oka and the original RCAP recommendations for Canada's new relationship with Aboriginal peoples that was reflected in the blueprint document *Gathering Strength: Canada's Aboriginal Action Plan* 1997.[83] I return here to the observation I make in the introduction, that Canada buried the RCAP recommendations save one: the RCAP recommendation to establish institutions and programs in the name of *healing*.

This chapter ends asking that we consider this moment when the "domestic" sphere becomes public. The shift in domestic violence law that accompanies the rise of victimology and psychological trauma also signals the movement from one order to another. It is a shift wherein the "private" domestic space of colonization also becomes the public space of trauma, where it painfully subscribes subjects for healing. This is also the moment where a powerful backlash arises to movements to empower the disenfranchised. In the next chapter I explore a plethora of "psy" techniques and New Age spiritualities that enter Indian Country practiced within disciplines of multiple self-help and psychological counseling programs as they become a healing industry in Canada and the United States. These programs entwine languages that are terms for development, personal development, and often spiritual healing. This activity may be seen as a site of triumphant action, where under Canada's thirty-year commitment to dismantling its welfare state and its embrace of neoliberal economics, Native peoples through their own report have made many inroads toward "healing," making significant gains in social well-being and education within self-determined goals. It is also a place where we might ask: what kind of nation is an Indigenous nation?

FIVE

Therapeutic Nations

*On January 7, 1998, Canada announced the creation of a 350-million
dollar Healing Fund designed to support communities in redressing
the tragic effects of the residential school system on generations of First
Nations peoples.*

—KATERIE AKIWENZIE-DAMM
AND CHERYL SUTHERLAND [1]

The Aboriginal Healing Foundation, headed by a Native who's who in
health, social work, and recovery, acknowledged their work as an extension
of grassroots work in communities. They had built on the back of work
that had been ongoing for over a decade. Charged with bringing the multiple healing needs of Aboriginal communities in line with government
mandates for awards (only physical and sexual abuse to be addressed) and
"best practices," they did an award-winning balancing act in a difficult situation.[2] Phil Lane Jr., an author of *Mapping the Healing Journey*, a survey of
best practices in the communities authorized by the foundation, posed the
challenges Indigenous peoples initially faced. Becoming sober and overcoming numbing behaviors were only first steps: "Since the early 1980s
. . . Aboriginal communities have been struggling with the challenge of
healing . . . it gradually became clear that alcohol and drug abuse was only
the 'tip' of a very large and complex 'iceberg,' the bulk of which remained
hidden beneath the surface of community life."[3] This widespread need had
been met head-on in the establishment of a network of therapeutic options:
"Aboriginal healing programs sprang up across the country addressing such
issues as addictions, sexual abuse, parenting, family violence, depression,
suicide, anger and rage and eventually the residential school syndrome."[4]
Phil Lane Jr. and Four Worlds had been in the field from the beginning.

Phil Lane Jr. represents the concept for community healing and reintegration with the symbol of a sacred circle in the Four Worlds literatures
that he and his colleagues Michael and Judie Bopp produced over many

years for the sobriety and wellness movements sweeping across Aboriginal Canada. These are plans for action. Their roots are both deep in Indigenous spirituality and in practical considerations of what it would take to heal peoples and nations.

In this chapter I explore the experience of communities that undertook the healing programs as they were presented in human development literatures. In a discussion of the quintessential experience of Alkali Lake, I discuss how human potential psy technique melded with human development philosophies to inform a vision for healing as nation building. I use the discussion I build here to contrast a related discussion I move to in the following chapter, a discussion about nation building that women had on the actual performance of Indigenous self-determination in Canada. A larger question that informs these chapters is how trauma as an overarching diagnosis related to questions of actually performed self-determination.

Healing and Development

Phil Lane Jr. and Four Worlds Development Project figure centrally in putting details to what *Breaking the Silence* can only outline. In a series of in-depth analyses that they undertook as a study for the Assembly of First Nations, called *Community Healing and Aboriginal Social Security Reform*, Four Worlds looked at what health and social security would mean in an Indigenous setting in Canada, "to re-conceptualize what social security actually means" in order to "promote and 'secure' a way of life that produces 'whole health,' broadly defined as human well-being and prosperity. Such a concept goes far beyond more money and program-based solutions."[5] It takes seriously and ups the ante on promises that Canada made in plans such as the Ottawa Charter for Health Promotion.[6] Lane and his colleagues Michael and Judie Bopp, drawing on their intensive participation with communities, leave almost no stone unturned, and almost no detail without comment. Canada, like the United Sates, provides for those who cannot provide for themselves. However, there have been differences. In a 1993 comparative study of social safety nets, labor researchers Rebecca Blank and Maria Hanratty observed that "Canada has a tradition of universal nonmeans-tested programs that is almost entirely absent in the United States. In addition, Canada's means-tested programs maintain broader eligibility and more generous benefit payments than those of the United States." Besides the above difference, as many have observed, Canada has universal health care.[7] Lane Jr. et al. warned that the present system could not serve

Aboriginal needs for real social security or safety. A storm was coming, in the form of economic reforms that they warned would undercut most government funding in the near future. The most feasible plan would be to embark on Indigenous plans for development; thus, funds for community healing would not be dependent on unreliable government fund transfers.[8]

Their sense of health is as expansive as their detailed plans for each aspect of healing both person and community. It would be exceedingly cynical to say that there is nothing in their plan that is not appropriate to the moment it was written in, in a moment that they themselves state well, in a moment when it would seem that they needed to define development before it defined them. Yet it bears many marks of a human development schematic, a conversation on human capital, ways that individuals' and communities' well-being might be thought in tandem with the more brutal aspects of capitalism in a new neoliberal moment.[9] Human development projects measure effects of development and chide corporations and world organizations on their human costs. Throughout the 1990s sexual abuse in residential schools became a prominent causal explanation for social fragmentation among Indigenous communities. Canada responded by settling a class action suit, establishing a formal international truth and reconciliation process. Here I begin to argue that this focus on alcohol, sexual abuse, and PTSD becomes informed by human development knowledges and technologies. Further, though, I propose that the Indigenous peoples of Canada's immediate concerns around personal and social damage attributed to the residential schools articulated something much larger that cannot be represented through healing as it is posed in therapeutic narratives. Indigenous concern with their social and personal damage points first to the power relations between Canadian and Aboriginal nationalisms, where indeed economic development is at the core. The destruction of their traditional land-based economies impoverished Indigenous peoples to levels not "acceptable" in First World countries, but their health was a non-issue up until a certain time. Development in Indigenous Canada has mostly been a voracious race to extract raw materials out of the land, poisoning water and making life in their homelands virtually impossible for many communities.

Thus, the abject conditions the peoples labor under to reproduce their lives reduced to one therapeutic causal frame has certainly been suspect among Indigenous scholars before.[10] Healing from trauma begins to be narrated as a prerequisite to self-determination. If the Indigenous don't heal, they may not be able to self-govern; in any case, they would need to heal to be self-sufficient. Self-determination became packaged in a deal wherein the Indigenous would heal from the past, the past dissolution of colonization while developing. This healing would occur while capitalist development might still displace one or require one's land—a little like accepting being bandaged by your armed assailant while he is still ransacking your house. While this might be a crude analogy, it puts some of the key terms out quickly. In the community accounts of healing Lane Jr. reports in the late 1990s, the significant analyses in play had become trauma, PTSD, or historical trauma. These diagnoses had also been joined to myriad other psychological designations. The concept of historical trauma as it emerged from Yael Danieli's Jewish Holocaust literatures or Maria Yellow Horse Brave Heart's specific account of Indigenous genocide, or their conceptual medical precursor PTSD as defined in war veteran's accounts, appears as effective explanatory cluster for the underlying social fragmentation and violence plaguing contemporary Indigenous communities. Healing becomes authorized in a "psychic turn," an increased use of psychotherapeutic languages and practices/treatment for sexual abuse, incest, and other sexual dysfunctions that emerge in startling numbers in mainstream western societies in the late 1980s, just as they did in the Aboriginal communities Phil Lane Jr. refers to above.

The Miracle at Alkali Lake: Healing as Transformation

The transformation of Alkali Lake in the 1980s is a keystone story, a story told widely in Indigenous recovery literatures. It was also reenacted by the community itself in *For the Honour of All: The Story of Alkali Lake*, a film made by esteemed First Nations filmmaker Phil Lucas and released in 1985.[11] In brief, Phyllis Chelsea became sober after her daughter Ivy refused to go home with her drinking parents. After a short time Phyllis's husband, Andy, joined her in sobriety, and they held out as a core group that eventually transformed the community. It is estimated that Alkali Lake went from a 100 percent alcoholism rate to what is now around 85 percent of the community achieving and keeping sobriety.[12] Even now, so many years later, it is moving to see the Alkali Lake community reenacting its own pain and rebirth in Lucas's film. The participants share their process by dramatizing the highlights as they saw them: the Chelseas' decision to get sober, the community picking Andy Chelsea as its chief, the Chelseas' lonely struggle to rid the community of alcohol: banning bootleggers (including relatives) and other measures some might see as draconian. The couple took control of social welfare payments and gave vouchers instead of cash to drinkers, vouchers that could be used for food and necessities but not for alcohol. There was the hard work of practicing sobriety, as others slowly made their decision to join them. There is the showdown with the local priest, an alcoholic who tried to rally factions of the community to oppose the sobriety movement. After the Chelsea family and their allies successfully challenged the authority of the Catholic church in their community, they also looked to other communities to bring Indigenous spiritual and cultural practices back in their midst. They borrowed practices from other non-Shuswap Native peoples to give Alkali Lake an enriched and substantive experience to replace drinking. They also were open to many lessons, self-transformation and self-organizing knowledges that they gained from a variety of human potential programs the community utilized, such as the California-based LifeSpring, which at one time a majority of Alkali Lake people attended. They shared the knowledge they had gained in their struggle. *For the Honour of All* is a training film made for this purpose. Through it, Alkali Lake had an enduring affective witness to Indigenous communities across North America.

But, as Phil Lane Jr. and others have pointed out, their real story is ongoing.[13] It has ups and downs and stalls. Hard victories won in one generation didn't keep subsequent generations entirely sober or drug-free. Thus, it is in the end an ongoing intergenerational struggle to define and redefine and practice what is "wellness." The storying of experiences in the community was an important part of their process. Narrating the story of their community was one of the myriad healing or community transformation techniques that Alkali Lake used. Lane Jr. explains:

> All story telling must be grounded in some intention. Stories are not merely a recitation of past events. In the recent marriage of participatory action research with community development practice, facilitating the telling of the "community's story" has emerged as a methodology for community analysis, visioning, planning, and evaluation. The community story process is essentially a method for systematizing what a community knows about itself concerning the past, the present and the desired or anticipated future. It is also a powerful builder of consensus and solidarity.[14]

Alkali Lake's storytelling figures as a communal technique wherein the community envisions itself. Involved early on in facilitating this and other First Nations communal storying, Four Worlds was first the Four Worlds Development Project, founded and coordinated by Phil Lane Jr. (Yankton Dakota/Chickasaw), an associate professor for sixteen years at the University of Lethbridge. John O'Neil, a professor and the director of the Northern

Health Research Unit at the time he wrote, called Four Worlds a National Native Alcohol Drug Abuse Program (NNADA) project, one of the "three most significant Aboriginal health initiatives in the country."[15] Others named are the Nechi Institute, headed by Maggie Hodgson, a coauthor of *The Spirit Weeps*, and the Alkali Lake Prohibition Strategy. Together, they had brought programs to Indigenous Canada that enabled the peoples to widely speak to the conditions in their lives. Phil Lane Jr., much visible in this account of Alkali Lake, had been part of the community healing movements from early in the 1980s. Those movements and Phil Lane Jr. figure in the historically dense configuration that is behind Alkali Lake's recovery, which I return to momentarily. I reflect on the complex show of human development and human potential technologies present in the story of Alkali Lake's transformation. Indian Country in Canada and the United States learned much about the processes called community healing from Alkali Lake, and also from another classic story, the Community Holistic Circle Healing (CHCH) program for incest and sexual abuse at Hollow Water, Manitoba, an Anishinabe (Ojibwe) First Nation. Each is a story wherein a new array of "best practices" was painstakingly eked out as the communities built and improvised on techniques for overcoming distrust, lack of communication, and family violence. Hollow Lake's holistic Circle Healing refers to circles of support for sobriety and self-responsibility that offered sex abusers restoration with the community rather than jail, after extensive self-work. The purpose was to reconcile perpetrator and victim and community, rather than incarcerate such a person, losing him or her to the Canadian jails already filled with Aboriginal men and women. It also established the community as an authority that could know when such a reconciliation was possible.[16]

In the beginning Alkali Lake served as the model. Alkali Lake and Hollow Water later developed ties through New Directions, a training program originating in Alkali Lake that Hollow Water took up and practiced. Thus, they forged lessons about lateral learning, ways that the "best practices" of communities could be shared with other communities and then be developed by those communities for their own unique experience. Alkali Lake and Hollow Water feature prominently in Four Directions International Institute's own story, first as the Four Worlds Development Project, and then as Four Directions International, an independent corporation that Lane Jr. founded in 1994. They figure heavily as its early success stories, ones that served as models as they went on to develop programs internationally. Its corporate résumé page describes its mission: "Four Directions International is dedicated to the development of sustainable economic enterprises that support wholistic educational, social, cultural, environmental, spiritual, and political development."[17] It lists activities in the Ukraine, Canada, Zambia, the United States, the Caribbean, and Central and South America. I highlight here how capacity building and nation building are linked to global and international development fields and as such represent the expansive relations that very local Indigenous communities now make in a globalized world through human development ideas and practice. I also want to begin to make a case for how the ideas and practices that Four Directions developed over the years have in part become institutionalized in Canada's reconciliation movement, even while Canada ignores the key tenets that Lane Jr. et al. make in their proposal for a radical, humane Fourth World development.

As I have shown, the narratives of community healing shifted in the mid-1990s to address trauma specifically. Sousan Abadian's research on trauma and community development after the miracle at Alkali Lake appears significant here. In 1999 Abadian, a doctoral student in Harvard's Political Economy and Government program, finished her 475-page thesis testing the theory of "unresolved trauma" as a variable in the success or failure of Indigenous development. That thesis, "From Wasteland to Homeland: Trauma and the Renewal of Indigenous Peoples and Their Communities," is a detailed microanalysis of the historical conditions that precipitated individual and communal trauma (displacement, residential schooling, and substance abuse) joined to community development theory and sophisticated economic analysis. She states her interest in testing the idea of "culture as treatment," which had emerged as a primary tenet of healing.[18] She also makes clear that she is not as interested in the "political" as in building an argument for "personal sovereignty."[19] But, aside from her "political" disavowal, it is a powerful economic analysis of the cost of trauma to human potential and economic development. Still, what remains erased by her disavowal of politics is her failure to specifically address what economic system she normatively assumes; her analysis assumes a liberal or classical liberal, or even a neoliberal, economic. This has ramifications for what she identifies as "culture as treatment." Abadian's scholarship gained credence in Aboriginal communities because it had been respectful and impeccable in following Indigenous research protocol within those communities, and thus her thesis and its analysis were (and still are) a valued and respected part of the planning process in Canadian First Nations healing programs. Her work also had credence and connection to a wider community of economists working on nation building in the United States.

Abadian's work was guided by her fifteen-year experience with Harvard sociologist Stephen Cornell and his collaborator, the economist Joseph P. Kalt, both initiators of precedent-setting research into American Indian national economic development.[20] Cofounders in 1987 of the Harvard Project on American Indian Development, Cornell and Kalt and their colleague Manley Begay have developed a sophisticated array of advisory tools on leadership and institution building in support of American Indian self-determination. The Harvard Project aims to "understand and foster the conditions under which sustained, self-determined social and economic development is achieved among American Indian nations."[21] Stephen Cornell introduced Abadian to Indian Country.

Sousan Abadian, an immigrant to the United States, grew up in the midst of conversations about global development. Abadian came from a Zoroastrian Iranian family that fled to India carrying memories of a people and a place dispersed. Her father, once a senior economist for the World Bank, gave her encouragement on her thesis project, as did many others. Abadian's husband, Ronald Heifetz, a lecturer on public policy at Harvard, founded the Center for Public Leadership at the John F. Kennedy School of Government. In Canada she affiliated with Phil Lane Jr. and the Four Worlds Centre for Development Learning, where she was "Community Healing Specialist."[22]

Her doctoral thesis based on Alkali Lake and other Canadian First Nations and US American Indian communities drew detailed correlations between the systemic destabilization of (mostly American Indian) Indigenous economies (ways of life) and the disintegration of their societies. It is this disintegration (anomie) at the most *intimate* levels that blocks the ability of First Nations to carry out self-determination in terms of constructing and maintaining meaningful institutions. The psychic pain carried and reproduced through generations is named "unresolved trauma" and is implicated in any future ability of First Nations to sustain "the benefits of economic and political development."[23] The bottom line would be whether individuals could achieve at a personal level sufficient psychic integrity (healing, identity) to sustain relations at other concentric levels of organization, that is, families, communities, or self-determining governing bodies, that is, "nations."

> [A] lack of productive resolution of individual and collective forms of trauma negatively affect social cohesion and cultural integrity in Native communities, distort institutions and the incentives to adhere to healthful ones, contribute significantly to the dearth of productive social capital, and generally, may be associated with a diminished capacity to govern effectively and utilize available economic opportunities; all of which in turn, aggravate and are associated with the substandard conditions in many Native communities today.[24]

Abadian thought that many Canadian and American Indian societies had come apart at the level of basic social relation, where sexual abuse among other abuses had produced individuals who lacked the capacity to trust or to make the kinds of relationships that formed coherent family relations, community, or meaningful self-determination. Unresolved, such trauma threatened a "diminished capacity to govern effectively." The link between individual dissolution and an inability to produce or maintain stable community and governance is profound. She reiterated recently "the most extreme types of collective trauma are sociocultural: It's not just an aggregation of individual traumas, but disruption of the fundamental institutions of society, and of its 'immune system' that can restore people and repair a culture."[25]

Abadian chronicles the rich mixture of Twelve-Step self-help therapies (Alcoholics Anonymous and, later, Al-Anon and Al-CoD [Alcoholics Co-Dependency]) that were made available to the Indigenous communities from the late 1960s on to treat alcoholism first. As individuals and communities became sober, deeper underlying issues regarding widespread sexual abuse and community members as sexual abusers arose. The influx of practices that have been characterized as human potential techniques in Indian communities provided forums and language to speak and proffered therapeutic practices to heal or transform behaviors. Phil Lane Jr. wrote of these healing techniques and belief systems, all joined under the rubric of healing, explicating their worth in motivating personal and social movement: "The human potential movement provided another sub-stream in the healing process . . . its origins in gestalt therapy, holistic health, eastern yoga, meditation and cultural development strategies, and in the performing arts (theatre, music, and dance applied to healing). From this sub-stream came a strong focus on health and wellness rather than sickness. The health promotion/determinants of health approach is now recognized by dominant culture health professionals as a legitimate strategy . . . [and] departure from the 'medical model' has much in common with Aboriginal community healing concepts and practices."[26] Alternative human potential therapies had more resonance with the community than did medical psychotherapy. Psychotherapy and psychiatry were associated with illness and individual dysfunctions. The human potential therapies stressed relations that were closer to Indigenous ideals for community relationality. For instance, Alkali Lake in the 1970s, at the height of its sobriety movement, had much success with a Canadian version of LifeSpring that utilized the precepts of Werner Erhard's Seminar Trainings (EST). Erhard believed that mass social change starts with the individual. Erhard's seminars had been wildly popular with adherents such as Cher and Yoko Ono. Erhard's teachings urged self-responsibility. LifeSpring was founded by John Hanley, who had worked with him. Abadian quotes from Furniss's observations:

> the [LifeSpring] training sessions utilized group therapy and confrontation techniques, and promoted the existentialist values of personal responsibility and positive thinking. Emphasis was placed on exploring and discussing the adequacy of certain behaviour patterns, and on overcoming emotional "blocks" that inhibited realization of one's goals and effective communication among family and friends. The individuals from Alkali Lake who participated in LifeSpring training . . . generally stated that through these trainings they learned how to communicate openly their thoughts and feelings to others, and how to listen to and care for others; in terms of personal growth the participants claimed to have emerged from the training with an increased sense of self-confidence and a more positive outlook on life.[27]

LifeSpring was dissolved in the early 1980s after lawsuits (one successful) accusing it of brainwashing and cultlike behaviors. But it was not widely seen in such a way. Alkali Lake formed its own training seminars, called New Directions, collaborating with LifeSpring personnel and adapting the seminars to a more specific Aboriginal practice. LifeSpring had not been free or cheap. It was four hundred dollars a head, and at one time Alkali Lake had sent most of its community to it. New Directions seminars, always free to community members, became (at least for a while) a source of income for the reserve, as Alkali Lake developed trainers and held training sessions for other communities.[28]

Another practice that the community participated in was Re-evaluation Co-Counseling, both a therapeutic technique for discharging negative emotion and a movement for personal and social reintegration. Re-evaluation Co-Counseling is "a process whereby people of all ages and of all backgrounds can learn how to exchange effective help with each other to free themselves from the effects of past distress experiences."[29] Barbara Helen-Hill identified co-counseling's healing from "internalized oppression" as one of many helpful therapies in her personal healing journey, narrated in *Shaking the Rattle: Healing the Trauma of Colonization*.[30] She also discusses William Glasser's reality therapy. Hill, who had herself become a counselor at the time she writes, wisely and succinctly surmises that all the "complex information on healing techniques boils down to a simple idea—healing emotional pain."[31]

Abadian, who studied the Alkali Lake community in the 1990s, had also participated in a number of alternative healing philosophies in a quest to understand personal and social transformation. She names some of these as: "East Indian yogic and tantric traditions (e.g., meditative traditions and Margo Anand's work at the Skydancing Institute), healing methods rooted in Jewish mystical Kabbalist traditions (e.g., Jason Shulman's Society of Souls and work done at Elat Chayyim), Roger Woolger's work on regression therapy, and Barbara Carpenter's (Network of Light) eclectic healing methods drawn from many nontraditional as well as traditional psychotherapeutic forms of healing."[32] While in Indian Country, Abadian had participated in sweat lodge and Sun Dance ceremonies.

Sousan Abadian's thesis draws heavily on the literatures produced in the sobriety movement to characterize "toxic" interpersonal relationships in Indian Country, such as codependency. Codependency is a concept widely circulated through the sobriety movement literatures, made available through texts by Melody Beattie and Pia Mellody, and even more widely popularized in the work of Anne Wilson Schaef.[33] Basically, codependence characterizes a cluster of behaviors in which showing excessive care for others without regard for one's own well-being is unhealthy "codependence." The codependent is emotionally addicted to external authority, letting someone else have inordinate power over his or her own life, or is addicted to "helping," taking care of others' needs in total blindness to personal cost. Codependent individuals have an "inner child" that must be developed into a more mature adult response. Thus, in addition to finding one's own pain, identifying it, and emoting it, a person on the road to healing would need to define healthy personal boundaries from others' needs.

This idea had some coherence in Indian Country, where caretakers had violated children's and adults' bodies and minds quite regularly. However, codependence broadly described here also had critics. In Indian Country, where interpersonal responsibility and dependence among extended families was common, this theory implied that reciprocal responsibilities were not always "healthy." For instance, if you chose to support your drinking siblings or parents by giving money, buying groceries, or letting them reside in your home, your behavior might be defined as "codependent." The concept was never established clinically. It never made the *DSM-IV-TR*, the *Diagnostic and Statistical Manual of Mental Disorders*. One critic, John Steadman Rice, a sociologist, observed in *A Disease of One's Own* that the concept "can be seen as part of a wider cultural shift from the ethic of self-denial to the ethic of self-actualization . . . a [shift to] a 'focus on' self."[34]

This practice in Al-Anon seems incompatible with AA, a shift from a surrender to a higher power, a defining characteristic of AA. Conventionally, though, AA is inherently social. Alcoholics need one another to stay sober. But, aside from AA, many of the techniques for healing in Indian Country were focused on such a "personal" healing or transformation. Rice asked, "How does co-dependency respond to the conditions to which these terms are used?"[35] He posed that codependency reflected a cultural shift from an individual concerned with society and social justice to one that takes "the self as the primary reference point."[36] He suggests that such a sea change completely redraws moral priorities. However, Rice also posits that Al-Anon draws its precepts from liberation psychotherapy but then offers no convincing account of liberation psychotherapy. All in all, the therapies involved are powerfully posed for individual development, to make the individual keenly aware of her or his own need.

Healing Culture

Sousan Abadian, as Phil Lane Jr. and others before her (even Cornell and Kalt in relationship to "nation building") profess, finds that such a personal healing would be meaningless without a "healing" of larger relations. I think it is important at this juncture to ask what Abadian means by "culture." What is the culture that she proposes as "culture as treatment" for the condition of trauma she complexly analyzes in Indian Country? Abadian draws on "culture as treatment" as a thesis present among Aboriginal peoples. There was a constant belief among surviving nations that their Indigenous cultures contained important prescriptions for living well, knowledges that were never totally extinguished by any colonial practice.

As a "participant observer" in Indigenous ceremony in Indian Country, Abadian notes how syncretic Indian spiritual ceremonial is across the communities, that is, how much ceremonialists had borrowed and incorporated from one another, even from Christian and other spiritual practices. She saw this as a very adaptive course of action in the reservations and reserves she visited. Cultural revitalization was a good thing, a protective against trauma, and perhaps even further trauma—as a "guard against the more rapacious and divisive forms of capitalist economic development."[37] She sees adaptive culture as a good defense.

On the other hand, what she sees as maladaptive is very telling. She posits a connection between "place" and spirituality among Indigenous peoples. Abadian understands that the land was imbued with sacredness by the Indigenous, a reverence that cultures might restore, which she posits would be individually and communally healing. Earlier in her thesis she holds that the split between economy and society is artificial, and that it is known that economic prosperity has a sociocultural basis. But that is as far as she can take it. This is best illustrated in her analysis of the Makah whaling revitalization. In Abadian's estimation, the Makah are practicing culture "inconsistent with basic realities" by seeking to revive the whale hunt in their present lives. It is maladaptive. Here, Sousan Abadian is an economist who doesn't recognize or acknowledge an economy. There is a profound connection between Indian peoples and their "food" in any place that hasn't been totally stripped. In most Indigenous communities, hunting or the gathering of plants was thought of in terms of an extended relationship that denoted responsibility—reciprocal responsibility, the necessity to take, but also the responsibility to maintain conditions in which everything else, be it fish or root, thrived too. This was the ideal and it is within such relationships that societies made law, disciplining individual action as part of their social organization, their governing.

The Makah were once part of relations on the west coast of North America (from the panhandle of Alaska to northern California) whose way of life and governing was "potlatching." Potlatching denoted in practice an integrated economy governed through great ceremonials where people both delegated responsibility and use of "resources" and distributed these responsibilities and the food and material items that resulted. The daily practices on the land, with the waters, with sea life, with one another—not just the ceremonies—were "culture." The ceremonies in Indian Country were originally given, inspired within those places and daily communion with spirits (land, animals, plants) with which the people had a close and necessary interdependency. Thus, the buffalo once central to the Lakota/Dakota ceremonial was "food" and "kin," that through its philosophy taught the *tiospaye* (the Lakota's primary kinship relationship), a set of relations informing all right acting in the world. What are the responsibilities to our relations, when we must eat our kin to live? It is only when the land becomes stripped through its development or its loss that the meaning of this sacred connection is lost to the people. If the connection between the people and "the land" as the site of the sacred is severed, then that connection is altered. Still, what people have done in the face of such primary loss is always instructive. The Lakota reaffirm their connection, even in the face of the nineteenth-century mass extinction of the buffalo, their primary sustenance. They and the buffalo were part of an interactive relationship informed and informing the ceremonial given to them by White Buffalo Calf Woman that sustained them from time immemorial. They remain true to these relations by remaining steadfast on their land. They have consistently refused to sell the Black Hills to this day. The Black Hills are basic to their idea of their "selves," their relations in that place, their relations in the "universe," and to their self-organization as societies, their "governance."

So Abadian separates expressions of deeper relations—that is, ceremonies, dancing songs and stories, or praying in certain ways—from the actual "economic" relations in a particular place, thus missing a primary point about what she seeks to prove. The "universal" religions of the book—Roman Catholicism, for instance—are mobile because they do not derive their spiritual authority from a relationship to any place on earth. These great patriarchal religions may have sacred places, and memorials to significant spiritual events, but these do not contain instructions on how to inhabit those places in relationship. The meaning of *Indigenous* as it is defined by all those cultures who identify themselves as such has always been in their relationship to a "land," that place they were in relationship to without anthropocentric bias, relationships that disciplined action and cohered Indigenous persons and societies. George Manuel, whose vision of development informed early articulations of indigenism, thought that any better lives for themselves could not be bought at the expense of their larger relations in any place.

Sousan Abadian concludes that the Makah need to adjust to new times. She only mentions the treaty of Neah Bay, the actual contract that the Makah entered into in 1855, renowned for its specific language about whaling in the context of a negative example of internal dissension in the Makah community discussion.[38] In this way she completely dismisses the chance to articulate what Indigenous economy actually does as social organization, as spiritual coherence. She goes on to read the Makah's attempts at exercising their treaty rights and their efforts to revive whaling as "blind cultural restoration," literally bolding her emphasis: *Ultimately, cultural elements can not survive into the future if they are inconsistent with basic realities*" [bolded in original].[39] What are these basic realities? Is it that the Makah's desire to put their living culture in relationship again with the whale does not agree with Abadian's personal conservation beliefs, beliefs that have cultural assumptions of their own? Or is it that she thinks, as a development professional, that the Makah should not exercise the treaty rights that define their spiritual, social, and political presence to the nation-state? Or, more to my point here, is it that culture is good as individual/community therapeutic practice but unimaginable as relational practices that inform governments, ways of living in places?

Like Lane and the Bopps, Souson Abadian is seeking to make her historical trauma analyses basic to development practices internationally. She is currently working on a book about American Indian communities and trauma, comparing them to other "postcolonial" societies. Her ideas are currently in circulation in development areas such as conflict resolution, where she argues that trauma is often the unseen condition that prevents reconciliation in global areas of fierce conflict—where she suggests Palestine and Israel are such a case.[40] What goes unanalyzed in Abadian's application of the trauma thesis are her own cultural assumptions about development. Further, even while western development in the forms that it is being proposed to the Indigenous proposes a good life in "healed individuals, communities and self-determination and/or 'reconciliation,'" the vision it contains may never support a sense of Indigenous culture. Culture in the sense I speak of it here is not the past but a living, enduring vision for a polity, one whose values could inform an Indigenous self-determination. It is Abadian's conclusion that "culture as treatment" is a good ingredient "in reconstituting the sociocultural and strengthening the spiritual," but in the end, any healing that occurred to move them forward would take place in "the 'dirty' work of individual psychological trauma recovery."[41]

There is another example that provokes much thought around a concept of "healing" in the sense I think Abadian uses it. The Innu Nation, as it presently calls itself, started with "self-determination." As part of the last intact, that is, holistic, hunting culture in North America to end its nomadic relationship with the caribou, the Innu settled into "village" life in the 1960s in approximately thirteen settlements. After Canada annexed their land in 1949 without Innu consent, the Innu came under intense pressure from church and state to settle down. The Labrador communities of Sheshatshiu and Utshimassits became the Innu Nation in 1990, with Quebec Innu settlements separated politically.[42] Canada did not extend the Indian Act, so Labrador, with few funds and a standard colonial bureaucracy, became responsible. It moved the people who finally settled in Davis Inlet (Utshimassits) twice. In Davis Inlet, the people were provided shacks with no running water, on land that couldn't drain—thus, without sanitation facilities. Worse, this Iluikoyak Island location cut them off from their hunting grounds most of the year, forcing many into welfare dependency. They were being encouraged to cut their ties to Nitassinan, their land. In the thirty-five years they lived there, they came apart. Sheshatshiu, located on the Labrador mainland, suffered similar conditions.[43] Their own description of this collapse is shared on the Tshikapisk Foundation website, an Innu project promoting cultural vitality: "The result was not the complete adoption of European mores envisaged by the social planners but rapid descent into a chaotic society in which all the underpinnings of social order had been removed."[44]

This history and dissolution has been the basis of intense academic and human rights interest over the years, as much a key framing story for trauma as Alkali Lake is. The healing is more complex here and hard to tell a story from. For one, it is difficult not to focus on the depth of the pain they exposed to the mass media in 2000, when Canada and the United States reverberated with the emotional knowledge of their children's mass suicide attempts.[45] Yet there is an accompanying story that shows their strength and resolve even as their worsening conditions become part of a diagnosis of anomie, trauma, and chaos. It still involves healing, perhaps in the sense of an adaptation to their new reality. In 1977, within ten years of their coming in from their life on Nitassinan, they moved to file a land claim. Following the Calder decision on Aboriginal land rights, the Innu organized themselves into the Naskapi Montagnais Innu Association in 1976 "to protect their rights, lands, and way of life against industrialization and other outside forces."[46] They went over a cliff of bureaucratic neglect, into a crevasse outside the Indian Act and reserve system. Yet between 1984 and 1998 they undertook a steady stream of highly articulate stands against state hegemony.

A partial list here cannot do justice to their effort: a campaign against the militarization of Nitassinan by NATO air force and bombing test runs, protests against hunting regulations on their land, a Freedom for Nitassinan walk across four provinces, a logging road occupation, and the removal of electricity meters to protest a hydroelectric dam. In 1992 Davis Inlet chief Katie Rich evicted the RCMP and a racist provincial court for a year and a half, before the province's threat to pull out of land negotiations ended the protest. In 1994 and 1995 they traveled to Geneva to protest their conditions to the UN Human Rights Commission and protested the Voisey Bay nickel mine . . . and on and on. Their Statement of Claim to Nitassinan was not accepted by Canada until 1990, and meanwhile their pain overflowed. The deaths by fire and by alcohol that finally spilled into the media in 2000 finally got Canada's attention.

In June 2001 Canada announced the Labrador Innu Comprehensive Healing Strategy, a five-year plan "initiated by Health Canada, Indian and Northern Affairs Canada, and Solicitor General to stabilize health, create safe communities and help the Innu build a better future."[47] It was comprehensive, since it included moving the people of Davis Inlet to a new community, Natuashish. In addition it committed Canada to a massive human development program to move both communities, Natuashish and Sheshatshiu, under the Indian Act so both could be governed under the band council system. This entailed building and developing western-style institutions (management systems) in both communities and instilling programs to treat their "trauma." The Nechi Institute was called on to train Innu in counseling. The original plan of 2001 was extended through 2010 for Indian and Northern Affairs Canada (INAC) and Health Canada. At that point their completed land settlement and First Nations funding kicked in. There had been diverse alliances made along the way—one with the archaeologists who had helped substantiate their long land tenure, who proudly announced their victory.

> Finally in 2008, after several hundred years of marginalization and almost fifty years of unsolicited industrial development in the Nitassinan, the Innu finally came to a land claim agreement, appropriately titled The Tshash Petapen (or "New Dawn"). . . . This claim was ratified by the Innu Nation on July 1, 2011, and was seen both as a major victory for all Innu inhabiting Labrador and as a message of hope by those residing in Quebec. Not only does it promise substantial financial restitution for the damage done to the native territory (in the form of 100 million dollars given over the following four years, three percent of the profits generated by the hydroelectric station, and training and business opportunities), it also gives land title to 5,000 square miles, hunting rights on an additional 22,000 square miles and the ability of the Innu to develop resources of their own accord within that territory as they decide."[48]

These arrangements appear stunningly advantageous, since they propose that while Nitassinan is too rich with resources to leave to Innu, they too can share in the capitalist development that was never in question. The Canadian Labrador Innu Comprehensive Healing Strategy undertook to transform the Innu on many levels, with healing as adaptation to "basic realities," in economics, in capitalism. Along the way many rallied to help; thus, it is a premier human rights advocacy story too. Are they better? Only they can say. As Sousan Abadian tells us, it is a long, long road. Here is a story of self-determination, destruction, and hope for a new kind of "self-determination," where the Indigenous can heal from their holism into the holism of capitalism.

A striking element of the Innu experience that partially separates it from other human development trauma narratives is its rapidity. These events unfold over a fifty-year period; thus, it is hard to evoke the long-span colonial story, or the residential-school narrative. Here three generations of Innu affected by the destruction of their "culture" are alive together and suffering. It's a straight-up story of the stripping of a way of life that once spiritually, emotionally, morally, socially, and economically organized a people. It's the story of their institutionalization.[49] It's also still the story of a people attempting to find anything as meaningful as what they lost.

Alkali Lake and the Hollow Water Community Holistic Circle Healing remain classic and often cited in many analyses of achievement in the areas of Aboriginal healing, in reintegration from fragmentation. They are a built-in feature of the Aboriginal Healing Foundation literature. Still, Alkali Lake went through a community conversation on the conflicts that arose from its status as a primary example of healing. Native communities remain poor and often still marginalized from any meaningful economic activities. For instance, Alkali Lake, the Esketemc First Nation, has been sober and with a strong will toward self-determination for twenty-five years. That community more than anyone has provided the experience that has come to be known as "the four seasons" of community healing.[50] *Breaking the Silence* established that a primary tenet of their healing would be largely out their hands. This was the safety of ever knowing what Canada as a nation-state would perpetrate on them in the form of unilateral economic and social interventions or neglect. Alkali Lake reported on the "glass ceiling" that loomed for them: "You can't really heal the people unless you can create security related to food, clothing and shelter. Unless we can address our *real economic development challenges*, complete healing remains out of reach."[51] Thirty years or more into its "healing," Canada had not been forthcoming with the substantial political empowerment or financial capability that would allow Alkali Lake to build on its hard-won stability. It wasn't that Alkali Lake was incapable of exploring new ideas; Alkali Lake citizens are a model for transforming themselves. It was that the changes affecting them were occurring on only one side of the relationship. Basically, the individual and communal healing of the people of Alkali Lake remained estranged from economic healing—for that, they would have to find their own economic development, the funds to develop. One was not the necessary outcome of the other.

Taking the Innu Nation as an example, it is understood that economic development is also not the final answer, either. The need to sustain ways of life that even minimally give a reason to live must negotiate finally with capital, with what can sustain them. Thus, "culture" is posed as "treatment" in human development literatures, and posed in Sousan Abadian's work as best when it is "adaptive" and "realistic" for a realistic adaptation to Canada's neoliberal development.

What happens, in this adaptation, to an Indigenous desire for autonomous self-determination? Is this vision confined to therapeutic governing, in nations that are positioned to help Natives adapt, to make a transition while the development goes on? What would it really take to materialize an ardent desire for self-determination into governance that could actually serve the peoples?

In an earlier moment, in the Indian activism of the '60s and '70s, healing had also been linked to cultural revitalization and political revitalization, one integral to the other. The destruction of Indigenous peoples' relationships to ways of life on their lands and their meaning, coupled with the emotional numbing that was part of their affective destruction in residential schooling, led to widespread dissolution just as surely as it had for the Innu. That disconnection had made it necessary to find practices to heal the affective voiding, the numbness that was their felt colonization. Alcohol was addressed as a symptom, but their true illness was thought to be their own rage turned against themselves and others in their attempt to break from the deep nothingness or inability to process feelings that many residential school survivors reported. In Canadian and US Indigenous contexts, healing from colonization, or decolonization, did mean looking to traditions, their own and others. There was a spiritual conversion, an experience that Jeannette Armstrong's Thomas Kelasket describes in chapter 3, that changed everything, because it transformed his worldview and his picture of himself and his family and community. But Thomas's and his peers' spiritual awakening was produced in relation to an assessment of their political options as well. There were relations between resurgences of Native spiritual practice and interests in self-determination. I make this connection not because I believe that spiritual practices were driving the political resurgence, but to say that increased political activities intertwine with soul searching for what is uniquely Indigenous peoples' strengths informed by cultural knowledges that do inform action. There was a reciprocal play between these activities. To practice a spiritually infused life with integrity implied that you would practice what you believed. At that time Indigenous peoples found profound attachment and meaning in their ways of life on the land and in a much larger sense of polity, just as their ancestors had. Practicing an Indigenous spirituality arose from the relations in a way of life, not separately.

But there was no direct link, and there was often a disconnect, between those who practiced these land-based Indigenous spiritualities and those who went to Ottawa or to Washington, DC, to argue for rights.[52] Still, there was a value forged in that resurgent moment, that self-determining peoples would honor themselves and act from their own histories and knowledges, a value that resonated profoundly. It is still the value. Activists fighting for political rights would first state the principles that informed their actions.

Thus, in 1988 Sharon Venne, an Anishinabe attorney, legal historian, and activist would first evoke the cultural and spiritual relations that Indigenous peoples have with land before she analyzed Canadian treaties and policies. She writes, quoting George Manuel: "The land is our Mother Earth. The animals who grow on that land are our spiritual brothers. We are part of that Creation that Mother Earth brought forth."[53] Were Indigenous "cultural" resurgences seen as practices of "health" in words that were not dependent on the therapeutic languages now so ubiquitous in our lives? It had been Indigenous women who first insisted on articulating holistic concerns, ones that necessarily included personal and familial concerns with economic well-being. A holistic sense of well-being as a goal embedded in community relations may have been politic and caring, but it was not therapeutic. It may have been politic to the larger sense of well-being in the community for families with more to aid families or individuals who were in need or incapacitated. For instance, in coastal First Nations, leaders were expected to aid those in need. Higher-caste individuals became noble by helping others in their extended families or through their extended clan relations that encompassed the community. Yet there was no sense of "pathology," that those in need were a specific "caste," one associated with a specific illness, much less one stemming from a western diagnosis of trauma." Women were integral to these Indigenous lifeways, from the beginning challenging any new articulation of indigenism that did not recognize the relationship between Earth and women and the well-being of any generation. Annette Jaimes expressed that "in a literal sense *indigenism* means to be born of a place, but for Native peoples, it also means to live in relationship with the place where one is born."[54] It is to live in kinship with all life. This first position was an inspiring moment that seemed bright with possibility. Between 1977, when the first Haudenosaunee walked into the United Nations headquarters in Geneva to argue for their continuing existence as nations, to this day, women play an important role in both articulating Indigenous nations and offering critiques of those same nationalisms. Women understood and stated unequivocally that nation as extended family entailed putting a focus on primary relations as politic and necessary.

In the next chapter, I pose what is at stake in omitting Indigenous women's vision when practicing self-determining autonomy, as opposed to a state-determination, as Roger Maaka and Augie Fleras so recently defined the possibilities.[55] This returns us to an earlier moment in Canadian history, and to what "women's rights" contestations meant to any notion of "nation." It also poses the question: why does it matter what *kind* of government we have?

SIX

What Will Our Nation Be?

Speaking for the sake of the land and the people means speaking for the inextricable relationship and interconnection between them.

—SIMON ORTIZ[1]

In the United States, Pat Bellanger, an Ojibwe from Minnesota, stated her community's interest: "To us, it is impossible to separate the fate of our children from the fate of our families—they are the same. We needed to come together as families. The women define the family and the family is the base of our culture and our culture, our families are under attack at every level, in every way."[2] Indigenous women imbued this concept of relations writ large with the sense of integral and reciprocal responsibility that their sense of "family" entailed, a sense that put them at odds with the rising white second-wave feminist movement's radical critique of women's subjugation in family. White feminists initially argued for abortion rights, and only later for "the right to choose" educated by the very different positions of Women of All Red Nations (WARN) and other women of color.[3] Indigenous women located "the fate of their children" at the center of their activism, because their struggle for their right to bear and raise their children was central to any future they had as peoples or nations. These positions were actually different sides of a similar issue. Radical western feminists argued for rights over their own bodies, which they saw usurped in national laws that forbid their decision to bear life or not. Obviously, for Indigenous women, it was the actual elimination of a decision, violating their bodies by sterilizing them without their informed consent. Then, even if they managed to have children, the state often took them, as it had for generations, either to schools or, at the time WARN wrote, to foster homes and adoption in white families. Either way the white male state sought control over women's reproductive powers.

In this chapter I track what healing means in two contexts, the one that I established in the last chapter as a language for the healing of nations steeped in community/personal development, and here in the language of women who argued for a radically different notion of nation. I do this because both of these discourses are a vision for community, for the heart and meaning of nation, not necessarily the nations called into being by a human-rights will to self-determination, but as the indigenous nations they already understood themselves to be. Women, the "heart of nations," as opposed to women as the abject heart of the dissolution of nations, come into focus in this chapter. I then shift to exploring how healing, community, and government is a conversation that Indigenous women have had and continue to have about what makes life generative, an expanded sense of potential for a people central to any vision of Indigenous nation.

As Our Bodies, Our Nations?

US national interests in population control in Third World countries tied to ideas of development supported Indian women's coercive sterilization in Indian Health Service facilities, a eugenics strategy aimed at poor women of color, a practice coupled with an alarming and escalating rate of out-adoption of Canadian and American Indian children to white families. While these out-adoptions also paralleled an unprecedented white adoption of Asian children where wars for democracy-development had raged, in particular the children of Korea (and, later, Vietnam), the loss of those children did not threaten Korea's ongoing existence in the same way.[4] "Without Our Children, There Can Be No Tribe," an Indian Child Welfare campaign slogan, symbolized the actuality of child loss to the American Indian nations. Yet these complex global connections to social engineering among "developing" peoples were related to their own lives and didn't go unnoticed. The focal points for Indigenous women's activism early on comprehended their oppression in ways that were immediately global as well as local. The penetration of global capitalism into the most essential areas of their lives as Indigenous women was historical and present, and their analyses took this into account. This "penetration" Andrea Smith, a member of WARN, equated with rape, as both a primary metaphor and an embodied practice. Smith articulates the relationship between a US-led global imperialism raping Mother Earth and Indigenous women in the same breath as part of the same violent militaristic patriarchal principles at work personally and globally.[5] WARN early on made the connections between sex, violence, and colonization.

Women of All Red Nations was an early and highly effective coalition of women activists from many fronts. A national conference of Native women in the Pacific Northwest organized by WARN in 1979 drew over 1,200 women. Listed as contacts were Katsi Cook, a Mohawk traditional midwife; Lorelei Means, Madonna Thunderhawk, and Vikki Howard from Education for Survival; Phyllis Young, working to research and present sterilization issues; Janet McCloud, a renowned fishing rights activist; and Pat Bellanger, a legal advocate for families. They gathered "to re-assess the direction, to formulate goals, to share methods, resources and skills."[6] They began to more finely tune their grassroots work in their communities, offering felt definitions of Indigenous governance and economy. They began to define and work for "women's issues" that they understood and posed as central to their actual survival as peoples. They located sexuality and reproduction as primary sites of their subjugation, which meant taking control of their bodies back from nation-state "health" interests, and their children from state welfare agencies. They sought education for themselves and their children and families that reflected accurate accounts of their history and contributions, and they fought to bring to the fore, reestablish, and practice their own unique cultural knowledges. WARN and grassroots community women's work were generative to an Indigenous vision of health and well-being that envisioned reciprocal, responsible human relationship to the Earth and all beings. Embracing a holistic dream of Indigenous community, for health and correct respectful relations between humans, between men and women, and for community, these women sought to identify sustainable ways of living in defiance of major onslaughts by corporate and nation-state classic liberal development projects that saw their homelands as "sacrifice zones."

Transforming this initial work, core women in WARN reorganized again in 1985, to become the Indigenous Women's Network (IWN). They announced, "Our vision was given to us by our Elders and the Original Instructions inherited by our Grandmothers. We understand that, in caring for Mother Earth, we care for ourselves. Women are the mothers of our Nations, and we share the responsibility of being life givers, nurturers, and sustainers of life with our Mother Earth."[7] The IWN, veterans of work in their local communities, moved to articulate the global Indigenous struggle to fight for Indigenous rights to land, life, and the health of the Earth from a United Nations human rights base. In doing so, they joined with Indigenous men in making a radical critique of capitalism as it had compromised them historically, but also, even more pressing, a felt analysis of the effects of globalization and development as they were experiencing it in the present. They initially saw the United Nations and its human rights agenda as a real alternative to working with the nation-states that continuously harmed them. Working on behalf of and as part of the first recognized Indigenous nongovernmental organization, the International Treaty Council, members of Indigenous Women's Network did the kinds of relational work that formed kinship across different fronts of resistance work. The IWN became an NGO, and their work expanded to include women from North and South America and the Pacific. Haunani Trask and Mililani Trask from Hawaii joined Janet McLeod, Nilak Butler, Winona LaDuke, Dagmar Thorpe, and Ingrid Washinawatok–Al Issa, among others, who articulated core Indigenous principles and provided role models for work in communities on the land (with a land base) and increasingly those without (urban).

In Canada, many of WARN's, and later IWN's, concerns, particularly child loss and sterilization, were articulated on similar fronts. But Indigenous women in Canada had first responded to conditions that were particular to Canada. In doing so, they revealed what I present here as a core conversation on envisioning nation that must inform all conversations on self-determination. Here, I must reprise some of what I have already introduced in this text. Unlike Indian nations located in the United States, who had treaty rights recognized in constitutional law, Canada's peoples did not. They had the Indian Act, and that act had been deeply invasive in pulling Indigenous societies into line with its patriarchal legal and social regulation. The 1876 Canadian Indian Act and subsequent gendered Indian policies had altered any once-reciprocal gender relations into well-entrenched western hierarchal patriarchal power relations that gave Indian men an inordinate power over Indian women, a history discussed at length in chapter 2. Indigenous communities had deep fault lines where the Indian Act had racialized, gendered, and forced them into heteronormative relations, cracks that split into factions when Canada patriated its own nation. In 1973 Canada had admitted to the Nisga'a that their land right (and by extension any Aboriginal land rights) had not been extinguished by the formation of the nation-state. In 1982 Canada included a constitutional clause (Section 35) that recognized Indigenous peoples' inherent rights. It is in the ensuing debates on the constitution of Aboriginal governments, on what these nations would be, that the old colonial fault lines so intensely show their power. What would their nations be, and what are their powers? Canadian women moved to instill Indigenous forms of governance and to restore respect for women's roles and contributions to a central place in the formation of Indigenous nations.

Canadian Indigenous women formed the Native Women's Association of Canada (NWAC) in 1974. At the time of the Canadian repatriation talks in the 1980s and early 1990s, NWAC nationally represented "status and non-status Indian and Métis women," struggling for women's inclusion at the table as Indigenous nationalism was being argued into Canadian constitutionality.[8] This struggle had come to a head as Indigenous women in Canada argued from their historical position as mothers of nations rejecting the intense inequalities that had stemmed from the Canadian Indian Act's gendered evisceration of Indian family and community. They argued from positions of shared gender power instituted in their roles as clan mothers and as once primary and honored negotiators for their historical Indigenous nations. Indigenous women argued for Aboriginal nations that foregrounded forms of customary law, laws that would inform governances that respected, honored, and afforded Indigenous women their rightful place.[9] That was never forthcoming, and NWAC had to fight Canadian legislators and government-funded and -sanctioned male Aboriginal organizations to even be present in the negotiations.

In her account of that political moment, "The Womb Is to the Nation as the Heart Is to the Body," Jo-Anne Fiske wrote that early constitutional and self-determination negotiations between men and women had been reframed by Canadian legislators' insistence on a rights discourse. At the reemergence of Indigenous political movement, men and women had to some extent shared a vision of women's traditional roles as the heart of their nations.[10] By the early 1990s they had been moved to conflict, as the primarily male Canadian legislative process drew Indigenous men into defining their own polities. Indian men began to portray Indian women as "women's libbers" who were divisively arguing for gender equity as personal rights, rather than with them for their nations' self-determination.

The core of this difference in these arguments between NWAC and AFN (among others) has large ramifications for the subject of healing and nation building I discuss in this chapter, because it records and analyzes a critical split in vision that has not been reconciled. I want to explicate the content of the women's position and why the men's position prevailed politically, specifically in national politics, while women's vision has been more or less deferred to the now more medicalized realms of "healing" ensconced in the community in social welfare and education. These women have made life possible in communities while making life possible in most homes. This split, I believe, has had far-reaching consequences.

The women originally dreamed of revitalized communities where men's and women's roles would achieve more equity, more balance. This was not a reality, since the actual experiences under Canada's colonial policies for over a hundred years had effectively put a new order in place. However, Indigenous peoples' still-vital social imaginaries located in their felt cultural values could inform their actual practice as "nations." Women's roles as life givers, as nurturers, and as teachers were very paramount in this visioning. Women drew strength from ancestors, from their grandmothers. Jeannette Armstrong, Okanagan author, activist, and director of En'owkin wrote, "in the part of me that was always there / grandmothers / are speaking to me / the grandmothers / in whose voices / I nestle / and / draw nourishment from / voices speaking to me / in early morning light."[11] Armstrong made her primary character in *Slash* an Indian man. She does so because among the roles she takes in her family (aside from storying their experience) is her role instructing her family in respectful relations. She speaks to men, to her brothers, through the struggles of Thomas Kelasket. These initial conversations that Armstrong reflects in her fictional work are respectful; they encapsulate a belief in colonized gender and community relations transformed as Thomas Kelasket understands his rage and opts to take a felt shared responsibility in his family and his community. One of the key decisions that provides a political landscape in *Slash* is the idea of accepting or rejecting inclusion in Canada's constitutionality. Armstrong posed this inclusion as boding a real loss of autonomy, intuiting what such a polity might ask in practice. Indigenous peoples believed in their inherent right to self-determination as given in creation. These were powers that were not derived from any state or western power, nor could they be granted by them. As cultural nations, they might still define themselves in ways that Canada would not. Armstrong's version of nation is envisioned with diverse life relations at its core, but perhaps, prophetically, her women often die. Two primary women characters in *Slash* die before the end of the novel, and in that Armstrong is a realist.

As Fiske points out, women did not hold views diametrically opposed to men's, and not all men were in opposition to what they envisioned. There were diverse views among men and women. The women shared "core issue . . . with male leadership: self-government, land entitlements, identity, economic well-being, etc."[12] As the constitutional talks heated up, Fiske notes that the "women's associations, NWAC, Aboriginal Nurses, Women of the Métis Nations grant[ed] priority to social concerns: family harmony, child welfare, health care, and education, all of which are seen as the foundation for community healing. Whether it is full political and social participation in their Nations or remedies for family violence, the goals of Métis and First Nations' women leaders are asserted in holistic terms."[13]

So how had men envisioned these emerging Aboriginal nations differently? Fiske noted that the primary differences formed around the stolid inequity already in place. The band governances that had formed within the Indian Act gave certain privileges to men, unquestioned citizenship, primogeniture, and first rights in the property and economic resources of the communities. If Canadian legislators could imagine Native polities at all, they saw them with their own order in place. Many Native leaders felt threatened by changes that women proposed. Fiske wrote, "Whereas women conceive of a community in which it can be said, 'the womb is to the nation as the heart is to the body,' men envision an Indigenous nation whose drum beat radiates from the quasistate powers of a constitutionally defined 'third order of government.'"[14] Fiske argues that any respectful conversation between female and male Indigenous leaders in Canada about the gendered constitution of their nations was short-circuited by "rights" arguments. The conversations that Indigenous women needed with Indigenous men to argue for nations that weren't carbon copies of western nationalism's patriarchal order were totally cut short. Women's vision encapsulated nations in which integral respectful reciprocal relations between persons regardless of gender, their families, and by extension all life forms informs a communal governance. This vision for an Indigenous governance constituted in principle and practice did not get a hearing. The conversations were forced into dominant Canadian legal rights discourses. Women's articulations on holistic governing were deferred to community health projects or were reduced and confined to conversations about "gender rights" and "sexual equality," which represented Canadian white women's more dominant critique of their own governance but did not represent Indigenous women's different concerns. Western constitutions and liberal rights arguments are both informed by the adversarial nature of western law. Thus, NWAC had been forced immediately into the position of defending their "right" to be at the constitutional talks. Fiske quotes Teresa Nahanee's estimation of their position: "What Aboriginal women have said . . . is that they have the right to give birth to the new government along with men. Aboriginal governments and Aboriginal justice will have a mother and a father or it [sic] will be an abomination rejected by women."[15] Nahanee directly addresses and names a top down male-headed hierarchy as an abomination. They knew that reinstating women and reciprocal relations would transform any polity in practice. Male leaders caught in the political games that were Canada's patriation talks consented to the women's exclusion and subordination at the negotiation table, not necessarily because they didn't understand the women's vision for a holistic nation, "as a large family, [as relations] between the Creator and Mother Earth," but because it represented a very different politic that they almost unanimously failed to imagine in practice.[16] Many of these men, even those who thought of themselves as "traditional," had been tutored by the political process that had empowered them, and they now moved to reinstate it.

Fiske argues that in the Canadian public eye the men opposed "outside" forces that these women purportedly brought to challenge their sense of self-determination. These "outside forces" were the human rights campaigns that Indigenous women appealed to in the early 1980s to change the sexist provisions in the Indian Act. The men had won initially because the Indian Act that gave them the rights to determine their own band memberships was excluded from the Canadian Charter of Rights and Freedoms. Then Canada was found in violation of the women's rights by the Canadian Human Rights Commission. Many male band leaders positioned the women as willing to defend their own "rights" while endangering the "rights" of self-determination. The Indian Act provision s.12 (1) (b) that the women had fought to overturn was the most heinous and blatant sexual discrimination regulation that Canada had enforced, a racialized feature of the Canadian Indian Act that pauperized and disenfranchised women and children from their own communities. While the passage of Bill 31-C had made it possible for disenfranchised women to be reinstated as "Indians," it did not reinstate them as members of their bands. Any redress from the long reach of s.12 (1) (b) was not successfully made until 2009, when Sharon McIvor finally pushed her case through. No remedy has yet been made in conjugal property law. That has been deferred to the bands. Male leaders have continuously seen women and families affected by Indian Act exclusion as a threat to self-determination, although it is now posed as more of an economic threat.[17] In 1991 NWAC adamantly refused that these men could represent the conditions that women lived within such a relationship.

> It does not matter which male-dominated organization appears before you to say they represent us. We are here. We are the women. We are entitled, and we do represent ourselves. We are not living in our communities because there is no land. We are not living in our communities because there is no housing. We have been shut out from our communities because they do not wish to bear the costs of programs and services to which we are entitled as Indians. We are telling you that this situation

will not change without our involvement in self-government and in the constitutional discussions. Our men could take the initiative and give us a place at the table. Have they done that? No they have not.[18]

After a lawsuit, NWAC did join in the negotiations but was summarily confined by the rights discourses in place. In the end it is a rights paradigm made necessary by the terms of the negotiation that finally trumped, excluding their fuller vision for Indigenous nations. Fiske, a white social historian and feminist, observed certain aspects of this lost chance to instill a radically different idea of nation-community. Given that patriarchal law and the western governments founded within it are synonymous with white male power as their unstated but assumed subject, this constitution forces women and "others" (all those not assumed) in this legal universal to argue for inclusion, to continuously argue for rights and reparations to augment and bring western governances into equity (equal rights) with this unstated but always assumed white male subject citizen. The women's appeal to UN human rights protection that the men resented is also ironically the same establishment that reconstituted these rights as the basis for international law in our time. But the UN has the same universal "rights of Man" enshrined in its practice and constitution. Indigenous women arguing for "women's rights" could be said to be part of the articulation of those rights within human rights law and not merely reliant on them. Human rights had been, prior to the 1970s, solidly heterosexual and sexist.[19] At the time of these patriation arguments, no rights yet extended to other gendered persons. Those rights, even now, would foundationally upset the core.[20]

Fiske observed that "a feminized nation transcends legal definition and jurisdictional restriction to truly be the teacher and keeper of tradition. The Nation is a higher good, a sacred unity," wherein it is already assumed everyone is included in the polity, in equity, and the governance maintains reciprocal relations that establish a "higher good," well-being, health, and prosperity as its value. Fiske also notes that this vision of the polity directly defies western law as patriarchal order: "Sacralization of women's sexual/reproductive powers in a commonwealth of equality defies legal boundaries, the foundation of male empowerment. Women penetrate the nation and upset the relations of sexuality and power."[21]

It is here that I must carefully clarify what is lost. I am not arguing that Indigenous women in their great variety represent one half of a western dichotomy, that they be reduced in a white male/female dichotomy to "good women" versus "bad men" stick figures. They did not argue for mothers to be central to governing; they didn't argue for a gynocracy.

They worked toward an Indigenous symbolic that does not see the polity organized around a white male subject *or* a female Indigenous one. They moved to transform the order. Indigenous women articulate a polity imagined in Indigenous terms, a polity where everyone—genders, sexualities, differently expressed life forms, the animals and plants, the mountains—are already included as the subjects of the polity. They are already empowered, not having to argue for any "right" to recognition; they form that which is the polity, that which is respected and in relation. That kind of polity would do more than "reform" any relations; it would bring us beyond "representation."

So how have these Aboriginal nations fared, "patriated" but with their mothers marginalized? Indigenous governances, in order to be "recognized" by the system, by the Canadian state, or any westernized governance, must have some recognizable form within that law, and thus any governances that are formed within it are not necessarily a surprise. It does not have to be so. I pause to reflect on this recognition to better specify and discuss what the ramifications were for Indigenous women marginalized in these nations and to think about what healing has been. I then suggest that while not revolutionary, the actual affective intensities, powers of transformation lodged within these women's (and some men's) understanding of society are moments of practice that can be glimpsed and reflected on.

What Is Lost and What Is Found?

Glen Coulthard, a Dene political theorist from Canada, speaks to his people's thirty-year struggle for recognition as a nation. His point is to unpack this "politics of recognition" that is currently so embedded in sovereignty language: "recognition of the nation-to-nation relationship between First Nations and the Crown; recognition of the equal rights of First Nations to self-determination . . . et al."[22] This sliver of language he pulls from the 1996 Report of the Royal Commission on Aboriginal Peoples, a document that since its release has often been held up as a blueprint for a new colonial/colonized relationship in Canada. Citing the proliferation of rights-based claims since the early 1970s, Coulthard challenges this "now expansive range of recognition-based models of liberal pluralism" to actually transform the colonial relationship. Arguing against Charles Taylor's influential essay "The Politics of Recognition," Glen Coulthard reads in Frantz Fanon insights that may recuperate Indigenous and Aboriginal societies from "recognition" in the "manageable" nationalisms that emerged. Coulthard reminds us that "recognition" by a nation-state like Canada does not produce any equal relationship. He posits that the Hegelian idea of reciprocity suggested in the concept of "recognition" does not exist. There can be no Canadian reciprocity with any First Nation, since the "master" in such a relationship can never actually recognize its "other" as any true equal. Thus, it is never equality that is achieved between such entities that have such vastly unequal powers and statuses. Moreover, the colonizer shapes and suits the terms of such a recognition to his own benefit. The relationships between Canada and the First Nations peoples remain such that Canada doesn't need the First Nations' recognition to carry out its business as usual.

Any recognition First Nations has achieved has led almost exclusively to a "strategic domestication" of the terms of that recognition. Coulthard cites the landmark decision in *Delgamuukw v. British Columbia* as an example where Canada recognized "any residual Aboriginal rights that may have survived the unilateral assertion of the Crown title" as long as none of those "residual rights" actually "throw into question the background legal, political and economic framework of the colonial relationship itself," that is, the state's ultimate sovereignty.[23] Coulthard excellently suggests ways Fanon anticipated the dual nature of economic and cultural/subjective colonization. Reading thusly, Coulthard suggests a transformative praxis, the performance of more radical acts of Indigenous-defined autonomous self-determination.

In keeping with Glen Coulthard's observation, I would add that any Indigenous nation at this moment in time visualized as an autonomy is challenged by the present neoliberal form it is forced to take, with its attendant bureaucracy and implied human and economic "development expectations." The bottom-line relationship between Canada and Canadian Aboriginal peoples is and shall always be land. Canada cannot exist without the lands that Aboriginal people still contest, particularly those in the North, where treaties are still being negotiated. Canada is a preeminent western capitalist nation-state and must develop and play the game of resource development to survive among other nation-states. The rise of neoliberalism beginning in the late 1970s coincided with the time that Canada as a modern nation-state reimagined its Aboriginal policies in keeping with revising if not eliminating its welfare state government to be in agreement with a revitalized global economy. Neoliberalism, Gabrielle Slowey says, "favours a system of policies and processes designed to assist the marketplace. . . . First Nations self-determination becomes more attractive than First Nations dependence on the state."[24] The reconstituted, "self-determining" Aboriginal nations are envisioned in part as a form that might be prepped to compete in the marketplace. The continuing devolution of services to self-determining Aboriginal nations (job training and welfare reform) puts responsibility on the community level of such "nations" to successfully fund their own operations as that function of the state recedes. In many ways, neoliberalism fits the desires of those Aboriginal leaders who see development-centered nationalisms modeled on capitalist nation-states as an answer to the continuing suffering witnessed to by Aboriginal peoples in healing forums. In this Canadian Aboriginal peoples articulate reconciliation as healing in their ongoing struggle for justice.

It's possible to see the changing political landscape in Canada since 1969 as one "concentrated on restructuring its relationship with First Nations" in an era when First Nations people "have their political rights, claimed their land and demanded renegotiated relationship." Canada needs a reconciled relationship with the Aboriginal peoples within its boundaries to settle land claims in order to provide "stable access to resources" and to fulfill demands in international markets for the players in northern development.[25] The business of "Indians" in Canada is still ensconced in the "Aboriginal Affairs and Northern Development Canada." Canada speaks the language of human rights in convening an in-house "truth and reconciliation commission" to practice a therapeutic national catharsis, while sidestepping any firm commitment to economic responsibility or constitutional reform that would secure Indigenous peoples in Canada more equal access to power.

So have Canadian Indigenous women taken a backseat in trying to steer these nations as they negotiate neoliberalism—in light of their own Indigenous vision for egalitarian, caring societies? In many ways we must see any success these polities do achieve, their ability to compete in "markets," founded in the intense amount of work and activism that Indigenous women actually *did*. This is in keeping with the global tendency to draw women's labor into the market as a cheap supply of labor. In Canada, while this is true, their influence is not necessarily minimal. You don't have to look long at any growth in these nations and in urban communities prior to and after 1992 to see women's huge influence, even while they are politically marginalized to the proverbial western "domestic" sphere. In addition to the roles women took in writing and founding presses, they performed a constellation of services for their communities and in public life. Marlene Brant Castellano, a Mohawk elder and highly esteemed educator, recounts that Aboriginal women provided significant leadership in all the fronts that they had identified as health and well-being in the communities: child welfare, health care, and education.[26] Castellano herself had held many key positions. Beginning her career as a social worker, she raised children, earned a degree, and became a professor. Castellano then served as a codirector of research for the Royal Commission on Aboriginal Peoples, and as a primary researcher in the Aboriginal Healing Foundation. Indigenous women had been part of building communication networks, made inroads as business women, and succeeded as entrepreneurs. They stood on the front lines in opposing destructive development, in organizing resistance and community education. They persistently informed the spheres of their influence with their different sense of nation. Occasionally, they led Native Nations.

Kim Anderson states, "For over a century, First Nations politics have been 'men's business.'"[27] In the twenty-plus years since the constitutional talks, a small but growing number of First Nations and Aboriginal chiefs were women (16 to 19 percent of 600 bands). She found little research available on what their experiences had been, but for her article she interviewed twelve female chiefs. Two of them were grand chiefs—Grand Chief Angie Barnes of the Akwesasne Mohawks and Grand Chief Denise Stonefish, Association of Iroquois and Allied Indians—meaning that Barnes and Stonefish each led a larger association of chiefs, who were all men. Two leadership strengths Anderson highlights among these twelve women are better communication skills and their focus on getting social issues to the table: "Women tend not to lose sight of the social issues in our community, where the male leaders are more focused on logging and fishing, not realizing that the health of our young people is important." They didn't attribute these characteristics to biological difference, but to their different focus.[28] They reported that men had a more difficult time confronting family violence issues, and that women reminded them that if the family and children were a priority, then they needed to put them high on the agenda in meetings, to "prioritize them."[29] Basically, they didn't define their interests as "women's issues"; they were concerned for "the overall health and well-being of their communities," an agenda that called for many approaches. They were good at seeing many interests and approaches included. While most of these women might not have identified with anything in the name of any feminism, they had some values that we can see across a spectrum of women's political positions on governing. They are more inclusive than exclusive.

Yet, overall, women were not represented. Anderson cited a national study by Judith Sayers and Kelly McDonald that found a "lack of women's representation in decision making . . . that concerns articulated by First Nations women (accountable governing structures, gender equality, and social issues) are not incorporated into the discourse on government and self-government."[30] The status quo held. Sayers and McDonald found women's representation sorely lacking in British Columbian treaty talks, resulting in the "glaring omissions" of family violence in male-dominated conversations on land and development. Undertaken to fill a gap, Anderson's interviews were her effort to ascertain what difference women's leadership might make.

As a whole, Indigenous men continued to dominate the politics of nation building and nation running, while depending on the great amount of work women did toward building emotional, social, and relational infrastructure in actual communities. Thus, it might be said that "nation building" appears as a segregated labor, where mostly male political leaders lead in national conversations and negotiations with the nation-state. Canada has consistently stalled on any significant negotiations of power, leaving the political sphere of self-determination (co-constructing polity and determining the powers of Indian nations) a sphere of forestalled action. Primarily, self-determination in band governments means devolution to Canadian-style devolution to municipal state-determined styles of governance. Presently, a more conservative neoliberal Canada lacks the political will to actually fund band governments for more autonomous self-determination.[31] Indigenous women and other feminist scholars have stepped up to confront what actually *is* in place.

Kiera Ladner perceives a "distance" between the spheres of self-determination action and articulation and the spheres of action and articulation for community wellness. She observes that while the "community wellness" is articulated as a given to achieving self-determination, the actual pursuit of self-determination is rarely informed by the "healing" knowledge/experiences generated in the communities. Ladner, Canada Research Chair in Indigenous Politics and Governance at the University of Manitoba, writes extensively about the complex gender politics that are present in pursuit of self-governance and self-determination. She also had occasion to ask what the relationship is between "community wellness" and self-determination. In her article "Understanding the Impact of Self-Determination on Communities in Crisis," she begins with a statement that clarifies her own sense of what governance is within Indigenous thought, an expression of "the way in which a people lives best together . . . as a part of the circle of life, not as superior beings who claim dominion over other species and other humans."[32] Thus, an Indigenous polity is inclusive, not rights-based with its already built-in lack. Ladner also points to historical evidence for the resilience in Indigenous governments, that even in the midst of disease, land loss, and the rise of another economic order as the settler-state began to encroach, Indigenous polities continued to adapt and provide order in the communities. They did not go down easily, and not until they were completely stripped by the Indian Act and the insertion of the heteronormative patriarchal western order in law. These indigenous governing systems had been replaced by the band council system, a system that had no jurisdiction, no authority, and no way of responding to people's needs.

Ladner asks us to remember that reserve band councils were not designed to govern: "regime replacement was designed to provide for easier federal control and administration. . . . That is, band councils were created primarily to serve as puppets . . . charged with the responsibility of providing local administration for Indian Affairs."[33] In that way they were particularly powerless to cope with the loss of their traditional economies, the damages the residential schooling wrought, or other destructive acts of colonization, thus often magnifying the social destruction in the communities rather than stopping it. Unfortunately, these band governments are more apt to create communities in crisis than to heal them. In Ladner's analysis, the *kind* of government in place has a direct relationship to the wellness of any community. Although revamped for this moment of less direct neoliberal administration, community control, and self-governance, band councils are still organized more for self-management than for self-government. Ladner is plainspoken about their limitation. They have "no decision-making ability that is not subject to the authority of the federal government, no inherent or constitutionally defined jurisdictions or responsibilities and no ability to generate revenue (delegated or otherwise) or to create the financial capacity to operate as a government"; thus, "Indian Affairs still exercises control through financial transfers, departmental administrative and accountability requirements, the use of third party management, and its ability to override all bylaws."[34] The band councils are still positioned as mid-level managers in the larger management of Indians and thus are ill equipped with the jurisdiction or power to respond to their people's needs. Money, or an influx of funds from development, doesn't necessarily fix anything. In illustrations of governments that gained jurisdiction in devolution with an ability to earn funds from development, Ladner observes that "even these communities with their seemingly endless financial resources" are thwarted from being more directly responsible to their people's needs by an Indian Affairs control "that sets priorities, controls budgets (including trust funds) and holds bands accountable (even attempting to do so when revenue is generated by the band)."[35] Many lack the trust of the people they are charged to govern, because they are so ill equipped to do so.

In a review of literature on this subject, Ladner sees a tremendous split. It is a wondrous split, considering the vigor of the discussions on healing as a prerequisite for development highlighted in the last chapter. Kiera Ladner, following the legal conversations on self-determination, saw something different: "the idea of community well-being and its relationship to governance has largely been overlooked in the indigenous governance literature, and no attention has been paid to the relationship between self-determination and communities in crisis. The reason for this is also simple, as the relationship is taken as a given and the literature has instead focused on pressing issues pertaining to the legal, political and constitutional justification for self-government and its scope and form. . . . Beyond the RCAP, there has been little written on the nuts and bolts of implementation."[36]

Ladner notes that an inordinate amount of discourse on self-determination in law is dedicated to Canada's multicultural angst around multiple polities. Such discussions had taken up over two decades of their Indigenous attention on self-determination. The literatures that were the communities' experiences with healing, as described for Alkali Lake, are absent for her, which means to me that the Healing Fund or NNADP community healing literatures are not seen as resources on this subject. One study that interests her is Chandler and Lalonde's 2008 study of suicide risk factors in communities. They found that suicides in communities went down when a number of "cultural continuity" factors were in place. Many have pointed out that the "cultural" factors that they name are features of self-determination, as Ladner does here.[37] Chandler and Lalonde pose several factors for increased community health: "self-government, involvement in land claims, band control of education, health services, cultural facilities, police and fire services."[38] She also mentions Cornell and Kalt and the Harvard Project, because it is there that she believes the researchers also provide evidence for the links between community wellness and good governance. She also sees that they equate wellness with "economic success (community well-being) and nation-building as practical sovereignty."[39] Given that Phil Lane Jr., Michael Bopp, and Judie Bopp produced thirty years of detailed accounts of healing projects in communities, how is it that these are not evidence of the governing that framed these experiences—or how the communities' healing transformed their governments? Alkali Lake did, but are there no other examples? Why would these literatures be so separate? If these experiences were not evidence for community healing as it produced the conditions for self-determining communities, what were they? Perhaps their meaning was being produced in support of something else.

Kiera Ladner, exploring the link between community wellness and good governance, then moves to a familiar question. She asks a question similar to the one that Sousan Abadian asks in the last chapter: "How is culture treatment [for traumatized communities]?" Ladner, in contrast to Abadian, and from her quite different perspective, asks what *Indigenous* governing systems have to offer to communities in crisis. If the present governments have enabled damage rather than ameliorated community crisis, what is the answer? She poses Indigenous polity as the *what*, in the question "*What* could be put in place?" if they could dump the Indian Act band-council state-determination governances. Ladner immediately grounds the discussion by reminding that Section 35 of the Canadian constitution affirms their inherent right to self-governance but does not define it. They did not lose the power to define it, in that "Self-determination is a right and responsibility vested in indigenous constitutional orders and as such contains all jurisdictions essential."[40] Ladner then quickly moves to examples where traditional governing became influential and what those examples have to offer.

The difference in these two positions speaks volumes. Abadian was unable to recognize cultures as living paradigms, with all their lived political and philosophical implications. For her, culture was a "therapy," a ceremonial life that shores up and gives meaning to individuals, adaptive or nonadaptive to "realities" that are left unnamed so that development can occur. Ladner does not see "culture" per se. She sees the way in which each people's long relationship with land, with one another, generate a specific order for them. This order is brought to the fore in crisis, because it is often in the breakdown or absence of the now-dominant capitalist order where the remnants of Indigenous governing practices still organize a first response. It is sometimes in crisis where transformation occurs. She sees a correlation between the communal examination that is sometimes present in crisis, peoples rearticulating what other orders are available to them, and the further possibility of change, of transformation. Affective, charged, emotional community participation takes place in these initial responses. Thus, it is often in "activism" that women take the leading roles in first mobilizations of non-state-directed acts of self-determination. Ladner notes "political mobilization" demonstrates "that increased self-determination (no matter its location) can positively affect community well-being even when it is the traditional leadership (in this case clan mothers and "traditional"/district chiefs) that show the vision and leadership and begin to [perform] responsible government."[41]

However brief these acts of community self-determination are, given how quickly the dominant usually responds to restore its order, the elements of traditional governance practices that shine through illustrate that "philosophy and leadership" are pivotal factors—that what *kind* of government matters; that traditional governing structures do play a part in either "enabling or disabling," depending on the actual vision in place. Ladner cites the Sainte Marie Tribe of Chippewa as an example of governing informed by "traditional teaching pertaining to clans, clan responsibilities of individuals within and to clans" that created "awareness of one's role within the collective." The focus was not on the negatives but on the reciprocal roles of caring between individuals that "transformed," "reducing both dependency and crisis and increasing community capacity and resiliency."[42]

There are several issues that Kiera Ladner brings up for me that I want to pull together as I begin to move on. Indigenous governing as it is imagined and sometimes practiced in the cracks that it is able to create in the dominant system both holds sociality in a place of compassion and incites it for movement. I elaborate more on this in the next chapter, but it is enough to say here that as incitement we could establish several examples, in both Canada and the United States. I could take a quick tour through the United States from the 1950s on—from Mad Bear Anderson through the Northwest fishing struggles, Alcatraz, and Wounded Knee—and see where Indigenous leaders, both men and women, intensely dream movement *and* community. Here, though, I call attention to where women articulating from a position of life *incite*, a word that in its French root means to "arouse toward." It is an affectively empowered moment. As Ladner poses in her argument, it is often in crisis that the people need to rearticulate themselves, to look for other order and sometimes, even if briefly, enact it. The potential is generative, and that moment Andy Smith has amply illustrated is a moment often filled with and fulfilled through alliances, likely and unlikely. The order that emerges from this incitation may not always be what was intended, but the order is changed. In Canada there are many instances that come to mind, but there is one example I wish to bring to the table. By remembering Ista I will bring my discussion back around to include the human development healing literatures that I discussed in the last chapter to ask one more question: what is this for?

In 2006 Jacinda Mack wrote a thesis to accompany her film, *Remembering Ista*, to reflect on social change in her community, the Nuxalk Nation in central British Columbia. She details how in the summer of 1995 the nation was thrown into what was, for them, a glaring international spotlight on their struggle to stop International Forest Products (INTERFOR) "from clearcut logging the sacred area of *Ista* within their ancestral territory." Ista is sacred because "Ista is the name of the first Nuxalk woman, as well as the place and *smuyusta* (creation story) that relate her to Tatau, the Creator, as well as the land and people who descend from her."[43]

Mack is compassionate toward the nation's experience; she holds all those involved in regard, even as she knows that they had been bitterly torn as a community from the conflicts that arose as they attempted to fight a multinational corporation. In part it is a conflict that has to do with tensions between two visions of governing where "[t]raditional Nuxalk government continues to exist in the hereditary chief system at the *House of Smayusta*, in direct opposition to the colonial structures of Canadian society, including the elected Nuxalk Band Council."[44] Pain and contention also arose when Forest Action Network (FAN) joined with the traditional government, causing an "acute social divide" between this alliance "and the status quo."[45] The Nuxalk still depended on the forest for subsistence and for spiritual substance. INTERFOR had caused extreme damage to the land and polluted areas that the stressed community relied on for food. Canada's resource extraction had no direct benefit to the community. She explains, "although multinational corporations such as International Forest Products (INTERFOR) have agreements with the Canadian governments to harvest millions of dollars worth of timber from Nuxalk Territory, the Nuxalk people themselves have not been consulted nor have they benefited in any way from these operations. In fact, the Nuxalk face near crippling poverty with a stable unemployment rate of over eighty percent for several generations."[46]

The community split when some disagreed with the traditional chiefs' decision to ally with FAN, the break illustrating tensions produced in the different responsibilities that traditional governance and the band councils represent. The House of Smayusta stood fast, and many were arrested. Cruelly, in the end Ista was logged as planned. Within the intervening years, Mack felt moved to make a film of their experience to "spark positive, reflective discussion within the Nuxalk and Bella Coola communities."[47] It is a decolonizing act made as a reflective tool for the communities involved. The film was distributed to the community.

Mack understood the events as moments when tensions *that were already there* became exposed in the crisis. She creates her film gathering from multiple participants in the hope of showing "community experience from many different perspectives in a non-confrontational way."[48] Many in the community had expressed even many years later that somehow they had not been fully informed about what was going on. She moved to give them information that portrayed no "singular Truth." Because she is known as a traditional member of the community with relations and she does frame the issue from the perspective of Nuxalk sovereignty, she knows that no such thing as objectivity is completely possible.

Here, what is striking to me about Jacinda Mack's account of her process from the perspective of Kiera Ladner's remarks is how the conscious
decolonizing methodology that she performs with her community is one
in which they must discuss what they did and why they did it. What order
is it that they have, and why do they have it? Mack locates sovereignty away
from the courts and the stark abstractions of law, or at least Canada's law.
She links their struggle to their Indigenous identity, one that represents
their rights and the global struggle for them. She moves to make the difference between Nuxalk sovereignty and what is available to them through
Canadian law explicit: "*Nuxalk Sovereignty is an active responsibility that
intertwines our history, language, families, and connection to the land
through complex and strict laws as related through our smayustas, songs,
dances, and potlatches.*"[49] In turn, Canada defines sovereignty legally,
in "certainty," as a title to land that Canada itself cannot produce to the
Nuxalk. Mack points out that the Nuxalk were never conquered, nor had
they ceded their land. She shared the affective import of her effort: "It is
important for me to acknowledge the tremendous emotional nature of this
work, as emotion often leads to insight that logic alone cannot. I can better
appreciate why people are hesitant to discuss Ista; it is deeply personal and
political."[50] The knowledge is felt.

It is in defense of Ista that they suffer the crisis of their colonization.
In turn, through Jacinda Mack's process, many in the community come
together to articulate an eloquent account of their process. It is a process
where Indigenous law can clearly state its difference from the "law" attached
to recognition. It is highly affective work in any capacity, deeply personal
and political as she witnesses. But the witness to her community is not
made as part of a witness to trauma. It is compassionate work taken up out
of a sense of what she could contribute to the healing of the community's
rifts, a tool of reflection, that each could examine individually or together,
to talk, argue, and remember what it had meant. In it she shares her process
and what she learns from it, how it changes her, teaches her, and weaves
her more deeply into the fabric of her community. I am deeply thankful
for Jacinda Mack's generous and thoughtful reflection, both "personal and
political," on the crisis and her own process of reflection.

Nuxalk people were called upon to examine their own knowledges to
generate a course of action, that involved the lived practice of their tradition at the same time that they must embrace what is theirs but not theirs in
the governance forms available to them in that historical moment. In short
flashes, like insights, there are glimpses of lived and imagined Indigenous
sociality, governance that imagines itself in expansive "compassion" not in

the sense of pity or tolerance but perhaps toward empathy. What would it really take to sustain all life in any place for eons? No English word will suffice. It is the process in a word that resonates in me from Jeannette Armstrong's long interview with the environmentalist David Hall as he sought to understand what she meant by *sustainable*, a meaning that she presented within an entirely different paradigm. "Sustainability" would have to involve everything, everyone, in respectful relations, it would have to involve those who make that commitment to begin moving together toward a future: naw'qinwixw.[51]

There is another story of their healing available, that while much less transparent bears evidence of this Nuxalk crisis, resolution, and moving on. As in the case of the Innu Nation, Canada also moved to offer healing strategy. In March 2000 Michael Bopp and Phil Lane of Four Worlds International offered the Nuxalk the first draft of a "comprehensive ten year plan for the healing and development of the Nuxalk Nation."[52] The Nuxalk band council successfully applied for and received a grant from the Aboriginal Healing Foundation. Bopp and Lane write that in 1996–97 they were approached by the band council to begin the task of "analyzing healing needs and recommending lines of action."[53] The healing plan that Bopp and Lane drafted began with the now-familiar litany of mass historical experiences, epidemic diseases, and highlights of colonization that preceded their present state, one that highlights trauma. Bopp and Lane offer that this account is not the Nuxalk's exact history but essentially an account of the historical forces that frame the nation's experiences. It is a huge litany of familiar symptoms, with alcohol and sexual abuse leading to the now also familiar diagnosis of trauma. Also familiar, almost to a word from their general literatures (available on their website), is this prescription:

> Healing therefore may be (strategically) described as a process of removing barriers and building the capacity of people and the communities to address the determinants of health. This work certainly involves overcoming the legacy of past oppression and abuse, but what that actually means in practice usually involves the transformation of our inner lives (i.e., one's established patterns and habits of thinking and feeling, as well as one's sense of identity, purpose and mortality), our relationships, and the social and environmental conditions within which we live. *Healing, as we will use the term, means moving beyond hurt, pain, disease and dysfunctionality, and establishing new patterns of living that produce sustainable well-being.*[54]

I have no knowledge of what the Nuxalk undertook within what Fourth World proposed as the process of "healing," nor do I think it is any of my business, but it still seems necessary to reflect on the larger process evoked again here. The Aboriginal Healing Foundation that administered the grants was under strict government guidelines about what these healing plans could address. They had to be about physical and sexual abuse suffered in residential schools. Certainly, none of the suggestions that Fourth World makes are "harmful"; they are just the template for a process, rather than the process itself. The techniques in place, the community story, and the rest that I discuss at length in the previous chapter are also ways of mobilizing the transformational forces released in crisis. But here a certain script is offered where "what happened" leads to a larger diagnosis of trauma with a prescription for healing. This diagnosis is most often identified with large-scale personal "healing" from dysfunctionality, rather than a discussion of "how we govern." Perhaps it did and thus I stand down in respect for what could belong only to the Nuxalk. I do note that this healing began at the moment that Jacinda Mack shared as a time of great Nuxalk pain at the end of their bitter struggle, when Ista is logged. Perhaps Fourth World had some part in their generative process to heal.

But what is this healing as it is now welded into healing from trauma? Does a diagnosis of trauma from their historical dismemberment empower them to evaluate or fight the forces that Jacinda Mack details as their grievances with a multinational corporation? Canada's mandate to develop the forest that once sustained the Nuxalk physically and culturally won't cease. Definitely, Four Worlds International is a realist about international capital, and what capacity building is necessary to negotiate a presence. Still, the larger goal of healing trauma, reconciliation, now pulls toward reconciliation with the state. It no longer necessarily informs stands against the state as it might have done in an earlier moment in Alkali Lake. The healing that is supported by reconciliation is adaptation to basic realities. What other than adaptation might inform Indigenous governments? Why does the *kind* of government matter? What kind of order does healing serve? These are the questions that Kiera Ladner asks and Jacinda Mack answers through her own process with her nation.

Marketwire announced in December 2010 that the Nuxalk Nation, after years of resistance, had signed the Coastal Reconciliation Protocol. "'We were very hesitant to sign the protocol with the Province, given that the courts have repeatedly ruled that the Province has no jurisdiction over unceded lands in what is currently known as BC,' stated Spencer Siwallace, the Nuxalk Nation's Elected Chief. 'But with Canada endorsing the United Nations Declaration on the Rights of Indigenous Peoples and the Province finally acknowledging that Nuxalk rights, title and interests exist, we are cautiously optimistic that the "new relationship" may have some merit.'"[55] And so the Nuxalk thus reconciled walk into their future assured by Canada's adoption of human rights protocols that they will not be further harmed. At the very end of its announcement, Marketwire quotes Siwallace again: "The Nuxalk do not acknowledge Provincial jurisdiction over Nuxalk Territory . . . we simply understand the reality of the current situation and the signing of this protocol is but a small step towards the implementation of complete Nuxalk control over our Ancestral Territory." As Jacinda Mack said, "Our story continues."

This chapter and the previous one pose readings of healing nations: one a human development approach entrenched in a vision of personal development and transformation, and the other a critical reflection on why the composition of government is integral to health, on how "What will our nation be?" matters.

In the next chapter, I take up a discussion of the biopolitical processes embedded in this healing linked to trauma to think about what psy interventions mean in Indigenous lives. These are the same technologies of the "self" that appear important to the development of a citizen-subject of neoliberalism. I offer some examples I think may be lived autonomous self-determination, lived examples of wellness and governing that utilize the interstices and cracks in neoliberalism's biopolitical "great society." I conclude by reflecting on the significance of present Indigenous feminism's offerings to these practices of self-governance and self-determination, to live lives that will walk us into a future none of us can know, but that we can and must attempt.

SEVEN

(Un)Making the Biopolitical Citizen

the caribou follows her desire / crosses the pipeline /
and the singing of wind rises in my ears

—DIAN MILLION[1]

On the website Self-Determination Theory, Edward Deci and Richard Ryan's words appear and dissolve, intermixed with pictures of smiling, healthy people. Their words introduce the power of self-determination as a theory for well-being: "To be self determined is to endorse one's actions at the highest level of reflection." This insight is followed by a second observation: "When self determined, people experience a sense of freedom to do what is interesting, personally important, and vitalizing."[2] Anthony Mancini, a project director for a study of traumatic grief at Columbia University, considers self-determination theory "a widely researched and empirically validated theory of human need fulfillment." Citing Ryan and Deci, he describes it as a "motivational theory that posits three fundamental human needs (autonomy, competence and relatedness to others)," which he observes "shows striking similarity to basic ideas on recovery."[3] In 2005 Charlene Crowe and Kim Ghostkeeper proudly announced the fifth Healing Our Spirit Worldwide (HOSW) Health, Healing and Self-Determination gathering, to be held in Edmonton, Alberta, the following year. The announcement heralded the HOSW as "a cultural celebration inviting the world to share holistic healing experiences of Indigenous Peoples in the movement toward healthy lifestyles . . . a celebration of health, healing and self-determination . . . a testament of the resiliency, courage, tenacity and the will of Indigenous Peoples everywhere to overcome the barriers to achieving self-determination in health, healing and addictions."[4]

Similarly, Sharon Parker, an international human rights lawyer, speaks confidently of "the right to self-determination, a fundamental principle of human rights law, ... an individual and collective right to freely determine ... political status and [to] freely pursue ... economic, social and cultural development."[5] Across a spectrum, from individual self-determination/ motivational and recovery literatures to Indigenous healing and principles in human rights theory, a shared common language posits optimism and concern. These documents can all speak some common language, constituting an issue I address here to return to some questions posed in my introduction. There I asked why in the last two decades sexual abuse became a primary site of affective articulation between states and Indigenous peoples for health, well-being, and Indigenous self-determination. To reiterate, what is indexical about this violence and the ways in which we witness it and speak it? Why is gendered sexual abuse so critical *now* to the discourse on our past colonization or our position within a global Indigenous politic, or to the politics of our self-determination? Why, additionally, is our political presence, a global presence, valorized now? What in particular is important about international Indigenous presence now? To begin to try to answer these questions, I must also return to the discussions that I illumine in my introduction. I wish to consider neoliberalism not only as a set of economic practices, but as a governance and an imaginary that infuses ways of life. It is here I would bring forward our Indigenous involvement with the biopolitic, as well as our affective attachments in such a biopolitic.

The Biopolitics of Healing

The kind of hope and optimism that can be attached to the above opening statements on self-determination has to be balanced with some knowledge of their attachments, histories, and valences. All are languages of the therapeutic as it poses movement beyond trauma in highly westernized nations. Self-determination articulated in the span from person to nation to international principle mirrors Phil Lane Jr.'s human development paradigm in Four Worlds literatures, bringing their reflexive relations into focus. The human potential movements that might now be associated with slightly embarrassing memories of Esalen and Timothy Leary were in fact highly successful. The human potential knowledges that provided a mixture of motivational and alternate spiritual mind-body practices for Aboriginal healing programs in Alkali Lake, for one, also successfully suffused western culture with their philosophy. They presciently foresaw or borrowed insights from a then-emergent western science paradigm on the innate self-organization of life, on chaos and complexity. In Ryan and Deci's approach: "SDT [Self-Determination Theory] is an organismic dialectical approach. It begins with the assumption that people are active organisms, with evolved tendencies toward growing, mastering ambient challenges, and integrating new experiences into a coherent sense of self."[6] It is a development theory infused conceptually with biological science, where social issues can be expressed in terms of maladjustments: "The darker sides of human behavior and experience, such as certain types of psychopathology, prejudice, and aggression are understood in terms of reactions to basic needs having been thwarted, either developmentally or proximally."[7] It gravitates Anthony Mancini, a psychological researcher to equate it with recovery, an area that he feels he must draw on to inform him. It already does, but he cannot place its resonance. Crowe and Ghostkeeper, speaking from a global Indigenous healing movement, pose health and life that would ground political self-determination, a political self-determination that Sharon Parker speaks of as basic. I would say these different voices do represent different interests at the same time they represent similar but nonidentically positioned rhetorical dances with the biopolitical. While self-determination as a political idea well predates the "psychic turn," it is like many knowledges that once informed sites of social justice now suffused by a new paradigm to produce new projects. So how can philosophies and practices that present themselves in such self-determined life-affirming languages also be linked to violence? Why in the presence of so much self-determination do we internationally experience an accelerated amount of death, destruction of life and life forms?

Michel Foucault first posed that western nations moved to develop styles of governing to produce certain lives rather than repressing "life" generally. In this moment, the biopolitical citizen self-manages his or her own "freedom."[8] In Nikolas Rose's analysis, the "free" subject of capitalism is now a consumer citizen with many choices that he or she makes in daily relations with a corporate advertising affectively attuned to both produce and serve desires. Rose articulates that liberal "freedoms" are based on power that does not rely solely on the capacity to dominate, because "to dominate is to ignore or to attempt to crush the capacity for action"; thus, "to govern is to act upon action. . . . To govern humans is not to crush their capacity to act, but to utilize it for one's own objectives."[9] Biopower radically diffuses across domains, socialities, and spaces, all organized to release a people's "capacity for action," to "make new kinds of experience possible, produce new modes of perception, invest percepts with affects, with dangers and opportunities, with saliences and attractions."[10] Those of us in the capitalist countries are used to "doing our own thing," creating radical differences in clothing, "lifestyles," music, cultural productions, and so forth—unless our lives transgress the larger projects of power in any given time, transgress the limits of what is deemed productive. Neoliberalism highly values the individuated citizen working on "oneself" to become more effective, vital, or productive. Rose poses the "psy"—the psychiatric disciplines and the now-verdant self-help therapies as neoliberal technique in this liberal production of freedom.

However, Rose also discusses the ways that different "populations" have and do now merit different technique. Liberal freedom's political social subject was formed earlier, in opposition to another, the savage. Western nations made distinctions between "the national spaces of advanced and civilized populations of citizens—even if their civility was potential—who warranted liberal forms of bio-political and disciplinary administration—and those of primitive 'peoples' who were 'regrouped and reconfigured according to somatic, cultural and psychological criteria that would make . . . administrative interventions necessary and credible."[11] Reserves and reservations, as Kiera Ladner pointed out, were designed to be temporary, to give Indians practice in using these democratic techniques of "freedom," within the tight supervisory control of Indian agents. Generally, Canada and the United States both conceptualized their own nations without the Native. The biopolitical is initially distinguished and inscribed in the race, gender, and sexuality of our bodies that remains an intense nexus of forces. That strict disciplinary space of the nineteenth and early twentieth centuries remains even as it was succeeded or coterminous with the rise of professional social sciences management, where mental hygiene education became a primary discourse on Indian mores and social life. Again race and sex figure heavily in authorizing social workers' invasive movements into Indian Country from the late 1940s on. Until 1960, when the newly organized international human rights movement began to find authority and institutional clout, nation-states managed "Indians" as a solely "domestic," internal "problem."

The struggles to claim Indigenous human rights also actively redefined *what* human rights *are*. In this moment of our inclusion as peoples with rights, the Indigenous do create new political and social spaces of "self-determination" that we seek to define. At the same time we are also called on to witness to and to define ourselves as the product of the state's violence as it presents in a rising tidal wave of self-immolating behaviors, where alcoholism and incest remain the top two indicators of Indigenous trauma. In the same arena Indigenous peoples seek to define terms of self-determination, outcomes of prior colonization are measured and diagnosed as trauma. This creates a site for our healing, our reconstruction and its management. This is actually a dangerous position. If we take seriously Australian Aboriginal people's recent violation by the Australian state, where the sexual abuse and incest that were diagnosed in a prior moment as trauma then became a policing rationale for their further colonization, we must be warned. The space of our medicalized diagnosis as victims of trauma is not a site wherein self-determination is practiced or defined. Caroline L. Tait reminds us that strong stands for self-determination arouse, in many Canadians, a "picture of urban and reserve aboriginal communities as 'nests of hopelessness.'" Contextualized thus by trauma syndromes, Aboriginal goals appear "misguided."[12] The site and projects that define and manage our trauma must be seen in light of biopower, and what it produces.

It is not my argument that there isn't a need to treat alcoholism and drug addiction or move to stop abusive behaviors. That is of utmost importance. What I do argue is that we should give attention to the biopolitical processes that are now abundantly available in the United States and Canada to "heal" the Native from traumas that are actually outcomes of power relations that remain our relations with states. States might not have the kind of "sovereignty" that they once imagined, but they remain in full force as systems of regulation over differently identified populations. Indigenous peoples are such "populations." Trauma and healing is a spiral narrative from personal fragmentation to national organization. I have posited that nations like Canada often pose self-determination as self-management in adaptation to capitalist realities. The rise of the psychiatric sciences and the therapeutic industry is striking in the West, as it is in Indian Country. Rose sees this as a science that arises to its highest prominence now to produce a particular kind of knowledge, a certain kind of individual, one that works to continuously manage one's own emotional and mental hygiene.[13]

Therapy for One, Therapy for All

Lauren Berlant points out how certain individuals, families, or communities positioned by race, poverty, sexuality, or a combination thereof are proffered as examples of states of "dangerous" health. In Berlant's essay "Slow Death," her example is obesity. She asks us to observe the way a "population" is identified and incited to work on its own "deviance." It is worth considering at some length. "Biopower operates when a hegemonic bloc organizes the reproduction of life in ways that allow political crises to be cast as conditions of specific bodies and their competence at maintaining health or other conditions of social belonging; thus this bloc gets to judge the problematic body's subjects, whose agency is deemed to be fundamentally destructive."[14] She moves on to identify the ways that people are marked or otherwise segregated "from zoning to shaming." These folks, positioned as they are in opposition to "social prosperity of one sort or another," make it so "[h]ealth itself can then be seen as a side effect of successful normativity, and people's desires and fantasies are solicited to line up with that pleasant condition."[15] Berlant's example of corpulence producing social anxiety about bodies immediately brings to mind the state's ongoing (dis)ease with uncontrollable Indian bodies, who are in "crisis," whose violence becomes marked for policing, but only after lots of media and a lack of policing. While the crisis is the ongoing effects of poverty and the continuing dissolution in communities in extreme marginalization from mainstream "freedoms," they are posed with the need to "heal." In US or Canadian societies where one self-manages, these behaviors are understood to be failures of will, of self-care, failure to self-manage one's passions for food or for alcohol, drugs, or sex. As subjects of the medical diagnosis of addiction, of poor health, and of suspect willpower, Indigenous peoples are subjects of a concern for their ability to self-control, to be autonomous, to be happy, well-adjusted members of a free society where one monitors one's own behaviors. Thus, we are heavily involved within psy technologies to teach us how.

Nikolas Rose clarifies the role and growth of psychology as a science and as a human technique, a technique for bringing forth more pronounced individuality. Psychology begins in the nineteenth century, "inventing the normal individual, . . . and in the first half of the [twentieth century] . . . it was a discipline of the social person." Today its role is to "elaborate complex emotional, interpersonal techniques by which the practices of everyday life can be organized according to the ethic of autonomous self-hood. Correlatively, freedom has come to mean the realization of the potentials of the psychological self."[16] Psychology is a complex of knowledges, of theory and practice, actually the site of many practices, that Rose conceives of as *techniques*, or technologies, "practices seeking certain outcomes in terms of human conduct."[17] As such these technologies have been allied with many different projects, most notoriously with disciplinary institutions (including residential and reform schools), prisons, and, of course, mental hospitals. Psy practices have also been allied with projects of torture, as well as those in liberation struggle. Psychology has also been (at least since the 1930s) integral to the training in management fields. I am reminded of

Eva Illouz's observation of psychology's early involvement in labor management.[18] Psychology has been studied as a "spirit," an ethos deeply intertwined with the emergence of modern western capitalist mass-consumer societies.[19] Psychology is particularly tight now with capitalist governance and corporate management informed through group and human development vocabularies and literatures that have common roots in the human-potential psy techniques—those same techniques that entered Indian Country in the 1970s. Rose poses that psychology has never been more prominent than now because its techniques have been optimum in producing an "enterprising culture" and new subjectivities, ways of being an "enterprising self." The "psychic turn" that Joseph Davis identified poses the rise of trauma as an ethos coinciding with Rose's characterization of a corresponding need to "heal," to reach for techniques with which individuals might optimize their capabilities, in order to "maximize advantage by strategies, tactics, costs and benefits."[20]

Rose posits that neoliberalism is thus "more than a phenomenon at the level of political or monetary philosophy. It constitutes a mentality of government, a conception of how authorities should use their powers in order to produce national well-being, the ends that they should seek, the evils they should avoid, the means they should use, and crucially the nature of the persons upon whom they should act."[21] The enterprising western citizen is urged to "achieve economy, efficiency, excellence and competitiveness . . . hence the vocabulary of enterprise links political rhetoric and regulatory programs to 'self-steering' capacities."[22] But this is only the most visible of neoliberalism's incentives for the production of a good life. We are deeply affectively attached to hopes for a good life. We are emotionally prompted over and over to want what may well be elusive. Health and prosperity are well beyond many peoples in the United States and Canada, the Indigenous included. Our narratives of healing are organized around our optimistic desire for a better life, for health. While many have observed that the Indigenous do not necessarily attach optimism to having lots of money, the desire for health and well-being, a desire for spiritual health and resilience, is an ardent attachment. Health arises here as an especially dynamic site—a site where, in Lauren Berlant's example in "Slow Death," health disciplines are identified and perhaps applied as people move to work on themselves as they are posed in their difference to the normed population's health. Keeping with the insight that biopower is productive, it may be good to see ways that it produces more complexly.

Paul Rabinow (whose example is the social implications of mapping human DNA in the Human Genome Project) observes how certain genetic conditions have given rise to whole networks of social interaction and identities where the commonality is illness. I would bring forward what he observes about diagnoses of illness as social catalysts (in his case a diagnosis of genetic disorder) and their potential for alliance or social networking in Indian Country. Rabinow characterizes these as "biopolitics from below," biosocialities, self-organizing generative collective forms of action and group identities that seek "channels of influence" to lobby in their own interest.[23]

Biosociality

At least from the 1950s on, Alcoholics Anonymous experienced exponential growth in American Indian and Canadian Native communities. AA posits a diagnosis of disease, one that is chronic, where no complete healing is possible. From a small beginning, Native peoples have now formed large, socially active networks for managing their lives around alcohol abstinence and healthy life choices. AA in itself is also a movement characterized as spiritually open-ended. It developed as a bridge between standard religions and psychotherapies, a trend coming into full bloom after World War II. Alison Falby found that several "interdenominational religious groups of the interwar period shaped the enormous sweep of psychotherapeutic mutual assistance movements that received their most enduringly popular expression in Alcoholics Anonymous."[24] Founded by Bill Wilson and Bob Smith in 1935, AA adapted methods that had been part of the Oxford Group experiments with group spiritual support in England and the United States. AA grew over time, with powerful results, developing a winning model that relied on its "emphases on confession and surrender of self (individualism being the modern psychological sin) to the 'Higher Power' of the group. A.A. also echoes the Oxford Group in its informality, its ecumenism, and its idea of conversion or a 'changed life' as a series of stages."[25] Its easily used forms of self-statement and release of self-control to a "higher power" does not require the practitioner to evoke a specific higher power. This flexibility allowed Indigenous peoples to adapt its framework to include specific Native spiritualities and ceremonies.

Still, AA offers narrative strategies and frames that can be overtly directive. In its model of self-speech, language is provided by AA literature and ritual that can be seen as coercive or not depending on the group. For instance, the ritual of identifying oneself immediately in a meeting as an alcoholic is self-speech that identifies one to the group and practices self-diagnosis.

Speech acts undertaken by individuals in AA can be highly scripted and directed by the individual culture of a particular group.[26] But even when such direction is considered, Mariana Valverde found in her research on AA in Canada that members practiced a type of self-care that removed the subject from the power relations inherent in a formal psychiatric patient–doctor relation. Members adopted "practices of truth-telling" that "have social and ethical effects that clearly differentiate them from the classic psychiatric 'confessional.'"[27] AA was the first peer support group in Indian Country, but not the last. In the late 1970s a plethora of different spiritual traditions, Jungian psychology, and self-help peer group interventions appeared in rural and urban communities, as described here in chapter 5.

Presently, some Native AA leaders see their practice as an extension of a series of abstinence-based spiritual revivals that have erupted periodically since contact times. Don Coyhis and William White, for instance, see their contemporary Wellbriety! movement in the context of the Handsome Lake Longhouse teachings (Seneca) in the early 1800s; John Slocum's (Sahewamish-Squaxin) establishment of the Indian Shaker church on the West Coast; and Quanah Parker's institution of the Native American Church.[28] Coyhis and White also reference the practices of many sober chiefs and leaders who preceded contemporary sobriety movements. In his account of the healing movement in Canada, Phil Lane Jr. agreed with Don Coyhis that easing government restrictions on practicing their own spiritualities was foundationally important. It was in the mixture of a sometimes pan-Indian spirituality and AA methods that Aboriginal people articulated great success at finding and keeping sobriety. Phil Lane Jr. also points to Canada's development of or heightened interest in health articulated as a larger social good that set a stage. Groups such as Wellbriety! can be understood as serious social movements, bringing into play social, medical, and psychiatric techniques for producing culturally competent wellbeing, in offering new social subjectivities grounded in well individuals and communities. Indian practices have actually successfully altered the practices of AA, as Indigenous peoples have successfully lobbied the global AA to adapt their nondenominational ecumenism to include specific and pan-tribal ceremonial practice in Indigenous groups.[29] Coyhis sees their practice as a fusion of Indigenous spirituality with western developmental and motivational psychology theory.

According to Coyhis, Erik Erikson studied Lakota philosophy and incorporated this into his theory of developmental psychology. Thus, the healing-forest concept in Wellbriety!, a plan wherein a critical mass of healers could be reached, who would then spread Wellbriety! practices, had dual roots in Lakota developmental psychology: "The Healing Forest is based on the social development stage model of Erik Erikson, who refined European American psychological principles through Native teachings; particularly the wisdom of the Oglala Lakota (Sioux) Tribe of South Dakota." Here, Coyhis moves to appropriate "Eriksonian developmental psychology" for Lakota culture, which he coins as "Eriksonian-Lakota." He posits a "stage theory of self-identity across the life span." An individual takes on particular tasks in his maturation, which unfolds in stages. Coyhis assures his readers that the "teachings of the Lakota are rich with a history of that dual knowledge."[30] In the last few years, other tribal healing groups have moved to publicize how their own cultural practices informed early psychological concepts, a move I see as both a partial truth and a way to appropriate a practice that has found usefulness, moving it from its position as "whiteman" knowledge into closer relations with Native lives. Wellbriety! has a very visible presence in both the United States and Canada and is considered a source of great energy in organizing communities' fights against addiction and family violence.

Maria Yellow Horse Brave Heart, Eduardo Duran, and Bonnie Duran mobilized *historical trauma* as diagnosis, with a course of treatments utilizing psy techniques available in the social sciences and resistance knowledges. Duran grounded his eclectic mixture of Jungian psychology, Buddhism, and trauma theory in liberation psychology and offered it up to the different cultural articulations in different communities. Eduardo and Bonnie Duran have been very successful in promoting healing, although it is a differently expressed psychology in Eduardo Duran's work that makes it powerful.

He speaks in terms that are familiar in communities as social justice liberation narratives. Many of the practices of the early social and civil rights movements were once informed by some blend of these knowledges. In articulation with the thought of Paulo Friere and others who practiced an intertwined liberation theology and liberation psychology, Duran is prominent in articulating colonization as a soul wound. Colonized communities actively perform healing as liberatory practices. He is also critical of more western-based psychological interventions into Indigenous communities. In his article "Liberation Psychology as the Path toward Healing Cultural Soul Wounds," Duran succinctly articulates that because culture is integral to person and community, the destruction of culture wounds the collectivity.[31] He posits that most psychological practices continue to participate in this wounding, rather than in healing. He thinks that western-based psychiatrists who wound are ignorant of oppression and their part in it. They aren't culturally knowledgeable enough to work with Indigenous clients, he believes, or they work toward a noncultural solution not based on the person's needs, needs founded in culture. Duran suggests liberation psychology as a treatment for "internalized oppression," and thus he seemingly builds on the tradition of Fanon and many others.

Both Eduardo Duran's and Bonnie Duran's thought, along with many other eclectic practices, informs the sobriety movements, most following philosophies that have human-potential-based personal transformation as social transformation as their basis. I highlighted these two thinkers in the "sobriety movements" to contrast their thought, but they actually have a more important element in common. The movements that gain ground in Indian Country are just as strongly spiritual movements as they are "developmental." Certainly, each is inclusive of the other. AA first enjoyed success in American Indian and perhaps Canadian Aboriginal communities because the program wasn't just about alcohol; it was about the spirit. Coyhis and Duran illustrate that psychology is a set of techniques that may be attached to differently articulated goals and aspirations than being a well-adjusted citizen of the state, yet trauma theory and its often accompanying human development goals do link these differently articulated practices. Still, when Alkali Lake experienced void and social chaos, it was AA that offered the only social organization available for a time. Wellbriety! dreams healing as reconciliation, that in order to heal, to be free, it is time—not to forget—but to forgive the oppressors. It is trauma placed in the past tense. Andrea Smith in her study of a Christian ethos of apology and reconciliation in Indian Country suggests the formula: "White people repent for genocide, the Indigenous repent for bitterness."[32] In order to heal what is imagined as past aggression must be reconciled; this view pictures the state as presently humane and benefic.

Trauma theory was first adapted in Indigenous settings by a number of western-trained American Indian psychiatrists, psychologists, and social welfare researchers.[33] They joined the huge influx of psychiatrists and psy practitioners that flooded western societies and Indian Country from the 1980s on. Today some professionally trained psychologists like Joseph P. Gone are tribal members who seek to indigenize psychiatry, to infuse or reframe these practices within community philosophies, to do a reverse appropriation of knowledges. Gone has proposed that there is resistance in communities against psy, but mostly against professional practices like his own rather than the informal "red road" therapeutic lay knowledges developed in the healing movements.[34] Psychology as western science is alien but suffused with a multicultural spiritual aura it integrates with local practice. Gone is critical of loosely defined psy knowledge. He does question and write about the role the psy sciences have in managing Indians in the present. He observes that "it may be that the missionary, military, and anthropology vanguard of the historic 'White–Indian' encounter has been displaced of late by the professional psychotherapists or credentialed counselors of the 'behavioral health' clinics who, armed with their therapeutic discourse and their professional legitimacy, are 'using a more shrewder way than the old style of bullets' to resolve the age-old 'Indian problem.'"[35] Although he doesn't necessarily see these as neoliberal techniques of self-management, his is definitely an Indigenous critique from inside the professional ranks of psychology.

The State of Culture

The "nation-state" is a development of culture, western culture that is now global and biopolitical. In neoliberal states the infrastructure that was previously used to deliver services is disappearing in the name of privatization. Capital is fluid and transnational, penetrating the state; in sync with moves to free capital, states destroy regulations and many forms of protection that prior "working-class" generations fought for, including collective bargaining in many places. Capital is deregulated but it micromanages. American Indian nations in the United States and the First Nations band councils in Canada always face instituting many of the same measures because the nation-state often compels them to emulate its practice for coherent relations. In Canada band councils are not evil; they do what they need to do to receive transfers of dwindling state monies into communities. The 2007 UN Declaration of Rights of Indigenous Peoples makes a strong statement supporting an Indigenous self-determination, where Indigenous polities might thrive infused with their own ways of life, creating conditions for Indigenous peoples to live in health and prosperity in representational forms they would make their own. Yet North America wavers and is slow to sign on.

In the United States the American Indian nations have sought to develop under an official US policy of self-determination. Stephen Cornell and Joseph P. Kalt's Harvard Project on American Indian Economic Development reports on the progress of this activity in *The State of the Native Nations: Conditions under U.S. Policies of Self-Determination*. Cornell and Kalt are the international authors of models for Indigenous development worldwide. But they caution that there is no guarantee that Indigenous self-determination in the model that American Indian nations have developed within for the last thirty years will stay in place. The policies of self-determination that have been in place since the Nixon administration are not unassailable. The clouds on the US horizon are important because US policy still has clout internationally. In their 2010 assessment of a growing conservative movement in US policy, Cornell and Kalt, two architects of self-determination policy, posit a growing trend: "signs of instability in the support for self-determination. The rising economic and political clout of Indian nations are often seen as threats at the local level to non-Indian governments. . . . The general trend of outcomes in the US courts has been a reining in, rather than an expansion, of tribal sovereignty over the last fifteen to twenty years."[36] Canadian band councils do not have these same powers that American Indian nations appear to have, although Canadian Indigenous people have negotiated new kinds of governing bodies and arrangements; the Nisga'a and Nunavut come quickly to mind. But these are polities that still must negotiate with the state and come under strict state regulation of their powers—and development is the keyword for this time. In no case has Canada come forward with the political agreements and initial funding that would have made the transitions empowered beyond devolution. Non-Aboriginal Canadians, like their counterparts in Australia, may apologize, but they are not supportive of Aboriginal self-determination.[37] Canada and the United States offer package deals for development that fall short of an autonomous Indigenous self-determination closer to that declared in the UN Declaration of Rights. Canada does not have to do more. Why?

Canada can point to the therapeutic reconciliation that it has put in place as progress for Indigenous nations within its borders. On the other hand, Canada can stall more autonomous self-determination efforts by Indigenous governments by negotiating their adaptive inclusions into its already expansive neoliberal multiculturalism.

For at least three decades, Canada has professed its allegiance to liberal multiculturalism. This was policy-driven in most western nations by capitalism as it expanded, pushed, forced, evicted, or enticed peoples across borders for work or for safety. Will Kymlicka attributes Canada's initial multiculturalism to leftist progressive democratic forces. Multiculturalism, rather than revolution, succeeded colonialism and paternalism.[38] There were voices among the Indigenous and Québecois that advocated for radical change, and multiculturalism was adopted through compromise by including moderate political factions to block radical ones. As Canada moved into neoliberalism, this initially moderate progressive project became neoliberal multiculturalism. Eva Mackey has argued that Canada mostly used cultural differences, appropriating them to their own nation-building project and without respect for Indigenous demands.[39] Kymlicka observes that the first neoconservative politicos had been adamantly hostile to multiculturalism, calling it a "politically correct" product of the nanny welfare state. After a while neoliberalism, with its focus on a smaller, less centralized state, saw how to incorporate it. The most crude method by which it did so was by seeing "ethnic" culture as product; thus, peoples' cultural dress, foods, and so forth could become marketable. As neoliberal thought grew more sophisticated, the World Bank and other neoliberal entities became involved by promoting culture as human capital, as labor, or as the potential for development of resources attached to cultural identity. In the Indigenous case, this is a human capital that came with territory, a rich sense of relationships, and natural resources. All very marketable. Kymlicka presents diverse cases, but I want to direct attention to two points he makes about Indigenism in neoliberal multiculturalism and to respond. First, Aboriginal self-determination wasn't abandoned in Canada's turn to neoliberalism, because Aboriginal rights had been embedded constitutionally. Kymlicka notes that Australian Aboriginals fared badly because they lacked this protection. Second, he rightly notes that in places like Bolivia, indigenism has appeared to use neoliberal political forms to come to power. This agrees with many others observing neoliberalism's adaptations to culture. I mention again Aihwa Ong's observation on a "promiscuous" neoliberal capitalism, how accommodating it is to different lifeways, different political styles, and different conditions.[40]

In Canada neoliberal multiculturalism wouldn't need to further empower Indigenous challenges to the state — only accommodate them and use them. The bottom line is always land and resources. This is the adaptation that the Indigenous in North America are really asked to make. Canada's reality lies closer to Patricia Richards's assessment of neoliberal racial politics: "the rationale behind neoliberal multiculturalism is less about changing racial hierarchies than it is about creating self-governing indigenous subjects that will not challenge the political-economic goals of the state."[41] Rauna Kuokkanen mostly finds a "neo-liberal agenda and construction of indigenous rights that seek to reduce and redefine indigenous rights to fit into a new model of market citizenship with a focus on economic development."[42] It is here that "culture as treatment" to enhance individual and collective capital gains context.

Multiculturalism once posed its worth in educating westernized peoples to respect cultural difference to reduce racism. In an Indigenous setting this is often done in the name of creating safety — for healing and reconciliation. Indigenous energy is expended in trying to translate. Maria Battiste and Sakej Henderson have urged us to move beyond trying to articulate "different" realities between Indigenous and western epistemologies, since there is no practical way to make comparisons.[43] At the time of Linda Tuhiwai Smith's elegant *Decolonizing Methodologies, Research and Indigenous Peoples*, which set the paradigm for seizing our own research agendas, I began to try to articulate the way in which Indigenous knowledges that we do produce now interact with western knowledge claims. I found three accounts over about a ten-year span that say something. Julie Cruikshank proved in her long relationship with Yukon elders that Indigenous oral narratives, "stories," had power to contest and sometimes redefine western historical knowledge as it moves to integrate or omit Native land tenure.[44] But Paul Nadasdy came to the jarring conclusion that most scientific projects' empirical effort to "integrate" Indigenous ecological knowledge into already defined western scientific "databases" radically altered that knowledge, because this effort abstracted it from what made it meaningful in the first place. Nadasdy found that "traditional ecological knowledge" could not be extracted and categorized to "enhance" western scientific information on land management. Nadasdy makes the point that integration "assumes that knowledge is an intellectual product that can be isolated from its social context." He observes that knowledge works in the world only when a thick index of social and material support provides a context for its "success." Worse, if Indigenous knowledge of the land did not fit the western researchers' ready categories, they would often ignore it or, worse yet, throw it away.[45] Thus, lifetimes of Indigenous experiential testimony ended up in waste receptacles because there was no connection. Indigenous knowledges inform an actually existing lived difference, not one reducible to western abstraction.

Stephanie Irlbacher-Fox picks up on this in her felt analyses of self-determination negotiations between the Dene and the Canadian government. Irlbacher-Fox, extremely cognizant and respectful of the effort of the Dene community, of Dene women, to teach her how to "find dahshaa," the ingredient that is transformative in tanning moose hides into the material that becomes amazing clothing suitable for the Yukon winters, acknowledges that in each step of this process *a way of life* is embedded: thick relations between all the elements, human, plant, and animal, in the place she resided. Living that, she found dahshaa an apt metaphor to contrast the Canadian government's preprepared package of concepts they brought to negotiating self-determination in Dene country. Dahshaa comes only in "enhanced awareness" in profound relationship with the great matrix of knowledge, patience, and hospitality of all involved. Dahshaa is contrary to the technical knowledge imported into the communities to "get a job done." The technicians and "self-determination" negotiators are unable to disconnect from the *need* to fit Dene lifeways into capitalism's necessity for "development." The negotiations for self-determination are always intimately connected to power; the knowledges at the negotiating table are not engaged in a dialogue, or even agreeing on similar paradigms. In Irlbacher-Fox's work Dene meanings are contrasted with the Canadian *need to know* how best to extract "resources," no matter what the eventual impact is on the matrix of life there.[46] From this I gather that if the interchange is very local without too much at stake, the exchanges are meaningful, but if they involve high stakes around territory, resources, or political power, the exchange becomes one of western coercion. Individuals can sometimes disconnect from that imperative and put what they learn to goals different from those necessary in negotiating treaties to assure western capitalism's orderly penetration of Dene lands and lives. Those people who commit to learn are those who may move in alliance with Indigenous epistemologies in these places against motivations of profit. In general, beyond the instances I discuss above, consumer citizens are attached affectively to pitying/adoring/hating/loving Indians, but they do not seek to know them, particularly if they cannot figure out how to consume them.

Indigenous peoples are widely aware that these people's interests in Indigenous cultures are often in the interest of their own self-care, to learn "healing" practices that they might undertake as individuals or as "lifestyles." I think the consumer citizen's "ignorance" is informed within the same affective, richly informed racial, sexual, and heteronormative knowledges that have always informed power relations in capitalist states, generation after generation, not individual aberration. It might change with the times but is enduring because it keeps these formative racial/gendered/sexed relations in place, active, established, and virile. There is no evidence that western capitalist cultures are motivated by altruism when they effect reforms in policies toward Indigenous peoples. I think there is accommodation when Indigenous peoples push back, and it is clear that the position of victim is not the best place to do that from. Thus, what can happen must happen from strength, where alliances are made, where people and communities act from specific mutual interest for some common goal, and not hold out that a dominant "culture" will magically transform if we educate its consumers on our "difference." I think that Indigenous cultures may represent the only living models for different economic and social systems on the planet, ways of life that have the power to challenge capital cultures, even when they are not pure or untouched by capitalism. We ourselves must take our "cultures" out of multicultural uses—to seriously see the active epistemologies they are that inform life and governing in particular places.

Healing Cultures

The multicultural experiments of Europe at this point are described as being in tatters, with racism and xenophobia common eruptions. As a nation that also adopted neoliberalism, Canada has hollowed out in practice more and more of the areas where it might once have met the self-determination demands of Indigenous peoples and has entered more fully into a largely symbolic arena of apology and truth and reconciliation. Canada moved to put forth what it considers to be important to this act, offering money in reparation for genocidal acts. To remind, this process was put into place to put Canada's vicious past behind it, to reconcile the state violence that constitutes its formation. Yet the state cannot also be a safe agent in the reconciliation, because it is still constituted through the same nexus of racialization, heteronormativity, and gender violence that it was formed in. Thus, its structural violence is the present and the future state. The Indigenous peoples of Canada are still at the epicenter of inordinate racism, gender violence, and poverty, and are mostly still managed within a colonial Indian Act. In a new global racial ethic, it is said there is no race, while race attaches to new projects. The Indigenous are more often portrayed in neoliberal multiculturalism to be a parochial and separatist identity-driven politic. Jodi Melamed observes, "Neoliberal multicultural-ism represents multiculturalism to be the spirit of neoliberalism"; thus, "[i]t justifies the removal of indigenous peoples from their lands by describing the entire world as the potential property of global multicultural citizens."[47]

Our epistemologies, our cultures, represent ways of thinking about the world truly different from capitalism. These epistemologies *are* the cultures that everyone is always referring to—they are ways of knowing, and I believe they are diverse, differently located, not always rural, never static, and do effect change. They do have strengths to differently define issues and offer different solutions to themselves and others. Mostly what I observe, because I go home to the North although I live in the South—is that while gripped in huge change, these Dena are still in relation with their land and the practices that sustain their daily life there. While not "pure," their lives are still informed largely by their own paradigmatic knowledges. It is not a symbolic practice, a practice that has to refer to somewhere else for its "authenticity." It's just *what they do*. What they do is of great beauty and cunning, because it's hard to live where it is very cold. In *Northern Athabascan Survival: Women, Community, and the Future*, Phyllis Fast, an Athabascan ethnologist, points out that "discourses related to social pathology are culturally potentiated to provide terms that fit mainstream American ideas of Native Americans."[48] While not ignoring the bleak statistics portraying Northern Athabascan health, Fast suggests that we look for a more nuanced and complex understanding. The Alaskan Athabascan peoples that Fast lived among and spoke to in the early 1990s attributed their social discord "to political and economic hegemony," not necessarily "illnesses" such as alcoholism and "outcomes" like suicide.[49] Phyllis Fast has mixed feelings about healing as it is presented in the trauma scripts: "freeze framing the conditions of Natives into one mode of being and one way of having reached that point."[50] Fast suggests there is a dissonance between community explanation and the common categories of pathology that dominate the conversation on contemporary Athabascan health. Gwich'in speak of values, *vat'aii*, and of *yinjih*, of survival and strength. These are ethical cores, values of northern Athabascans that are practiced and perceived in everyday personal and communal actions across and against the medical languages that demarcate modern Native experience. These values exist, not necessarily in an unchanging oral tradition or in an unchanging world, but at the nexus of change, in the moment-by-moment struggle to live Gwich'in meaning into another day.

But not everyone in rural communities has this knowledge. We mostly know the horror stories, where it is all stripped and Natives live in abject poverty, a poverty not just material but spiritual. Indigenous poverty *is* being totally stripped of the knowledges that informed you how to live in your place, knowledges that give the spiritual affective strength to want to live. The wound that Indigenous peoples refer to is not only the stripping of those knowledges but the results when you are also positioned by racialization and gender violence, how your body is marked and read in another epistemology as a threat, and you are without access to alternate meaning or another way of being. The healing stories are sometimes triumphant, a people's rich account of how they regenerated their own ways of life from an utter void. Still, their expectation is that they restore their cultures to govern themselves as Indigenous, with their governing reflecting these knowledges and ways of life. That is where the big disconnect is. The healing narrative within reconciliation and the nation-state's actual agenda do not coincide.

At the same time there are multiple intense and meaningful "cultural" activities, performances of culture in all aspects of Indigenous life, mobilized for many reasons and actions, many in the name of health and development. Indigenous peoples are increasing rather than decreasing activities wherein we have faith that our articulation and practice of our own epistemologies are good ways of doing things. But these activities are all over the place, with some harnessed to biosocialities in the name of healing from the traumas of residential schools, some in reconstructing polities, and some mobilized as attractions within capitalist tourism development projects. Indigenous epistemologies inform education across a wide spectrum of life present in rural and urban health programs, community-based schools, treatment centers, and some college classrooms. Indigenous peoples have no easy agreement (and no easy agreement will ever be possible) on what the potential of our own knowledges represents or what power they have. In some places this is because there is confusion between race and culture, although I think these are not now experienced separately—but there is sometimes confusion over what race is, and how it informs culture.

I see this confusion in its most bloody splendor in the places where it is more difficult to show cultures as different epistemologies that inform practices (ways of life, law, governing). I confront this in the actuality of our attempts to teach culture problematized by racialization/sexualization as power in urban settings. How deep must we make the actual resources (parents, teachers, knowledges) to bring children into their cultures where they are a barely visible "minority"? How to totally prepare them to handle the force of the virulent racism and gender violence mobilized against their efforts? How do we support them through a time when it may be hard for them to imagine their budding language and performances of culture *are* meaningful outside of the immediate pressure of their peers? Isolation isn't possible. We must confront that they will always face the "intense pathologizing of Native peoples generally, evident in policy discourses and portrayals of Native youth as antisocial, deviant criminals with a propensity for violence and gang involvement, [that] conjures up an image of them as 'ignoble' beings, individuals deserving of little empathy but much surveillance from dominant society."[51]

There is a founded basis for believing that teaching grounded, connected practices as self-disciplines and as ways of knowing and seeing the world does counter kids' vulnerability to these forces. Many kids understand only their racialization—where "Indian" is mobilized without culture. But that "Indian" is attached to the worst articulations of racist, sexist, homophobic normativity that western nation-states can dish out. Our cultures are not food choices, window dressing, or weekend endeavors. Sometimes there is a fear of youth or confusions around whether cultures are living resilient organic practices or precious vaults wherein culture must be preserved as a static "thing"—weak, fragile, and dying—to be preserved as a museum piece. Each elder that dies does take their knowledge with them, but I must support that we can trust the youth to generate and practice cultures, relations with the land, relations with all life forms, ways respectful of women, men, and children into the future. How might we honor languages and songs but not turn a deaf ear when hip-hop is a resistance language that youth and the peoples adapt in order to culturally participate. I want to face the fear that we lose culture by performing it differently. I want to directly confront the message that our cultures are dying because we live them differently. But it is this "we" and "our" that also loom huge in these conversations.

In general I have thought that Gerald Taiaiake Alfred is magnificently cognizant of the power of Indigenous epistemologies as disciplines, as vital ways of perceiving and acting as Indigenous peoples in the world.[52] What I don't hear in his otherwise brilliant thought is how we might—other than to condemn as lost or as duped—engage the actual multiplicity that is. Other powerful discourses, religions, and healing practices continuously intersect and transform our cultures. While I wish to remain in relationship with an indigenism informed by a living relationship to land, to lives lived in honor of these relations, I don't live at home. Current demographic studies cite 60 percent of the Indigenous peoples in North America as living in cities. We know this means off the reserved lands, while our ancient relations are with much larger areas—that often include such urban areas. It is said we are disconnected, but we are disconnected only if we do not know or make our relations known or fight to make relations. It is said we can't produce the ways of life we once had, yet no spirit is static. It's not so much about the specific technologies as about the spirit of what we do to live and the choices we make. It is said we are going down the identity road to multiculturalism's great highway. I think race becomes confused with spirit and content. What does the radical "difference" that is "us," that exists in any of us, mean? What and whom do the identity wars serve? The Indigenous will be transformed by our lived experiences with imperial globalization—experiences we cannot control just by tighter and tighter attempts to regulate identity—while not prepared to have a deeper conversation about what is at stake in inclusions and exclusions. I believe that Indigenous epistemologies, if they are not thought of as static or rigid but as the truly amazing adaptable practices that they are, can weather these huge debates. Taiaiake Alfred has mostly left the subject of gender to the women; thus, his otherwise astute accounts of colonization miss some important aspects of what has taken place. I am definitely not suggesting or calling for a dialogue on what any "true" practices are. I ask a different question: what do our practices serve? In part I would say that some aspects of "cultures" have been harnessed by the biopolitical state in the service of managing our health and well-being at the community level—in keeping with their promise to human rights organizations to cause us no overt harm—but that could never be the whole story.

Cultures, not as a monolithic "culture," also hold the intense imaginary affective dreaming power of the people's will to live and thrive. These cultures hold a sense of polity that poses opposition to the necrotic forces of capitalism, knowledges that keep the land in connection to us even when we are not able to live there or learn directly from that experience. It is in the fragile and also powerful way that a little "culture" can totally generate different ways of perception that can and do inform peoples; it is the space where we create and negotiate multiple subjectivities, and the stuff we create as Dena or Lummi or Nuu-cha-nulth.

The Canoe Way

In the 1960 world of the Coast Salish, now the Pacific Northwest of the United States and the southwest coast of British Columbia, political "turmoil" and a resurgence of powerful spiritual practices took place. New "babies," initiates to the Coast Salish smokehouses, rose in numbers startling to mainstream social scientists studying Indian assimilation.[53]

As part of many resurging cultural practices in the watersheds of the Salish Sea and farther north, Indigenous peoples got their canoes out of the backyard and put them in the rivers and in the coastal waters again. New canoes were carved for a new time. They took to the waters with a different purpose than the racing that had been a mainstay cultural activity in their pre–World War II and early 1950s communities to evade government regulations. Even though many still raced canoes, this was an activity that paled in comparison to what the original role of the canoe was in their culture.[54]

The canoe was the primary means of transportation in these regions for a time beyond any western calculation. There had been canoes of all sizes for all jobs—huge ones for transporting large numbers of peoples to potlatches and swift streamlined ones for war. There were small ones for everyday use and specialized ones for different jobs. The canoe is a superb Indigenous technology. The Coast Salish people's canoe as a way of transportation and their knowledge of the rivers and coastal waters enabled the growth of the first settler states in their homelands. The canoe's use declined in part because Indigenous movement and trade, Indigenous economies, became severely curtailed (not stopped) by colonial regulations, regulations that also suppressed the potlatch ceremonies and smokehouses, along with fishing and gathering in usual and accustomed places.[55] Slowly these regulations were fought and lifted, so that after 1950 a little life began to return. In the Puget Sound area, the Coast Salish fought a successful treaty rights struggle, forcing the state of Washington to recognize their rights to fish in their "usual and accustomed" places. They won a protracted war that had taken place on riverbanks and in the streets and in the courts. Across the "border" huge flurries of political organizing geared up to articulate the treaty rights that Canadians had neglected to make with most of British Columbia's Indigenous peoples.[56]

The Canoe Way has "origins" in all these activities, although the canoe journeys as the spectacular practices of Coast Salish culture in late summer all over Puget Sound and beyond are credited in their contemporary form to Emmett Oliver, who organized the first Paddle to Seattle in 1989. The Journey has grown exponentially since then to include paddlers from southeast Alaska, Hawaii, Northern California, and the entire west coast of Canada. Recently, Maori have participated, as well as Indigenous peoples from Central and South America. It has included Ojibwe and other canoe traditions.

These practices perform exemplary acts of generative cultural activity; youth, elder, and adult interactive participation; activities that organize Indigenous cultural practices year-round in all the communities that participate. They are integral and inclusive. Organized in "families," each group, mostly dedicated to particular Coast Salish and coastal nations, draws in a wide mixture of individuals. Some are tribal nation members, although because so many are related in some way throughout the region, many tribes may be present in one canoe. There are non-Natives of many races and persuasions; those with urban or rural experiences; people who are on a healing path; those whose cultural knowledge is not certain; and those with much experience and cultural practice. Shasta Cano-Martin, executive director of the Lummi CEDAR Project, says, "The Canoe families are not always 'families,' but we talk about how when we get in the canoe and travel together, we become like a family."[57] The families model inclusiveness. Each year such a family forms around a core group with enough experience and resources to put the canoe in the water to train and to finally make a Journey.[58]

There are now hundreds of these families, and never fewer than eighty canoes, who participate. Each canoe with its paddlers and support crew can represent as many as fifty people involved in direct ways, and hundreds indirectly. Each year a Coast Salish or coastal community in Washington or British Columbia hosts the event, and each year the canoes set off on their Journey from their homes, traveling over hundreds of miles of rough coastal waters and rugged strait currents to reach the host. Traveling in groups, each stops and does protocol in the many other communities along the way. The communities on the route both send their canoes and host smaller protocol events with food, dancing, singing, and rest, the honoring offered to each canoe and to the people and the Journey. Each community officially honors itself by giving permission to visitors to come to its shores. Communities do so to honor each other, to imprint their ancient relational and national boundaries over and across those of nation-states.

This is a contemporary practice of the potlatch that at one time was the governing organization of this entire area, melding everyone in practices of ceremony and strict protocol for the taking of fish and other beings for sustenance. The potlatches organized the distribution of responsibilities for the land and waters in different regions and in elaborate ceremony gifted, danced, and sang individual communal responsibilities into law all over.[59] Up until the early twentieth century, the peoples of the Coast Salish Sea from coastal southeast Alaska, Tlingit territory, to Northern California potlatched. They traveled in canoes to different communities so that everyone witnessed and participated in claims to wealth articulated as responsibilities to particular food-producing areas and the fair distribution of those resources.[60]

The Canoe Way is often portrayed as a healing activity akin to the Wellbriety movement that I discussed earlier. It is true that everyone makes a personal journey that is also part of the journey of each family. The Canoe Journey does offer a discipline and a practice for healing. It is a spiritual practice, but it also does more, in the sense that it is not ever imagined so instrumentally—it is like other cultural performances informed by practices in particular places and spiritualities. It is not separate from posing an order and governance. This was expressed early on by a number of influential elders. Reflecting on the Paddle to Bella Bella in 1993 that followed the first Paddle to Seattle, Frank Brown of the Heiltsuk portrayed the emotional, spiritual, and disciplining knowledges of the Canoe Journey.

> One lesson from the canoe culture is that people will not move ahead unless they all take ownership of the work required to get what they need as a crew or community. This example transfers from the canoe teachings to our everyday lives. Let us use these canoe teaching metaphors as powerful reminders of what we must do to govern ourselves. Preparing to

welcome each other, voyaging on the ocean, we find what is similar to us all. That is called healing. Our lesson is to reevaluate our whole thinking process about our society and how we relate to each other. Ultimately, we discover new ways to obtain the most efficient of governmental means, what our people have always used to sustain ourselves, called consensus.[61]

The Canoe Journeys have since the 1980s truly brought the Coast Salish peoples into a closer union, working in greater alliance than they have in over a century, and perhaps in a new way—in a union formed around many common goals. The inner waters that form parts of the Georgia Strait, the Strait of Juan de Fuca, the southern waters around Vancouver Island, and the Puget Sound were officially designated the Salish Sea, in part because these peoples asserted it. They also are asserting their responsibility to artic- ulate sustainable practices in the bioregion, in sustaining interdependent life without an anthropomorphic focus. In 2008 after a joint regional policy meeting that included over 350 Coast Salish elders, chiefs, chairmen, and environmental staff, they announced a commitment. In an international negotiation with Environment Canada, the US Environmental Protection Agency, the Province of British Columbia, and Washington State, they took their place as comanagers of their ancient homelands, articulating their particular interest: "We, the indigenous peoples of the Salish Sea, honor and respect our sacred trust to restore, preserve and protect our culture, treaties, aboriginal rights and the land, air and waters of the Salish Sea. Our sacred trust has been given to us from our ancestors and defines our role as protectors of our Mother Earth. We are entrusted with the protection and sustainability of environment and natural resources of our ancestral lands, watersheds, and estuarine waters of the Salish Sea."[62] The Salish have made their ancient responsibility to their lands and water the reason for acting across nation-state borders to protect their elders and their children. To protect their heritage in their elders and their future in their children, they move to protect their land: "Defending and protecting our ancestral lands and waters, we seek to acknowledge our sacred alliance so we may work together as one proud nation."[63] This is a statement that claims its own authority beyond that of treaties but protects the treaty—by articulating their rights as sacred and part of what they seek to protect, by assuming them and performing them. It is also a statement that reaches out inclusively to portray that their responsibility should be shared, should be everyone's.

The peoples of the Salish Sea journey to each others' homes each sum- mer to honor their shared heritage and to practice ways that are informed by the abundant life in an environment that once made them secure in ways that no policing in any nation-state could imagine. The Canoe Journey offers the individual Coast Salish peoples practices in daily life that work to continue it and sustain it and instill an order that cannot be achieved solely by policing. Shelly Vendiola, a Swinomish/Filipina educator involved in organizing the Lummi CEDAR Youth Empowerment and Training program, portrays exactly how the knowledges in the Canoe Way give youth support to practice their cultures at the same time that they teach them skills to confront rampant racism and other issues and conditions endemic to their lives. First, they are brought into community with elders, learning who they are, their stories, relations, languages, and responsibilities. She shares that "in addition to acquiring a greater understanding of cultural identity, youth learn peacemaking strategies, such as undoing racism and oppression, prejudice reduction, anger management, violence reduction, effective communication, and basic mediation and conflict resolution skills." She offers further that "they learn various approaches to community organizing." The canoe teachings of pulling together and being in balance physically, mentally, emotionally, are incorporated into the community organizing process.[64]

I think this is a good example of how cultural practices inform more than individual identity, becoming integral—as Frank Brown said, "powerful reminders of what we must do to govern ourselves," what these peoples pull for, and why they must pull together. Thus, instruction on how to live on Earth as peoples informed by a long knowledge of place and respectful relations therein is a living practice.

Food Sovereignty

It is easy to build on the first Coast Salish example in this section, because the Northwest Indian College located at Lummi has a wonderful program that teaches Indigenous epistemologies, ways of knowing, that like most Indigenous cultures are knowledges of the land, of the foods, and of the multiple practices of abundance that indigenism is synonymous with. While the focus of the Diabetes Prevention through Traditional Plants Program of the Northwest Indian College is located at Lummi and serves that community, its responsibility is to a much larger Indigenous community in the region: "Northwest Indian College [NWIC] is the only accredited tribal college in the Pacific Northwest. [Located] in Lummi Nation near Bellingham, Washington . . . [it also] serve[s] extended campuses . . . located at four reservations in Washington (Swinomish, Muckleshoot,

Port Gamble S'Klallam, and Tulalip) and one in Idaho (Nez Perce). . . . During the 2008–2009 year the College provided academic courses to 1,254 students. Students came from 101 tribes and First Nations bands throughout the United States and Canada."[65]

The Traditional Plants Program that NWIC provides is informed by rich research that has been a cooperative effort of Indigenous and non-Native researchers in the region over many years. This research was driven by more than their own particular interest in Indigenous plants. Elise Krohn and Valerie Segrest in Traditional Foods of Puget Sound Project's final report said that their project used but expanded on the University of Washington's Burke Museum staff reports from archaeological sites in the region detailing ancient artifacts found there, including evidence of food practices. Krohn and Segrest noted how valuable the Burke research was, but also that it was available only in spreadsheets, making such knowledge not practical or useful to daily lives in the communities.

Diabetes, as a primary and often silent killer in Indigenous communities, is known to be a recent occurrence; thus, diabetes prevention is certainly becoming an important focus in community health education. In positing that traditional foods take their place in preventative health strategies, Indigenous peoples also assert their epistemological frames on what those foods mean and a whole world of differently theorized practices. "Food" profoundly organizes a sense of Indigenous polity; thus, any discussion of food is always a profoundly political one.[66] Through such a conversation on diabetes, NWIC intersects with prevention programs at many levels of tribal, civil, state, and nation-state governance across the United States and Canada. It is also through a discussion of food sovereignty that the project articulates within an international rights conversation on food security. A discussion of traditional foods and the knowledges that are involved in growing, procuring, or understanding their significance opens up a space that brings together many threads of concern that I have discussed in this text. I will only briefly walk through some of these connections.

I might, because I am from the North, look to places like Alaska and Canada, the circumpolar north, as places where Indigenous peoples still sometimes live directly off their lands, to give examples of how "food" organizes life. In communities that still depend primarily on hunting large animals such as whales or caribou, the activities to procure this "food" and others inform and generate spiritual practices, senses of family, communal roles, responsibilities, and order. This effort takes place informed by an entire gamut of emotions, wherein felt human accomplishment or defeat is part of the seasonal cyclical integration of human, animal, and land, all spirits that inform one another. We do empathic intense dreaming from these places that are less integrated into capitalism, although those places are very rare at this point—while we, I, do not idealize their struggles.

We might only get glimpses, but it is these ways, these epistemologies thus formed, that still, even as remnants, organize indigenist interests now. It is this same empathic intense dreaming that organizes indigenism as a fight in the name of the rare places where peoples are still attempting to live in holistic practices on their land, to live their cultures. At the same time we understand that even while all may not be able to do this, it is our responsibility to defend these cultural practices in whatever form they can still exist without putting them in mental or emotional formaldehyde. In practice this has meant that while we are defending land and cultures, we are defending that our values might inform not just ourselves but a larger world of "capitalism" and its cultures. It is an indigenist position that the capitalist philosophies presently informing global development practice are destructive rather than generative to the fragile conditions that maintain "life as we know it" on this planet.

This global destruction is of course the site of the "wound." Nancy Turner wrote that "within the past few decades there has been a growing movement worldwide toward recognition of the importance and validity of traditional, or local, knowledge. This movement is both ethical and practical." Indigenous peoples were oppressed "in many ways, removed from their lands, or restricted within small areas of their traditional territories, or sometimes outside of them, forbidden to speak their language or practice their culture, including the use of traditional resources and traditional land and resource management." Turner posits that "the loss of indigenous knowledge is a loss to all humanity."[67] She speaks to traditional knowledges, not as abstract ideas but as grounded practices, whose loss is a loss to humanity because these practices hold the key, she believes, to ways of life that could sustain all life rather than destroy it. This belief, with all the alliances it entails, organizes a majority of ethical practices that are now globally called "environmental" or "ecological" activism, whose various interests do not always, like Nancy Turner's, coincide with those of Indigenous communities attempting to practice their ways of life as food sovereignty. As I explained earlier in this chapter, those who want to "extract" so-called TEK (traditional ecological knowledge) can be as violent as anyone with respect to what they want. Environmentalism is often an uncomfortable but necessary alliance for Indigenous peoples.

A huge case in point would be those animal rights and environmental forces that physically and affectively converged on the Makah in their first treaty-organized whale hunt in nearly a century.[68] These forces fight for the "rights," for the inclusion of the nonhuman within the protection of law, yet do not question what that law is. Environmentalism as a mission contains many wide and various projects that do and sometimes do not understand what the cultures that generate and nurture "sustainable" knowledges pose as law. In that way, environmentalists miss another order of relations that is available to humans living with other life forms, another order of "law." In many ways there is still a disconnect between needing to "save the planet" and what the subjugation of Indigenous peoples and their knowledges (cultures) has served and continues to serve, what is foundational about this subjugation to continuing capitalism as usual.

Many western environmentalists place Indigenous peoples on the fringes of their interests, because our knowledges and peoples are positioned as racially and epistemologically hybrid, or impure; we are not the "real Indians." Likewise, those real Indians lived in the past, rather than in our now as the contemporaries of modern nation-states. We aren't the real generators of our ancient knowledges. As contemporary Indigenous nations that must negotiate with international regulatory commissions with our treaty rights, who are required to use high-powered rifles to ensure humane hunts (in the case of whales), we are not the pure Indigenous hunters of old. This reveals the fallacy in an old capitalist developmental worldview that positions us all in a serious mistake.

It is in a western conception of progress, the philosophy behind global capitalist development where Indigenous peoples are positioned in an anthropological past rather than as contemporary peoples practicing from radically different worldviews (not monolithic). The practices and cultures of capitalism that see themselves as the sole vision for humankind's "progress" are synonymous with those polities, that were formed and informed within the *rights of man*, constituted for and around the subject of western law, traditionally a racially white, heterosexual male figure. This figure, whether or not it has been constituted to be more inclusive in the last fifty years by granting and recognizing the "rights" of those originally excluded—the female, the racial others, other genders, the differently abled—still operates in a position of absolute authority. Such a figure has no capacity to represent the nonhuman. Indigenism as a philosophy argues that humans are embedded in a web of larger relations that is life. *Life* cannot be reduced to the property relationship implied by *resource*. Human and nonhuman relations cannot be figured in a representational system that is configured through the primacy of property and the rights-bearing property owner.

This same figure has been synonymous with a capitalism that envisions its trajectory in a teleological progress, a progress that refutes challenges to its vision of unlimited growth as a cultural practice. Capitalism is a practice that evades any criticism of its own limits, posing itself as global rather than as a specific practice of western culture that still seeks to colonize other lifeways, that is, other models for living. Other lifeways and polities are posed as fundamentalist and backward in this vision. Indigenous peoples are primitives who are slowly being brought from their backward state into the present. Their ways of life are, as Sousan Abadian informed us, "inconsistent with basic realities."

Yet it is to these same Indigenous lifeways that many in the West want to turn for ideas to inform their own intense dreaming that has generated more and more nightmares these days. This is usually a utilitarian interest, one that mostly wants to "extract" TEK to make a newer and better model of sustainable capitalism. Indigenism contains glimpses of other ways of living, of governing our conduct, for different purposes, that are not chained to the grandiose visions of a "sustainable" but ever-expanding voracious development. Thus, indigenism is posed and poses itself as knowledges and cultures opposed to the unbridled knowledges of capitalism, while not separate from, or untouched by, their forces.

Nancy Turner articulates her perception of Indigenous worldview loosely as a "belief in the spirituality and innate power of all things; respect for other life forms and entities; ideological systems that enforce sustainable use of resources (social sanctions, sharing); concepts of interactive relationships with other life forms; and close identification with ancestral lands."[69] That is, everything is alive and has the capacity to affect, and because of that, respect is practiced, so as not to unduly cause such harm or affect that might invite negative relations, a respect that is reinforced in customs that govern every aspect of daily practice in relation, with everything. That is the ideal in the philosophy, that all imperfectly strive for when it is in practice in a particular place.

Thus, bringing traditional food practices back into Indigenous lives is to bring with them certain philosophies. For Elise Krohn and Valerie Segrest's Traditional Foods of Puget Sound Project, this is to produce practical knowledge for the wider communities and families that each student has relations with. In the project the organizers took archaeological data and informed it with the rich oral knowledges, stories, and memories of those who attended that begin to inform places and practices that had been severely curtailed by government regulation, by land loss, boarding school interruption to traditional teaching, and neglect as families tried to survive in labor economies. Each student who gains new or better appreciation for the plants, fish, and animals and the philosophies they entail as food or medicine will touch many families and communities. Krohn and Segrest hope that food gathered or grown in respect will be healing and reinforce daily food practices that will prevent illness. They know it is not diabetes alone that affects them, but many health issues, particularly those "illnesses" associated with poverty, poor living conditions, stress, and subjugation. They also know that growing and securing traditional foods involves the worldview and philosophies that I suggest above. Likewise they know that these same practices transgress many nation-state laws and cultural mores.

There is a growing recognition among young people of the centrality of food to Indigenous existence. In 2011 Michelle Daigle, a member of the Constance Lake Cree, shared her research interest in her traditional food systems with a symposium of Native American Students in Advanced Academia (NASAA) at the University of Washington in Seattle. Daigle proposed a thesis entitled "The Restoration of Traditional Food Systems: A Pathway toward the Regeneration of an Indigenous Existence." She posits that food practices as ways to heal specific injuries are important, but that in actuality ancient food traditions are integral to culture, "regenerating our ancestral knowledge systems, our sacred relationships with all of our relations and our cultural practices which uniquely define us as Nistam Eniniwak (the Cree expression for Original Peoples)." She relates the rising health risks in her community and others across the continent. She also notes that a renewed interest in restoring traditional foods had mostly highlighted health concerns. She seeks its wider significance: "While [traditional foods are] . . . of great value to the future physical well-being of our communities, I will propose that the restoration of our food systems becomes much more than simply a good source to a healthy diet and nutrients."[70] Our "foods," our lands, or how the earth shares food, is of vital interest to us all right now. Our health is important, but health bespeaks a quality of life, and food ways are now put in a key positioning for our survival internationally. While the "Traditional Foods of Puget Sound Project" joins in alliance with the Burke museum's archeological staff to share knowledges, NWIC asserts its authority to translate data back into Indigenous practice. The NWIC is part of a movement that is not separate from the Canoe Way; they are integral to each other as each community goes through the seasonal cycle of ceremonies to celebrate the spirits of the fish and the foods, to dance in honor of them and their cultures in potlatches all up and down the southwestern coast of Canada and the Puget Sound.

This movement is also closely related to larger movements all over the Northern Hemisphere and beyond, practices of self-determination where concerns for food sovereignty illuminate the interconnection among food, land, culture, health, and autonomy.

Food sovereignty is self-determination practice and thus brought to the fore as a primary human rights issue. An International Indian Treaty Council (IITC) pamphlet, *Food Sovereignty and the Rights of Indigenous Peoples*, articulates the support human rights law might give in local assertions of self-determination.[71] Assertions of food sovereignty articulate what "food" is, ways of life, and protecting the lands and places that sustain them. The International Indian Treaty Council, the first Indigenous NGO accepted into the United Nations, remains thirty-four years later a strong advocate for enforcing treaty rights as human rights in the Americas. In their short pamphlet they state the political significance of food in this international rights setting: "the denial of the Right to Food for Indigenous Peoples not only denies us our physical survival, but also denies us our social organization, our cultures, traditions, languages, spirituality, sovereignty, and total identity; it is a denial of our collective indigenous existence." Citing the "Declaration of Atitlan," a first Indigenous Peoples' Global Consultation on the Right to Food and Food Sovereignty held in Guatemala in 2002, they cite the ongoing major insults to Indigenous life in the twenty-first century as conditions that Indigenous face any place on the planet: the "[l]ack of access to Traditional Lands, Water and Natural Resources; Imposed development including deforestation, mining, drilling and damming; Environmental contamination; 'Free Trade Agreements' and food imports; Introduction of genetically modified food and seeds; Large-scale industrial agricultural methods; Loss of language, cultural practices, and ways of transmitting traditional knowledge to new generations; Impacts of climate change and false 'solutions' including bio/agro fuel production."[72] The IITC contests these practices, referencing a promise to a "right to a standard of living adequate for the health and well-being of himself and his family . . . including food" that is secured in the Universal Declaration of Human Rights in 1948. The IITC also cites the language, "In no case may a people be deprived of its own means of subsistence," that exists in Article 1 in Common, of the International Covenants on Civil and Political and on Economic, Social and Cultural Rights. They assert, "The rights to land, water, and territory, as well as the right to self-determination, are essential for the full realization of our Food Security and Food Sovereignty."[73] The lack of access to their lands to procure food or the efforts by nation-states to develop lands that destroy foods, or the massive neoliberal deregulation of capital and environmental laws that have been part and parcel to "Free Trade Agreements," and the trade wars are among the direct assaults we live daily—now, not only in a past. It is within human rights that Indigenous peoples cite their right not only to live and thrive as peoples but to become the critique, the basis for an articulation of rights that are deterrents to unbridled capitalisms. To deter "business as usual" is literally a life-and-death proposition. The traditional "food systems," once the heart of alternative economies, organized ways of life and governing. They now become an intensely dreamed opposing imaginary to capitalist culture in international discourse. Fifty years ago no nation-state would have imagined this.

Indigenous Women Articulate Mental Health in the Abject Heart of Neocolonialism

In this text I spend time on working beyond the place where Indigenous women are posed as the abject victimized subjects of our present neoliberal states. I do so because I want to celebrate and raise my hands to the work that Indigenous women do to practice a different politic than the one created in classic liberal and now neoliberal universal law. The threat to our bodies and spirits is extremely brutal and pervasively present. We are more likely to be brutalized than anyone else—except those differently gendered, or Two-Spirit, or Trans peoples—in every place we exist, including our own homes. It is most usually men who brutalize us, and though there are statistics pointing to many of these men being non-Native, I certainly don't think it safe or realistic to assume it's not our own fathers, brothers, and husbands who do this as well. We know it is. We are rightly campaigning to put laws in place to enhance our chances of safety, and to seek justice for ourselves and our families. We are not safe because our societies, our local communities, or the nation-states are not safe. To simply posit this violence as a man-versus-woman dichotomy is to pretend that this is not the system. The abject heart of colonialism and neocolonialism, and their practice of capitalism, is *gendered violence*. Gendered violence is perpetrated by individuals and polities in times when heteronormative order is threatened, and likewise when there is a threat to the power still invested in a racialized white male universal subject. We live in such a time when these structures of power are under enormous social pressure to change. Thus, I think that such violence is not incidental but common to the stresses that race, gender, and sexuality play in ordering and reordering power in our times. Those who colonized and those who were colonized have engaged in a therapeutic ethos to ameliorate these stresses. Yet this therapeutic ethos has often lent itself to a reconciliation that does not change the colonial structures but adapts the colonized to the colonial systems as they change. I have argued that Canada and the United States (along with Australia and New Zealand, less mentioned) once constituted themselves in power that is synonymous with the white heterosexual male that remains their now unspoken but still normalizing political subject.

The Indian Act in Canada performed the violent evisceration of Indigenous traditional nations (cultures, ways of life, economies) whose polities had made women integral to their actual practices of governing. It is still this heteronormative racialized order instilled in the core of Indigenous lives by a society that benefits from it that enables Indigenous women's brutalization and murder. This is so because we are symbolic and significant in being the absolute antithetical to the normal constitutive subject of western universal law. We share this with other racialized women. But I would posit that it is we as Indigenous women who still embrace knowledges that poses Indigenism against the practices of capitalist development. Differently practiced Indigenisms are knowledges that organize resistance and alternatives to the unbridled religion that is capitalist progress. It is the western nations' continuing belief in their Manifest Destiny, posited as a teleological progress, that informs these same states' incessant development. This "development" produces a profit that provides conditions of life, heightened senses of utopia for a very few—while killing, either directly or slowly, other peoples who might pose different answers to why it is we live. We die from acts that could be likened to the autoimmune effect of a social body attacking a felt biological nemesis. I want to elaborate on this specifically here.

Capitalism seeks to "colonize" life, to use life, to become one with the forces that life is at the same time it abandons lives it does not promote. The neoliberal transformation of capital coincides with the explosion of scientific knowledges to manipulate the biologic, molecular biology, cell biology, and microbiology. It invests itself monetarily and philosophically in the development of immortal cell lines, tissues, and stem cells. These become industries, seeking to harness matter's reproductive powers in the biologic to a capitalist intense dream to exceed its own limit.[74]

Capitalism as it is practiced might be likened to an organism highly selfish, jealous of competition, seeking ways of life to capitalize on them. It permeates cultures to promote and offer fantasy lives and ways of life that appear infinitely intoxicating, promising. Capitalism works by attaching our fondest desires to visualize and hope for futures that it cannot or does not produce for everyone.[75] Capitalism has no culture, has no creed; it "ceaselessly revolutionizes and expands . . . it could do nicely without meaning at all . . . whatever local meanings it provides are derivatives of whatever axioms happen to be in place."[76] Capitalism is a vampire on our cultures. It is a desire to become all, infinite, and at one with itself, exempt from limit, producing death for those it uses up or that are not of value to it. Our blood is its currency. And thus in the purported loss of a realized alternative socialist imaginary (which was never an alternative, but only an alternate capitalism), there are many forces that would ally with an Indigenous philosophy and practice at this time, and many alliances have been made already—some in the name of health and some for justice. But I posit here that we think outside the biopolitical imperative for healing as reconciliation with capital, with development as business as usual. However fragile international declarations are, a moral line has been created. Indigenism contains seed for imagining what else our nations might be. And while that is a dark star to peer at, it is also exactly why many Indigenous have so tenaciously opted to continue to fight in belief and action that our lifeways may pose something other than illness and death. What would our governances be if they already assumed that all life, all life's "vibrant matter," rather than such an impossible universal subject, formed their primary responsibility?[77]

Two issues I address at this juncture. One is *that it matters what kind of governments that peoples choose to constitute*, as many women have pointed out. The other is how this argument formed in Indigneous feminism— though for me these two are one. I think an era of human rights represents profound opportunities and challenges for any Indigenous governance, or ways of life as they are now formed for a self-determination posited in a rights language. Ladner asks us to understand that it matters what kind of governing we perform. To remind, she believes that governance "is an expression of the way in which a people lives best together . . . as a part of the circle of life, not as superior beings who claim dominion over other species and other humans."[78] This would mean an expansive plural polity that did not have white, heteronormative male figure as logos. Rights are multiplied across inclusions as afterthoughts that vex but never displace this subject. This is the universal subject whose unspoken centrality to the "rights" of man still fuels the big philosophical theoretical debates of this century and the last. The era of human rights begins when this universal figure becomes questioned, first for the savagery displayed in the performance of absolute sovereignty, a sovereignty in which Germany could murder its own people after imagining their Jewish alterity as an enemy ontology that had to be purged from its pure state. Human rights as a universal law seeks security in inclusion of all its imagined others, while it cannot replace its "self" with any true "we" inclusive enough to produce life rather than a necropolitic. Thus, it is also the site of frantic projects to protect life, police life, and heal trauma in the name of human rights. Whatever powers of self-determination that can be eked out must be fully cognizant about what it means to exclude women, other gendered peoples, or our relationship and responsibilities to what sustains us, because governing arises from those relations. It is this thought in Indigenous feminisms that informs me in this text, that posits that the nurturing inclusiveness that is often modeled as an ideal in kinship teaches us that we form one another and create social and spiritual relations that we extend and that are extended to us in radiating bursts of affective interrelations that also include nonhuman relations. That is a basis for polity. It is a powerful model that interrupts absolutely—one I came to know and share within our individual and collective struggles; to articulate something we understood as Dena, or Nimipu, or the Peoples. It was within these practices that the questions I have asked here came to be important for me. It was in these questions that I attempted here that I also came into articulating and understanding the position that I am holding as an Indigenous feminist, in order to perform a critique that I again claim as suggestive rather than definitive. In doing so, my position thus informed my arguments here where I seek to push many boundaries of current definition. Thus, I believe that it is in the practice of Indigenous philosophy and its differently performed polities that we produce and find self-determination performing into strength those practices that do vex and move nation-states in these new times. May our peoples walk on into their futures. *Basi chu.*

Notes

Chapter 1

1. Dian Million, unpublished poem, 2005.

2. Nancy K. Miller and Jason Tougaw, eds. *Extremities: Trauma, Testimony, and Community* (Urbana: University of Illinois Press), 2002, 1–2.

3. The original name of the commission as it appears in the 2007 Indian Residential Schools Settlement Agreement.

4. *The Report of the Royal Commission on Aboriginal Peoples*, vol.1: *Looking Forward, Looking Back* (Ottowa: Royal Commission on Aboriginal Peoples, 1996), 15.

5. Priscilla B. Hayner, *Unspeakable Truths: Facing the Challenge of Truth Commissions* (New York: Routledge), 2001. See also Teresa Godwin Phelps, *Shattered Voices: Language, Violence and the Work of Truth Commissions* (Philadelphia: University of Pennsylvania Press), 2004.

6. Joanna Rice, "Indigenous Rights and Truth Commissions," *Cultural Survival Quarterly* 35, no. 1 (2011).

7. Hayner, *Unspeakable Truths*, 135.

8. Claire Moon, "Healing Past Violence: Traumatic Assumptions and Therapeutic Interventions in War and Reconciliation," *Journal of Human Rights* 8, no. 1 (2009): 72.

9. Yael Danieli, ed. *International Handbook of Multigenerational Legacies of Trauma*, Plenum Series on Stress and Coping (New York: Plenum Press, 1998); Eduardo Duran et al., "Healing the American Indian Soul Wound," in *Intergenerational Handbook of Multigenerational Legacies of Trauma*, ed. Yael Danieli (New York: Plenum Press, 1998); Shoshana Felman and Dori Laub, *Testimony: Crises of Witnessing in Literature, Psychoanalysis, and History* (New York: Routledge, 1991); Laurence J. Kirmayer, Robert Lemelson, and Mark Barad, eds., *Understanding Trauma: Integrating Biological, Clinical, and Cultural Perspectives* (Cambridge: Cambridge University Press, 2007); Spero Manson, Janette Beals, Theresa O'Nell, Joan Piasecki, Donald Bechtold, Ellen Keane, and Monica Jones, "Wounded Spirits, Ailing Hearts: PTSD and Related Disorders among American Indians," in *Ethnocultural Aspects of Posttraumatic Stress Disorder*, ed. Anthony J. Marsella, Matthew J. Friedman, Ellen T. Gerrity, and Raymond M. Scurfield (Washington, DC: American Psychological Association, 1996).

10. To see the global reach of "trauma" as an explanation for disparate injuries and multigenerational grievance, see Danieli, *International Handbook of Multigenerational Legacies of Trauma*.

11. Didier Fassin and Richard Rechtman. *The Empire of Trauma: An Inquiry into the Condition of Victimhood*. (Princeton, NJ: Princeton University Press, 2009), xi.

12. Moon, "Healing Past Violence," 71.

13. The United Nations Declaration on the Rights of Indigenous Peoples begins, "*Affirming* that indigenous peoples are equal to all other peoples . . . " A copy can be downloaded at http://www.un.org/esa/socdev/unpfii/documents/DRIPS_en.pdf. The international concept of "self-determination" is constantly evolving. Anaya states it first as "grounded in the idea that all are equally entitled to control their own Destinies." S. James Anaya, *Indigenous Peoples in International Law* (New York: Oxford University Press, 2004), 75.

14. Elizabeth A. Povinelli, *The Empire of Love: Toward a Theory of Intimacy, Genealogy, and Carnality*, ed. Dilip Gaonkar, Jane Kramer, Benjamin Lee, and Michael Warner (Durham, NC: Duke University Press, 2006), 227–28.

15. Roger Maaka and Augie Fleras, "Contesting Indigenous Peoples Governance: The Politics of State-Determination vs. Self-Determining Autonomy," in *Aboriginal Self-Government in Canada: Current Trends and Issues*, ed. Yale D. Belanger (Saskatoon: Purich, 2008), 69.

16. Maaka and Fleras, "Contesting Indigenous Peoples Governance," 74.

17. Marlene Brant Castellano, "Renewing the Relationship: A Perspective on the Impact of the Royal Commission on Aboriginal Peoples," in *Aboriginal Self-Government in Canada*, ed. John H. Hylton (Saskatoon: Purich, 1999), 109.

18. Bonita Lawrence, "Gender, Race, and the Regulation of Native Identity in Canada and the United States: An Overview," *Hypatia* 18, no. 2 (2003): 3.

19. Michael Ignatieff and Amy Gutmann. *Human Rights as Politics and Idolatry* (Princeton: Princeton University Press, 2001), 4.

20. Ibid., 5.

21. Ibid., 6.

22. Ibid., 8–12.

23. Randall Williams, *The Divided World: Human Rights and Violence*. (Minneapolis: University of Minnesota Press, 2010), xv.

24. Susan Koshy, "From Cold War to Trade War: Neocolonialism and Human Rights," *Social Text* 58 (Spring 1999): 1.

25. Robert H. Jackson, *Quasi-States: Sovereignty, International Relations and the Third World*, ed. Steve Smith, Cambridge Studies in International Relations (Cambridge: Cambridge University Press, 1990). While I do not agree with Jackson's politics, I do agree that the sovereignty that "decolonizing" polities achieved was always embedded in the actions capitalist western nations took to maintain their hegemony, the relationship between the "developed" and the "developers."

26. Jacques Rancière, "Who Is the Subject of the Rights of Man?," *South Atlantic Quarterly* 103, nos. 2/3 (2004): 297–98.

27. "Where all order in a state has disintegrated and its people have been delivered up to a war of all against all, or where a state is engaging in gross, repeated, and systemic violence against its own citizens, the only effective way to protect human rights is direct intervention, ranging from sanctions to the use of military force. . . . The armed forces of the Western powers have been busier since 1989 than they ever were during the Cold War, and the legitimizing language for this activity has been the defense of human rights." Ignatieff and Gutmann, *Human Rights as Politics and Idolatry*, 37.

28. Didier Fassin and Mariella Pandolfi, eds., *Contemporary States of Emergency: The Politics of Military and Humanitarian Interventions* (New York: Zone Books, 2010), 13.

29. Achille Mbembe, "Necropolitics," *Public Culture* 15, no. 1 (2003): 30.

30. Fassin and Pandolfi, *Contemporary States of Emergency*, 13.

31. Vanessa Pupavac, "Pathologizing Populations and Colonizing Minds: International Pyschosocial Programs in Kosovo," *Alternatives* 27, no. 4 (2002): 489–90.

32. Jackson, *Quasi-States*.

33. Fredrick Cooper and Randall Packard, eds., *International Development and the Social Sciences: Essays on the History and Politics of Knowledge* (Berkeley and Los Angeles: University of California Press, 1997), 2.

34. Frantz Fanon, *Black Skin, White Masks* (New York: Grove Press, 1967); Etienne Balibar and Immanuel Maurice Wallerstein, *Race, Nation, Class: Ambiguous Identities* (London: Verso, 1991); Jodi Melamed, *Represent and Destroy: Rationalizing Violence in the New Racial Capitalism* (Minneapolis: University of Minnesota Press, 2011). Together these texts represent good accounts of race as it transforms through different periods.

35. Cooper and Packard, *International Development*, 8.

36. Ingrid Washinawatok, "International Emergence: Twenty-One Years at the United Nations," *Indigenous Woman* 4, no. 2 (2001): 12.

37. George Manuel and Michael Posluns, *The Fourth World: An Indian Reality* (New York: Free Press, 1974).

38. Glen T. Morris, "The International Status of Indigenous Nations within the United States," in *Critical Issues in Native North America*, ed. Ward Churchill (Copenhagen: International Work Group for Indigenous Affairs, 1989), n36.

39. Washinawatok, "International Emergence," 14.

40. Ibid.

41. Internal colonization was described in the United States for blacks and Indians in Robert Blauner, *Racial Oppression in the United States* (New York: Harper and Row, 1972).

42. "Indians" in different places posed a conundrum, because they sometimes challenged the nationalisms of emerging "postcolonials." See Roxanne Dunbar-Ortiz, "The Fourth World and Indigenism: Politics of Isolation and Alternatives," *Journal of Ethnic Studies* 12, no. 1 (1984): 79–105. See also Philip A. Dennis, Roxanne Dunbar-Ortiz, Bernard Nietschmann, Stedman Fagot Muller, and Jorge Jenkins Molieri, "The Miskito–Sandinista Conflict in Nicaragua in the 1980s," *Latin American Research Review* 28, no. 3 (1993): 214–34.

43. Manuel Castells, *The Power of Identity*, vol. 2, *The Information Age: Economy, Society and Culture* (Oxford: Blackwell, 1997), 72.

44. Ibid., 77.

45. For astute analyses of these nationalisms in Canada from an Indigenous perspective, see Gerald Taiaiake Alfred, *Heeding the Voices of Our Ancestors: Kahnawake Mohawk Politics and the Rise of Native Nationalism* (Toronto: Oxford University Press, 1995). See also Gerald Taiaiake Alfred, *Wasáse: Indigenous Pathways of Action and Freedom* (Peterborough, ON: Broadview Press, 2005). In the United States, read Vine Deloria and Clifford M. Lytle, *The Nations Within: The Past and Future of American Indian Sovereignty* (New York: Pantheon Books, 1984).

46. David Harvey, *A Brief History of Neoliberalism* (Oxford: Oxford University Press, 2005), 3.

47. Nancy Fraser, "Feminism, Capitalism and the Cunning of History," *New Left Review* 56 (March/April 2009): 100.

48. Michael T. Clark, "Wither the Nation-State?: The Subaltern and the Redeployment of Latin American Nationalism in the Era of Globalization," *Disposition: American Journal of Cultural Histories and Theories* 19, no. 46 (1994), 28.

49. Fraser, "Feminism," 107.

50. Harvey, "*Brief History,* 23.

51. Nikolas Rose, "Community, Citizenship, and the Third Way," *American Behavioral Scientist* 43, no. 9 (2000), 1395.

52. Ibid., 1399.

53. Ibid., 1400.

54. Wanda Vrasti, "How to Use Affective Competencies in Late Capitalism," in British International Studies Association Conference, University of Leicester, December 2009 (accessed September 12, 2012), http://bisa.ac.uk/index.php?option=com_bisa&task=view_public_papers_author_char_search&char_search=V.

55. Aihwa Ong, "Neoliberalism as a Mobile Technology," *Transactions of the Institute of British Geographers* 32, no. 1 (2007): 4–6.

56. John Lavoie, John O'Neil, Jeff Reading, and Yvonne Allard, "Community Healing and Aboriginal Self-Government," in *Aboriginal Self-Government in Canada,* ed. Yale D. Belanger (Saskatoon: Purich, 2008). Almost ten years earlier, O'Neil and colleagues had reported very similar findings. See John O'Neil, Laurel Lemchuk-Favel, Yvon Allard, and Brian Postl, "Community Healing and Aboriginal Self-Government," in *Aboriginal Self-Government in Canada,* ed. John H. Hylton, 130–56 (Saskatoon: Purich, 1999). This continuing lack of interest in funding or finding funding for Aboriginal health initiatives is also documented throughout my arguments in this text.

57. Maaka and Fleras, "Contesting Indigenous Peoples Governance," 73.

58. Australian Human Rights and Equal Opportunity Commission, *Bringing Them Home: Report of the National Inquiry into the Separation of Aboriginal and Torres Strait Islander Children from Their Families* (Sydney: Human Rights and Equal Opportunity Commission, 1997). A copy may be obtained online at the commission's website in the Aboriginal and Torres Strait Islander Social Justice section, http://www.humanrights.gov.au/social_justice/bth_report/index.html.

59. Melinda Hinkson, "A 'National Emergency' in Australia: The Howard Government's Intervention in Northern Territory Aboriginal Affairs," *Indigenous Affairs,* no. 4 (2007): 38. Also see Rebecca Stringer, "A Nightmare of the Neocolonial Kind: Politics of Suffering in Howard's Northern Territory Intervention," *borderlands e-journal* 6, no. 2 (2007): accessed June 11, 2009, http://www.borderlands.net.au/vol6no2_2007/stringer_intervention.htm; Jon Altman and Melinda Hinkson, eds. *Coercive Reconciliation: Stabilise, Normalise, Exit Aboriginal Australia* (Melbourne: Arena Publications, 2007); Irene Watson, "In the Northern Territory Intervention: What Is Saved or Rescued and What Cost?" *cultural studies review* 15 (2009): 2; and Deidre Howard-Wagner, "From Denial to Emergency," in *Contemporary States of Emergency: The Politics of Military and Humanitarian Interventions,* ed. Didier Fassin and Mariella Pandolfi (New York: Zone Books, 2010). The actual report is Rex Wild and Pat Anderson, *Ampe Akelyernemane Meke Mekarle "Little Children Are Sacred": Report of the Northern Territory Board of Inquiry into the Protection of Aboriginal Children from Sexual Abuse* (Darwin: Northern Territory Government, 2007), http://www.nt.gov.au/dcm/inquirysaac/pdf/bipacsa_final_report.pdf.

60. Stringer, "Nightmare of the Neocolonial Kind," 1. The agendas of the intervention are drawn from the abstract for brevity but are well detailed in the article.

61. Will Kymlicka, "Neoliberal Multiculturalism," keynote, Eminent Speakers at the Faculty of Arts Lectures, University of Ljubljana, Slovenia. Video recorded March 2011 (accessed September 1, 2012), http://videolectures.net/ffeminent_kymlicka_neoliberal/.

62. Amnesty International, *Maze of Injustice: The Failure to Protect Indigenous Women from Sexual Violence in the USA* (New York: Amnesty International USA, 2007); Amnesty International, *Canada: Stolen Sisters: A Human Rights Response to Discrimination and Violence against Indigenous Women in Canada*, October 4, 2004 (accessed November 29, 2007), http://www.unhcr.org/refworld/docid/42ae984b0.html.

63. Rauna Kuokkanen, "Globalization as Racialized, Sexualized Violence," *International Feminist Journal of Politics* 10, no. 2 (2008): 216–33.

64. James D. Wilets, "Conceptualizing Private Violence against Sexual Minorities as Gendered Violence: An International and Comparative Law Perspective," *Albany Law Review* 60 (1996), 991.

65. Michel Foucault, *The History of Sexuality*, vol. 1, *An Introduction* (Paris: Gallimard, 1976), 145.

66. Thomas Lemke, *Biopolitics: An Advanced Introduction*, Biopolitics: Medicine, Technoscience, and Health in the 21st Century, ed. Monica J. Casper and Lisa Jean Moore. (New York: New York University Press, 2011), 38.

67. Bruce Burgett, "Sex, Panic, Nation," *American Literary History* 21, no. 1 (2009), 68.

68. Andrea Smith, *Conquest: Sexual Violence and American Indian Genocide* (Cambridge, MA: South End Press, 2005).

69. Elizabeth Woody, "In Memory of Crossing the Columbia," in *Dancing on the Rim of the World: An Anthology of Northwest Native American Writing*, ed. Andrea Lerner (Tucson: University of Arizona Press, 1990), 247.

70. Sean Patrick Eudaily, *The Present Politics of the Past: Indigenous Legal Activism and Resistance to (Neo)Liberal Governmentality*, ed. Frank Wilmer. Indigenous Peoples and Politics (New York: Routledge, 2004), 12.

71. Elizabeth Cook-Lynn, "How Scholarship Defames the Native Voice . . . and Why." *Wicazo Sa Review* 15, no. 2 (2000): 92.

72. Andrea Smith, *Native Americans and the Christian Right: The Gendered Politics of Unlikely Alliances* (Durham, NC: Duke University Press, 2008), xiii.

73. Gloria Bird, "Breaking the Silence: Writing as 'Witness,'" in *Speaking for the Generations: Native Writers on Writing*, ed. Simon J. Ortiz (Tucson: University of Arizona Press, 1998), 28.

74. Hanssen describes the agon again as "reciprocal incitation and struggle." Beatrice Hanssen, *Critique of Violence: Between Poststructuralism and Critical Theory* (London: Routledge, 2000), 13.

75. Jeannette Armstrong and D. E. Hall, *Native Perspectives on Sustainability: Jeannette Armstrong (Syilx)* [Interview transcript], 2007. Retrieved from the Native Perspectives on Sustainability project website: www.nativeperspectives.net. The quote is a few moments from 48:25. The complexity, simplicity, and beauty of *naw'qinwixw* should be heard in its original. I urge readers of this book to read/listen to Armstrong and Hall's entire conversation.

76. Lemke, *Biopolitics*, 119.

77. Sunni Patterson, "We Know This Place," *American Quarterly, In The Wake of Hurricane Katrina: New Paradigms and Social Visions* 61, no. 3 (2009): 719.

78. Jordan T. Camp, "'We Know This Place': Neoliberal Racial Regimes." *American Quarterly, In The Wake of Hurricane Katrina: New Paradigms and Social Visions* 61, no. 3 (2009): 694.

79. Robin D. G. Kelley, *Freedom Dreams: The Black Radical Imagination* (Boston: Beacon Press, 2002), 8, quoted in Camp, "'We Know This Place,'" 693.

80. I acknowledge that I am richly informed by Andrea Smith's enunciation of *performance* that she attributes to the articulation of Justine Smith as the way indigenism sees "Native communities as bounded by practices that are always in excess but ultimately constitutive of the very being of Native peoples themselves . . . performances by definition are not static." Andrea Smith, *Native Americans and the Christian Right,* xxv–xxvi. See Justine Smith, "Indigenous Performance and Aporetic Texts," *Union Seminary Quarterly Review* 59, nos. 1–2 (2005): 114–24. This has also been the way I see the reflexive, always changing result of our struggle, our enunciation of culture, our performance of culture and how it changes us. I have been reluctant to use *performance* to theoretically articulate this movement because of its connotation of "acting," and the horrendous conversations that erupted over the characterization of Indian identities and nationalisms as "imagined communities." I stride forth emboldened by these women's use of this word, because it is a useful theoretical shortcut to express something beautiful and complex. We have the potential to create liberatory practices, performing them inside and outside and exceeding any particular articulation of "nation."

Chapter 2

1. Amnesty International, *Canada: Stolen Sisters: A Human Rights Response to Discrimination and Violence against Indigenous Women in Canada,* October 4, 2004 (accessed November 29, 2012), http://www.unhcr.org/refworld/docid/42ae984b0.html, 1.

2. Amnesty International, *Stolen Sisters*; Amnesty International, *Maze of Injustice: The Failure to Protect Indigenous Women from Sexual Violence in the USA* (New York: Amnesty International USA, 2007).

3. See their research in *What Their Stories Tell Us: Research Findings from the Sisters in Spirit Initiative* (n.p.: NWAC, 2010), http://www.201.nwac.ca/. Also available is the appeal for support after the Harper government moved to defund their work: http://www.nwac.ca/sisters-spirit-supporters.

4. Sandra Lovelace successfully challenged Canada for sex discrimination in a human rights court. In 1981 the UN Committee ruled that Canada had broken the International Covenant on Civil and Political Rights. Lovelace tells her story in her own words in Jane Silman, *Enough Is Enough: Aboriginal Women Speak Out (as Told to Jane Silman)* (Toronto: Women's Press, 1987). Also see Anne F. Bayefsky, "Applying International Human Rights Law: Indigenous Women," *Canadian Yearbook of International Law* 20 (1982): 244–65.

5. Amnesty International, *Maze of Injustice,* 2.

6. Ibid., 3.

7. See the National Congress of American Indians Resolution #MIC-06-008, "Resolution Requesting the Federal Government Adequately Fund Law Enforcement and Courts on Reservations" (June 2006), National Congress of American Indian (accessed September 1, 2012), http://www.ncai.org/attachments/Resolution_SJQZvWynouItoZYDsIIEtyZJlysYiCOKZUAiGKsZdLUPgdeIxrrD_MIC-06-008_Law_Enforcement_Courts_Funding.pdf. US Native nations were subject to increased

drug trafficking and crime without resources, or often power, to protect their citizens. NCAI began to lobby heavily for increased funding and increased jurisdiction that resulted later in the Tribal Law and Order Act (2010) that I discuss in my text.

8. Sarah Deer, "Sovereignty of the Soul: Exploring the Intersection of Rape Law Reform and Federal Indian Law," *Suffolk University Law Review* 38, no. 2 (2005), 465.

9. Ibid.

10. Sarah Deer, "Toward an Indigenous Jurisprudence of Rape," *Kansas Journal of Law and Public Policy* 121, no. 79 (2004): 121–54.

11. Sarah Deer, "Decolonizing Rape Law: A Native Feminist Synthesis of Safety and Sovereignty," *Wicazo Sa Review* 24 (2009): 149–67.

12. Ibid. Jennifer Denetdale is also a good resource for articulating this sexism as it insinuates customary law. See Jennifer Nez Denetdale, "Chairmen, Presidents, and Princesses: The Navajo Nation, Gender, and the Politics of Tradition," *Wicazo Sa Review* 21, no. 1 (2006): 9–28. Also see Jennifer Nez Denetdale, "Securing Navajo National Boundaries: War, Patriotism, Tradition and the Dine Marriage Act of 2005," *Wicazo Sa Review* 24, no. 2 (2009): 131–48.

13. Larissa Behrendt, "Consent in a (Neo)Colonial Society: Aboriginal Women as Sexual and Legal 'Other,' *Australian Feminist Studies* 15, no. 33 (2000). Also see Sherene H. Razack, "Gendered Racial Violence and Spatialized Justice: The Murder of Pamela George," *Canadian Journal of Law and Society* 15, no. 2 (2000): 91–138; and Rosemarie Stremlau, "Rape Narratives on the Northern Paiute Frontier: Sara Winnemucca, Sexual Sovereignty, and Economic Autonomy, 1844–1891," in *Portraits of Women in the American West*, ed. Dee Garceau-Hagen (New York: Routledge, 2005).

14. Kristin Bumiller, *In an Abusive State: How Neoliberalism Appropriated the Feminist Movement against Sexual Violence* (Durham, NC: Duke University Press, 2008). Funding and the taming of grassroots movements is critically discussed in *The Revolution Will Not Be Funded: Beyond the Non-Profit Industrial Complex*, ed. Incite! Women of Color Against Violence (Cambridge, MA: South End Press, 2007). A pointed article in this collection underlining Bumiller's observations is Alisa Bierria, "Pursuing a Radical Anti-Violence Agenda Inside/Outside a Non-Profit Structure," 151–63.

15. Luanna Ross, *Inventing the Savage: The Social Construction of Native American Criminality* (Austin: University of Texas Press, 1998).

16. Behrendt, "Consent," 365. See also n92.

17. In nineteenth-century western societies a distinction between "public" male space and private male "domestic" space is made—where domesticity is the woman's sphere of action but legally the man's private domain inviolable by the law; hence, "a man's home is his castle."

18. Kathleen Jamieson, "Sex Discrimination and the Indian Act," in *Arduous Journey*, ed. J. Ponting (Toronto: McClelland and Stewart, 1986).

19. John Sheridan Milloy, *A National Crime: The Canadian Government and the Residential School System, 1879 to 1986* (Winnipeg: University of Manitoba Press, 1999).

20. Mark Rifkin, *When Did Indians Become Straight? Kinship, the History of Sexuality, and Native Sovereignty* (New York: Oxford University Press, 2011). Rifkin's is an excellent explication of the strict US heteronormative formation in the face of the more varied Indigenous forms of kinship, sexuality, and belonging. Also see Julia V. Emberly, *Defamiliarizing the Aboriginal: Cultural Practices and Decolonization in Canada* (Toronto: University of Toronto Press, 2007).

21. Ann Laura Stoler, "Tense and Tender Ties: The Politics of Comparison in North American History and (Post) Colonial Studies," *Journal of American History* 88, no. 3 (2001): 843.

22. Milloy, *National Crime*, 296.

23. Michel Foucault, *The History of Sexuality: An Introduction*, vol. 1 (New York: Random House, 1990), 103.

24. Ann Laura Stoler, *Race and the Education of Desire: Foucault's History of Sexuality and the Colonial Order of Things* (Durham, NC: Duke University Press, 1995), 97.

25. Stoler, "Tense and Tender Ties," 832.

26. Ibid.

27. Jo-Anne Fiske, "Ordered Lives and Disordered Souls: Pathologizing Female Bodies of the Colonial Frontier," in *New Perspectives on Social Deviance*, ed. Lori Beaman (Scarborough, ON: Prentice Hall Allyn and Bacon Canada 2000).

28. Elizabeth Furniss and Cariboo Tribal Council, *Victims of Benevolence: The Dark Legacy of the Williams Lake Residential School* (Vancouver, BC: Arsenal Pulp Press, 1995), 124. Chief Beverly Sellars's (Soda Creek First Nation) entire speech to the First National Conference on Residential Schools, June 18, 1991, in Vancouver, BC, appears in Furniss's text, pp. 21–128.

29. Joan Sangster, *Regulating Girls and Women: Sexuality, Family, and the Law in Ontario, 1920–1960* (Toronto: Oxford University Press, 2001), 313.

30. Joan Sangster, "She Is Hostile to Our Ways: First Nations Girls Sentenced to the Ontario Training School for Girls, 1933–1960," *Law and History Review* 20, no. 1 (2002): 59–96.

31. Ibid., 45.

32. Ibid., 52.

33. Lauren Berlant, *Cruel Optimism* (Durham, NC: Duke University Press, 2011), 65.

34. Diamond Jenness, "Canada's Indians Yesterday. What of Today?," in *As Long as the Sun Shines and Water Flows: A Reader in Canadian Native Studies*, ed. Ian L. Getty and Antoine S. Lussier (Vancouver: University of British Columbia Press, 1983), 163. In his article reprinted from 1954, he "found a deep-rooted prejudice against them . . . which was noticeable everywhere from the Atlantic to the Pacific."

35. A. Richard King, *The School at Mopass: A Problem of Identity* (New York: Holt, Rinehart and Winston, 1967), 90.

36. Ibid., 65.

37. Niels Winther Braroe, *Indian and White: Self-Image and Interaction in a Canadian Plains Community* (Stanford, CA: Stanford University Press, 1975).

38. Ibid., 87.

39. Ibid., 5.

40. Ibid., 4.

41. Ibid., 180.

42. Howard Adams, *Prison of Grass: Canada from the Native Point of View* (Toronto: New Press, 1975).

43. Niels Braroe found moral assessment common to keeping racialized populations widely distinct even when he thought the distinction was not distinct to an outsider, that is, Sami from Laplander in his example. This complex of racialized social knowledge that intricately informed settler societies is well documented. See Elizabeth Furniss,

The Burden of History: Colonialism and the Frontier Myth in a Rural Canadian Community (Vancouver: University of British Columbia Press, 1999).

44. Thomas J. Scheff, "Socialization of Emotion: Pride and Shame as Causal Agents," in *Research Agendas in the Sociology of Emotions*, ed. Theodore D. Kemper (Albany: State University of New York Press, 1990).

45. Ibid., 281.

46. Elspeth Probyn, "Writing Shame," in *The Affect Theory Reader*, ed. Melissa Gregg and Gregory J. Siegworth (Durham, NC: Duke University Press, 2010).

47. Jane Blocker, *Seeing Witness: Visuality and the Ethics of Testimony* (Minneapolis: University of Minnesota Press, 2009), 105.

48. Ibid., 106.

49. Ibid.

50. Giorgio Agamben, *Remnants of Auschwitz: The Witness and the Archive*, trans. Daniel Heller-Roazen (New York: Zone Books, 2002), 107, quoted in Blocker, *Seeing Witness*, 111.

51. Nick Crossley, "Emotion and Communicative Action: Habermas, Linguistic Philosophy and Existentialism," in *Emotions in Social Life: Critical Themes and Contemporary Issues*, ed. Gillian Bendelow and Simon J. Williams (New York: Routledge, 1998), 26–27.

52. Ibid., 35.

53. I explore the concept of intense dreaming most fully in my essay, "Intense Dreaming: Theories, Narratives and Our Search for Home," *American Indian Quarterly* 35, no. 3 (2011): 314–33.

54. Eva Illouz, *Cold Intimacies: The Making of Emotional Capitalism* (Cambridge: Polity Press, 2007), 4.

55. Ibid.

56. Andre C. Drainville, "The Fetishism of Global Civil Society: Global Governance, Transnational Urbanism and Sustainable Capitalism in the World Economy," in *Transnationalism from Below*, ed. Michael Peter Smith and Luis Eduardo Guarizo (New Brunswick: Transaction, 1998), 44n4. Using "neo-liberal constitutionalism," coined by Stephen Gill, Drainville observed states at the core of the reorganization made "the move toward construction of legal or constitutional devices to remove or insulate substantially the new economic institutions from popular scrutiny or domestic accountability."

57. James L. Nolan Jr., *The Therapeutic State: Justifying Government at Century's End* (New York: New York University Press, 1998), 179.

58. Lauren Berlant, "The Epistemology of State Emotion," in *Dissent in Dangerous Times*, ed. Austin Surat (Ann Arbor: University of Michigan Press, 2005), 47.

59. Ibid., 49.

60. Will Sanders, "Ideology, Evidence and Competing Principles in Australian Indigenous Affairs: From Brough to Rudd via Pearson and the NTER," *Australian Journal of Social Issues* 45, no. 3 (2010): 307–31.

61. Deer, "Sovereignty of the Soul," 465.

62. Elizabeth Ann Kronk, "The Emerging Problem of Methamphetamines: A Threat Signaling the Need to Reform Criminal Jurisdiction in Indian Country," *North Dakota Law Review* 82, no. 4 (2006): 1253. Kronk notes that "74 per cent of the ninety-six Indian law enforcement agencies nationwide indicate meth as their 'greatest threat.' This is

backed up by the National Congress of American Indians, "Methamphetamines in Indian Country: An American Problem Uniquely Affecting Indian Country" (2006), and numerous other congressional hearings and task force reports. One issue was that drug cartels "used" Indians, prompting calls for greater border security operations within Indian nations that bordered or were adjacent to the southern militarized border with Mexico.

63. White House, "Remarks by the President before Signing the Tribal Law and Order Act," July 29, 2010, transcript (accessed August 30, 2012), http://www.whitehouse .gov/photos-and-video/video/signing-tribal-law-and-order-act#transcript.

Obama states that "crime rates in Indian Country are more than twice the national average and up to 20 times the national average on some reservations." However, it is a traditionally dressed American Indian woman who stands next to him as he signs.

Chapter 3

1. Pierre Machery, *A Theory of Literary Production*, trans. G. Wall (London: Routledge and Kegan Paul, 1978), 79.

2. Janet Silman, *Enough Is Enough: Aboriginal Women Speak Out (as Told to Janet Silman)* (Toronto: Women's Press, 1987). The struggle to abolish the sexist provision in the Indian Act is narrated in the women's own voices. The Tobique Group were Lilly Harris, Ida Paul, Eva Saulis, Mavis Goeres, Joyce Sappier, Bet-te Paul, Juanita Perley, Shirley Bear, Glenna Perley, Carolyn Ennis, and Sandra Lovelace Sappier.

3. Silman, *Enough Is Enough*, 241.

4. Kathleen Jamieson, "Sex Discrimination and the Indian Act," in *Arduous Journey*, ed. J. Ponting (Toronto: McClelland and Stewart, 1986), 127.

5. Maria Campbell, *Halfbreed* (Toronto: McClelland and Stewart, 1973).

6. Hartmut Lutz, Jeannette Armstrong, Beth Cuthand, Maria Campbell, Jordan Wheeler, Lenore Keeshig-Tobias, Tomson Highway, Beatrice Mosionier, Thomas King, Greg Young-Ing, Ann Acco, Howard Adams, Daniel David Moses, Lee Maracle, Emma LaRocque, Ruby Slipperjack, Joy Asham Fedorick, Basil Johnston, and Rita Joe, *Contemporary Challenges: Conversations with Canadian Native Authors* (Saskatoon: Fifth House, 1991), 42. In her 1989 interview with Hartmut Lutz, Campbell noted that a great deal was cut from her novel not only to shorten it but for it to be "acceptable" to a Canadian audience: "The decision was made by the publisher—without consulting me!"

7. Howard Adams, *Prison of Grass: Canada from the Native Point of View* (Toronto: New Press, 1975). Howard Adams was the first Métis man in Canada to earn a PhD. He received his degree from the University of California, Berkeley.

8. For an account of racialization in the United States as internal colonization, see Robert Blauner, *Racial Oppression in the United States* (New York: Harper and Row, 1972). For an account of internalized oppression used among feminist organizers advocating for legal remedy for child abuse, see Nancy Whittier, *The Politics of Child Sexual Abuse: Emotion, Social Movements, and the State* (New York: Oxford University Press, 2009). I revisit this use in a later chapter.

9. Bobbi Lee, with Don Barnett and Rick Sterling, *Indian Rebel: Struggles of a Native Canadian Woman, Life Histories from the Revolution* (Vancouver, BC: Liberation Support Movement Information Centre, 1975).

10. Lee Maracle, *Bobbi Lee: Indian Rebel* (Toronto: Women's Press, 1990).

11. Jeannette C. Armstrong, ed., *Looking at the Words of Our People: First Nations Analysis of Literature* (Penticton, BC: Theytus Books, 1993), 29.

12. Helen Hoy, *How Should I Read These? Native Women Writers in Canada* (Toronto: University of Toronto Press, 2001).

13. Beatrice Culleton, *In Search of April Raintree* (Winnipeg: Pemmican Publications, 1983).

14. Ruby Slipperjack, *Honour the Sun: Extracted and Revised from the Diary of the Owl* (Winnipeg: Pemmican, 1987).

15. Hartmut Lutz, ed., *Approaches: Essays in Native North American Studies and Literature* (Augsberg: Wibner, 2002), 209.

16. Jeannette C. Armstrong, *Slash* (Penticton, BC: Theytus Books, 1988).

17. Ibid., 200–201.

18. Ibid., 208.

19. Emma Larocque, "Preface, or Here Are Our Voices—Who Will Hear?," in *Writing the Circle, Native Women of Western Canada*, ed. Jeanne Perreault and Sylvia Vance (Norman: University of Oklahoma Press, 1990), xvii.

20. Ibid.

21. Ibid.

22. Ibid.

23. Maurie Alioff and Susan Schouten Levine, "Interview: The Long Walk of Alanis Obomsawin," *Cinema Canada 1987*, quoted in ibid.

24. LaRocque, "Preface," xxvii.

25. Gloria Bird, "Introduction, or the First Circle—Native Women's Voice," in *Writing the Circle: Native Women of Western Canada, an Anthology*, ed. Jeanne Martha Perreault and Sylvia Vance (Norman: University of Oklahoma Press, 1990), ix.

26. Ibid.

27. Jeannette Armstrong, "The Disempowerment of First North American Native Peoples and Empowerment through Their Writing," in *An Anthology of Native Canadian Writing in English*, ed. Daniel David Moses and Terry Goldie (Oxford: University of Oxford Press, 1992), 209.

28. Scott Trevithick, "Native Residential Schooling in Canada: A Review of the Literature," *Canadian Journal of Native Studies* 18, no. 1 (1998): 49–86.

29. Ibid., 50.

30. Ibid., 52.

31. Ibid., 56.

32. Ibid., 61.

33. Ibid., 63.

34. Louise Moine, *My Life in a Residential School* (Saskatchewan: Provincial chapter I.O.D.E. in cooperation with the Provincial Library of Saskatchewan, 1975); Isabelle Knockwood and Gillian Thomas, *Out of the Depths: The Experiences of Mi'kmaw Children at the Indian Residential School at Shubenacadie, Nova Scotia* (Lockeport, NS: Roseway, 1992).

35. Trevithick, "Native Residential Schooling," 65. His exact quote is: "I think we felt very sorry but she had done a terrible thing [—in trying to burn down the school—] and she *deserved* to be punished (Moine 1988:10, Moine's emphasis)." He cites Moine's 1975 memoir in the bibliography but spells her first name wrong. The date in the text itself, 1988, is not listed in the bibliography.

36. Ibid.

37. Ibid., 65.

38. Ibid., 66.

39. Ibid.

40. Richard White, "Using the Past: History and Native American Studies," in *Studying Native America*, ed. Russell Thornton (Madison: University of Wisconsin Press, 1998), 217.

41. Ibid., 229.

42. Ibid., 233.

43. Ibid., 234.

44. Ibid.

45. Ibid., 236.

46. Gail Guthrie Valaskakis, "Indian Country: Negotiating the Meaning of Land in Native America," in *Disciplinarity and Dissent in Cultural Studies*, ed. Cary Nelson and Dilip Parameshwar Gaonkar (New York and London: Routledge, 1996), 151. It was Gail Valaskakis's position that "Native studies is a topic, not a methodological approach; and although it draws heavily on its anthropological and historical roots, writing about Indians incorporates all the disciplinary boundaries of the fields, which are absorbed within it." My position is that Indigenous studies is the place where an Indigenous methodology will emerge from the myriad works and peoples as the field grows. At this point it is a site wherein we claim our ethical positioning with Indigenous projects.

47. I am not a postmodern "relativist." My historical sense is most in agreement with Michel-Rolph Trouillot, *Silencing the Past: Power and Production of History* (Boston: Beacon Press, 1995). Trouillot rejects any strictly positivist notion of history as a clean and retrievable "place," sternly resisting the notion that history is irretrievably "nothing," where one history is as good as another, depending on what point of view you take. Trouillot's theory of history suggests we look at the acts of doing history as interactive articulations between the chaos of historical process (everything that occurs) and our acts of telling, the space between the "happened" from *that which is said to have happened*. "Nowhere," Trouillot says, "is history infinitely susceptible to invention." All peoples dictate differences between stories that carry the weight of a *"something that happened* and those that do not." The quotes are from Trouillot, *Silencing*, 8, 13.

48. Angela Cavender Wilson, "American Indian History or Non-Indian Perceptions of American Indian History?" in *Natives and Academics: Researching and Writing about American Indians*, ed. Devon A. Mihesuah (Lincoln: University of Nebraska Press, 1998).

49. M. Annette Jaimes, ed., *The State of Native America: Genocide, Colonization, and Resistance* (Boston: South End Press, 1992).

50. Claude Denis, *We Are Not You: First Nations and Canadian Modernity* (Peterborough, ON: Broadview Press, 1997).

51. See Lilian Friedberg, "Dare to Compare: Americanizing the Holocaust," *American Indian Quarterly* 24, no. 3 (2000): 353–80.

52. Jeffrey C. Alexander, "On the Social Construction of Moral Universals: The 'Holocaust' from War Crime to Trauma Drama," *European Journal of Social Theory* 5, no. 1 (2002): 5–85.

53. Jeffrey K. Olick and Charles Demetriou, "From Theodicy to Ressentiment: Trauma and the Ages of Compensation," in *Memory, Trauma and World Politics: Reflections on the Relationship between Past and Present*, ed. Duncan Bell (New York: Palgrave Macmillan, 2006), 75.

54. Dian Million, "Telling Secrets: Sex, Power and Narratives in Indian Residential School Histories," *Canadian Woman Studies/Les Cahiers de la Femme* 20, no. 2 (2000): 92–104.

55. Justine Smith, "Indigenous Performance and Aporetic Texts," *Union Seminary Quarterly Review* 59, nos.1/2 (2005): 115.

56. Kay Schaffer and Sidonie Smith, *Human Rights and Narrated Lives: The Ethics of Recognition* (New York: Palgrave Macmillan, 2004), 1.

57. Ibid.

58. Ibid., 5.

59. Ibid.

60. Ibid., 6.

61. Ibid.

62. Ibid., 5.

63. Ibid., 7.

Chapter 4

1. *The Report of the Royal Commission on Aboriginal Peoples* (Ottowa: Royal Commission on Aboriginal Peoples, 1996), 359.

2. Audra Simpson, "Commentary: The 'Problem' of Mental Health in Native North America: Liberalism, Multiculturalism, and the (Non)Efficacy of Tears," *Ethos* 36, no. 3 (2008): 376.

3. Elizabeth Furniss and Cariboo Tribal Council, *Victims of Benevolence: The Dark Legacy of the Williams Lake Residential School* (Vancouver, BC: Arsenal Pulp Press, 1995), 125. Bev Sellars's entire unedited speech is available as an appendix to Furniss's text, pp. 121–28. For the sake of brevity, I offer excerpts from what can be appreciated fully only by reading the original.

4. Ibid., 126.

5. Suzanne Fournier and Ernie Crey, *Stolen from Our Embrace: The Abduction of First Nations Children and the Restoration of Aboriginal Communities* (Vancouver, BC: Douglas and McIntyre, 1997).

6. Furniss and Cariboo Tribal Council, *Victims of Benevolence*, 128.

7. G. K. Gooderham, "Prospect," in *The Education of Indian Children in Canada: A Symposium Written by Members of Indian Affairs Education Division, with Comments by the Indian Peoples*, ed. L. G. P. Waller (Toronto: Ryerson Press, 1965), 95.

8. Diamond Jenness, *The Indians of Canada*, 6th ed. (Ottawa: National Museum of Canada, 1963), 261.

9. Henry Zentner, "Reservation Social Structure and Anomie: A Case Study," in *Indian Identity Crisis: Inquiries into the Problems and Prospects of Societal Development among Native Peoples* (Calgary: Strayer, 1973), 3.

10. A. Richard King, *The School at Mopass: A Problem of Identity* (New York: Holt, Rinehart and Winston, 1967), 90.

11. Ibid., 91.

12. David Ashley and David Michael Orenstein, *Sociological Theory, Classical Statements* (Boston: Allyn and Bacon, 1990), 130.

13. Wolfgang Jilek, *Salish Indian Mental Health and Culture Change: Psychohygienic and Therapeutic Aspects of the Guardian Spirit Ceremonial* (Toronto: Holt, Rinehart and Winston of Canada, 1974). See also Wolfgang Jilek, *Indian Healing: Shamanic Ceremonialism in the Pacific Northwest Today* (Surrey, BC: Hancock House, 1982).

14. Jilek, *Indian Healing*, 50.

15. Harold Cardinal, *Unjust Society: The Tragedy of Canada's Indians* (Edmonton: M. G. Hurtig, 1969). The white paper was a policy statement wherein Canadian premier Pierre Trudeau proposed ending the Indian Act.

16. Cardinal writes in 1969 as president of the Indian Association of Alberta and as a board member of the National Indian Brotherhood. George Manuel in 1974 was the president of the National Indian Brotherhood. Howard Adams, PhD, was a revered Métis activist.

17. Cardinal, *Unjust Society*, 60.

18. Ibid., 53.

19. Ibid.

20. Howard Adams, *Prison of Grass: Canada from the Native Point of View* (Toronto: New Press, 1975), 182.

21. Ibid., 144.

22. George Manuel and Michael Posluns, *The Fourth World: An Indian Reality* (New York: Free Press, 1974).

23. Ibid., 9.

24. Ibid., 217.

25. Ward Churchill, ed., *Marxism and Native Americans* (Boston: South End Press, 1983).

26. See Ronald Niezen, *The Origins of Indigenism* (Berkeley and Los Angeles: University of California Press, 2003); Alcida Rita Ramos, *Indigenism: Ethnic Politics in Brazil* (Madison: University of Wisconsin Press, 1998). There is a literature that articulates this from an *indigenous* point of view: Akwesasne, ed., *Basic Call to Consciousness* (Rooseveltown: Akwesasne Notes Mohawk Nation, 1978). Also see Haunani-Kay Trask, *From a Native Daughter: Colonialism and Sovereignty in Hawai'i* (Monroe, ME: Common Courage Press, 1993).

27. Susan Koshy, "From Cold War to Trade War: Neocolonialism and Human Rights," *Social Text* 58 (Spring 1999): 1–32.

28. Gerald Taiaiake Alfred, *Wasáse: Indigenous Pathways of Action and Freedom* (Peterborough, ON: Broadview Press, 2005).

29. I revisit this in chapter 7 when I discuss Kymlicka's take on neoliberal multiculturalism.

30. Charlotte Hooper, *Manly States: Masculinities, International Relations, and Gender Politics* (New York: Columbia University Press, 2001).

31. Curt Taylor Griffiths, J. Collin Yerbury, and Linda Weafer, "Canadian Natives: Victims of Socio-Structural Deprivation?" *Human Organization* 46, no. 3 (1987): 277.

32. Ibid., 278.

33. James L. Nolan Jr., *The Therapeutic State: Justifying Government at Century's End* (New York: New York University Press, 1998).

34. This was considered a major shift in most western nations. Some of my sources: Nolan, *Therapeutic State*; Joseph E. Davis, *Accounts of Innocence: Sexual Abuse, Trauma, and the Self* (Chicago: University of Chicago Press, 2005); Lorraine Wolhuter, Neil Olley, and David Denham, *Victimology: Victimisation and Victims' Rights* (London: Routledge, 2008); Kristin Bumiller, *In an Abusive State: How Neoliberalism Appropriated the Feminist Movement Against Sexual Violence* (Durham, NC: Duke University Press, 2008), and Nancy Whittier, *The Politics of Child Sexual Abuse: Emotion, Social Movements, and the State* (New York: Oxford University Press, 2009).

35. Tony Martens, Brenda Daily, and Maggie Hodgson, *The Spirit Weeps: Characteristics and Dynamics of Incest and Child Sexual Abuse with a Native Perspective* (Edmonton: Nechi Institute, 1988).

36. Christine A. Courtois, *Healing the Incest Wound: Adult Survivors in Therapy* (New York: Norton, 1988).

37. Martens, Daily, and Hodgson, *Spirit Weeps*.

38. See Rupert Ross, *Returning to the Teachings: Exploring Aboriginal Justice* (Toronto: Penguin Canada, 2006). See also Bruce G. Miller, *The Problem of Justice: Tradition and Law in the Coast Salish World* (Lincoln: University of Nebraska Press, 2000). Rupert Ross explains different worldviews between Canada's criminal justice system and an emerging Indigenous justice as reconciliation. Indigenous justice did not see a perpetrator as a criminal but as a family or community member in need of reconciliation with the community and family. Ross and Miller both analyze how difficult it was for Canada to accept this different focus even though it is informed by the same logic that forms Canada's reconciliation, or reconciliation projects. However, Indigenous women have argued that "restorative justice" was not Indigenous. Andrea Smith argues that such justice often ignores safety issues for victimized women. See Andrea Smith, *Native Americans and the Christian Right: The Gendered Politics of Unlikely Alliances* (Durham, NC: Duke University Press, 2008), 57. She cites Ross Gordon Green, *Justice in Aboriginal Communities* (Saskatoon: Purich, 1998), and conversations with the Aboriginal Women's Action Network.

39. Mariana Valverde, "Experience and Truth Telling in a Post-Humanist World: A Foucauldian Contribution to Feminist Ethical Reflections," in *Feminism and the Final Foucault*, ed. Dianna Taylor and Karen Vintges (Urbana: University of Illinois Press, 2004), 83.

40. Joseph Davis calls this move the "psychological turn," where the social justice goal in women's grassroots articulations for social justice for *survivors* begins to be usurped by a particularly professionalized and medicalized diagnosis, *trauma*. See Davis, *Accounts of Innocence*.

41. Courtois, *Healing the Incest Wound*, ix.

42. Ibid., 5.

43. Judith Herman, *Trauma and Recovery: The Aftermath of Violence—from Domestic Abuse to Political Terror* (New York: Basic Books, 1992), ix.

44. Bonnie Burstow, "Toward a Radical Understanding of Trauma and Trauma Work," *Violence Against Women* 9, no. 11 (2003): 1293.

45. Ibid., 1299.

46. Ibid., 1298.

47. Robert Elias, *The Politics of Victimization: Victims, Victimology, and Human Rights* (New York: Oxford University Press, 1986).

48. A good entry into this literature is Shoshana Felman and Dori Laub, *Testimony: Crises of Witnessing in Literature, Psychoanalysis, and History* (New York: Routledge, 1991).

49. Yael Danieli, ed. *International Handbook of Multigenerational Legacies of Trauma* (New York: Plenum Press, 1998).

50. Spero Manson, Janette Beals, Theresa O'Nell, Joan Piasecki, Donald Bechtold, Ellen Keane, and Monica Jones, "Wounded Spirits, Ailing Hearts: PTSD and Related Disorders among American Indians," in *Ethnocultural Aspects of Posttraumatic Stress Disorder*, ed. Anthony J. Marsella, Matthew J. Friedman, Ellen T. Gerrity, and Raymond M. Scurfield (Washington, DC: American Psychological Association, 1996).

51. Laurence J. Kirmeyer, Caroline L. Tait, and Cori Simpson, "The Mental Health of Aboriginal Peoples in Canada: Transformations of Identity and Community," in *Healing Traditions: The Mental Health of Aboriginal Peoples in Canada*, ed. Laurence J. Kirmeyer and Gail Guthrie Valaskakis (Vancouver: University of British Columbia Press, 2009), 24.

52. Ibid.

53. Michael B. Salzman, "Cultural Trauma and Recovery: Perspectives from Terror Management Theory," *Trauma Violence and Abuse* 2, no. 2 (2001): 1.

54. Maria Yellow Horse Brave Heart and Lemyra M. DeBruyn, "The American Indian Holocaust: Healing Historical Unresolved Grief," *American Indian and Alaska Native Mental Health Research Journal* 8, no. 2 (1998): 1. See also Maria Brave Heart-Jordan and Lemyra DeBruyn, "So She May Walk in Balance: Integrating the Impact of Historical Trauma in the Treatment of Native American Indian Women," in *Racism in the Lives of Women: Testimony, Theory, and Guides to Antiracist Practice*, ed. Jeanne Adleman and Gloria M. Enguidanos-Clark (New York: Haworth Press, 1995).

55. Eduardo Duran, *Transforming the Soul Wound: A Theoretical/Clinical Approach to American Indian Psychology* (Meerut, India: Archana, 1990); Eduardo Duran and Bonnie Duran, *Native American Postcolonial Psychology* (Albany: State University of New York Press, 1995); Eduardo Duran, Bonnie Duran, Maria Yellow Horse Brave Heart, and Susan Yellow Horse-Davis, "Healing the American Indian Soul Wound," in *Intergenerational Handbook of Multigenerational Legacies of Trauma*, ed. Yael Danieli (New York: Plenum Press, 1998).

56. Eduardo Duran, Judith Firehammer, and John Gonzalez, "Liberation Psychology as the Path toward Healing Cultural Soul Wounds," *Journal of Counseling and Development* 86, no. 3 (2008): 288–95.

57. Burstow, "Toward a Radical Understanding," 1297.

58. Maggie Hodgson, *Impact of Residential Schools and Other Root Causes of Poor Mental Health (Suicide, Family Violence, Alcohol and Drug Abuse)* (Edmonton: Nechi Institute on Alcohol and Drug Education, 1990).

59. Martens, Daily, and Hodgson, *Spirit Weeps*, 1.

60. Ibid., 107.

61. *Report of the Royal Commission on Aboriginal Peoples*, vol. 1, *Looking Forward, Looking Back* (Ottawa: Royal Commission on Aboriginal Peoples, 1996), 360.

62. Furniss and Cariboo Tribal Council, *Victims of Benevolence*, 124.

63. Assembly of First Nations, *Breaking the Silence: An Interpretive Study of Residential School Impact and Healing as Illustrated by the Stories of First Nations Individuals* (Ottawa: Assembly of First Nations 1994). Wilma Spearchief and Louise Million were the primary researchers and writers of this report.

64. N. Rosalyn Ing, "Dealing with Shame and Unresolved Trauma: Residential School and Its Impact on the 2nd and 3rd Generation Adults" (PhD diss., University of British Columbia, 2001).

65. Ibid., 10.

66. Ibid., 18. The "Non-Assimilable" were "Orientals [the racialization used by Ing, reflecting the older literature], East Indians, Asians, South Asians, and Blacks."

67. Ibid., 45.

68. Ibid., 52.

69. Ibid., 72.

70. Ibid., 85.

71. Danieli, *International Handbook*.

72. The entries on or by the Indigenous are Marie-Anik Gagne, "The Role of Dependency and Colonialism in Generating Trauma in First Nations Citizens," in Danieli, *International Handbook of Multigenerational Legacies of Trauma*; and Duran et al., "Healing the American Indian Soul Wound."

73. Assembly of First Nations, *Breaking the Silence*.

74. *Breaking the Silence* immediately cites Ing, Furniss, and Knockwood, as well as many others.

75. Assembly of First Nations, *Breaking the Silence*, 5.

76. Ibid.

77. Ibid., 112–19.

78. Joshua Breslau, "Cultures of Trauma: Anthropological Views of Posttraumatic Stress Disorder in International Health," *Culture, Medicine and Psychiatry* 28, no. 2 (2004): 114.

79. Ibid., 115.

80. Byron J. Good, "Mental Health Consequence of Displacement and Resettlement," *Economic and Political Weekly* 31, no. 24 (1996): 1505.

81. "Ottawa Charter for Health Promotion," International Conference on Health Promotion: The Move towards a New Public Health (November 17–21, Ottawa, 1986).

82. Assembly of First Nations, *Royal Commission on Aboriginal People at 10 Years: A Report Card*, (Ottawa: Assembly of First Nations, 2006). See also John Lavoie, John O'Neil, Jeff Reading, and Yvonne Allard, "Community Healing and Aboriginal Self-Government," in *Aboriginal Self-Government in Canada*, ed. Yale D. Belanger (Saskatoon: Purich, 2008).

83. *Gathering Strength: Canada's Aboriginal Action Plan* (Ottawa: Indian and Northern Affairs Canada, 1997).

Chapter 5

1. Katerie Akiwenzie-Damm and Cheryl Sutherland, *Residential School Update* (Ottawa: First Nations Health Secretariat, Assembly of First Nations, 1998).

2. Marlene Brant Castellano, "A Healing Journey: Reclaiming Wellness," in *Final Report of the Aboriginal Healing Foundation* (Ottawa: Aboriginal Healing Foundation, 2006), 5–8, 112.

3. Phil Lane Jr., Michael Bopp, Judie Bopp, and Julian Norris, *Mapping the Healing Journey: The Final Report of a First Nation Research Project on Healing in Canadian Aboriginal Communities* (Ottawa: Aboriginal Healing Foundation, 2002), 10.

4. Ibid.

5. Four Worlds International, *Community Healing and Aboriginal Social Security Reform: A Study Prepared for the Assembly of First Nations–Aboriginal Social Security Reform Strategic Initiative* (accessed September 1, 2012), http://www.4worlds.org/4w/ssr/INTRO105.html.

6. "Ottawa Charter for Health Promotion," International Conference on Health Promotion: The Move towards a New Public Health (November 17–21, Ottawa, 1986).

7. Rebecca Blank and Maria Hanratty, "Responding to Need: A Comparison of Social Safety Nets in Canada and the United States," in *Small Differences That Matter: Labor Markets and Income Maintenance in Canada and the United States*, ed. David Card and Richard Freeman (Chicago: University of Chicago Press, 1993), 191.

8. "Ottawa Charter for Health Promotion."

9. An excellent report on Human Development as a sphere of humanitarian activity is Sabina Alkire, "Human Development: Definitions, Critiques, and Related Concepts,"

in *Oxford Poverty and Human Development Initiative Working Papers* (Oxford: Oxford Department of International Development, 2010).

10. Roland D. Chrisjohn and Sherry Woods, *The Circle Game: Shadows and Substance in the Indian Residential School Experience in Canada: A Report Submitted to the Royal Commission on Aboriginal Peoples* (Penticton, BC: Theytus Books, 1997).

11. Phil Lucas, *For the Honour of All*. 57 minutes: Native American Public Broadcasting Consortium, 1985.

12. Sousan Abadian, "From Wasteland to Homeland: Trauma and the Renewal of Indigenous Peoples and Their Communities" (PhD diss., Harvard University, 1999).

13. Lane et al., "Mapping the Healing Journey," 26.

14. Four Worlds International website, *Community Healing and Aboriginal Social Security Reform*.

15. John O'Neil, Laurel Lemchuk-Favel, Yvon Allard, and Brian Postl, "Community Healing and Aboriginal Self-Government," in *Aboriginal Self-Government in Canada*, ed. John H. Hylton (Saskatoon: Purich, 1999), 138.

16. See note 38 in chapter 4.

17. Four Worlds International, "Corporate Resume" (accessed September 1, 2012), http://www.4worlds.org/4w/corporate/CORPRESUME.html.

18. Abadian, "From Wasteland to Homeland," 17.

19. Ibid., 20.

20. Stephen Cornell and Joseph Kalt, "Pathways from Poverty: Economic Development and Institution Building on American Indian Reservations," *American Indian Culture and Research Journal* 14, no. 1 (1990); Stephen E. Cornell, *Accountability, Legitimacy and the Foundations of Native Self-Governance* (Cambridge: Harvard Project on American Indian Economic Development, Malcolm Wiener Center for Social Policy, John F. Kennedy School of Government, Harvard University, 1998); Stephen Cornell and Joseph P. Kalt, "American Indian Self-Determination: The Political Economy of a Policy That Works," *Harvard Kennedy School Faculty Research Series 2010*, Harvard Kennedy School, John F. Kennedy School of Government. Unpublished working paper.

21. Harvard Project for American Indian Economic Development, "Overview" (accessed September 1, 2012), http://hpaied.org/.

22. Abadian, "From Wasteland to Homeland."

23. Ibid., 452.

24. Ibid.

25. Quoted in Craig Lambert, "Trails of Tears, and Hope," *Harvard Magazine*, March/April 2008.

26. Four Worlds International, *Community Healing and Aboriginal Social Security Reform*.

27. Elizabeth Furniss, "A Sobriety Movement among the Shuswap Indians of Alkali Lake" (master's thesis, University of British Columbia, 1987), 68, quoted in Abadian, "From Wasteland to Homeland," 404–5.

28. Andie Diane Palmer, *Maps of Experience: The Anchoring of Land to Story in Secwepemc Discourse* (Toronto: University of Toronto Press, 2005), 55.

29. Re-evaluation Counseling Communities, eds., *Heritage* (Seattle: Rational Island Publishers, 1982). Also see Nancy Whittier, *The Politics of Child Sexual Abuse: Emotion, Social Movements, and the State* (New York: Oxford University Press, 2009), 51–52.

30. Barbara Helen-Hill, *Shaking the Rattle, Healing the Trauma of Colonization* (Vancouver, BC: Theytus Books, 1995).

31. Ibid.

32. Abadian, "From Wasteland to Homeland," 30 f22. Abadian's participant observations coincide with the era when numerous Indigenous peoples complained that they were being overrun with New Age spiritual appropriation. While I did not substantiate the connection, the timing seems suggestive that not everyone enjoyed the influx of alternative practitioners. I don't include Sousan Abadian as such an intruder, since it appears she made lasting relations in the communities she visited.

33. Melody Beattie, *Codependent No More: How to Stop Controlling Others and Start Caring for Yourself* (New York: Harper/Hazelden, 1987); Pia Mellody, *Facing Codependence* (New York: HarperCollins, 1989); Anne Wilson Schaef, *When Society Becomes an Addict* (San Francisco: Harper and Row, 1987).

34. John Steadman Rice, *A Disease of One's Own: Psychotherapy, Addiction, and the Emergence of Co-Dependency* (New Brunswick, NJ: Transaction, 1998), 11.

35. Ibid., 205.

36. Ibid.

37. Abadian, "From Wasteland to Homeland," 448.

38. Ibid., 430.

39. Ibid.

40. Lambert, "Trails of Tears, and Hope."

41. Abadian, "From Wasteland to Homeland," 447.

42. Innu Nation (accessed September 1, 2012), http://www.innu.ca/index .php?option=com_content&view=article&id=10&Itemid=7&lang=en.

43. Colin Samson, James Wilson, and Jonathan Mazower, *Canada's Tibet: The Killing of the Innu* (London: Survival International, 1999).

44. Tshikapisk Foundation (accessed September 1, 2012), http://www.tshikapisk.ca/ home/mission.htm.

45. "Help Us to Help Ourselves," *Globe and Mail*, December 7, 2000. The ongoing crisis well told in their own words is Innu Nation and Mushuau Innu Band Council, *Gathering Voices: Finding Strength to Help Our Children* (1995).

46. Innu Nation website.

47. Aboriginal Affairs and Northern Development, "The Labrador Innu Comprehensive Healing Strategy," Labrador Innu Chronology of Events (accessed September 1, 2012), http://www.aadnc-aandc.gc.ca/eng/1100100016951/1100100016952.

48. Jordan Graham and C. Michael Hogan, "Labrador Innu Land Claims and the Indigenous Archaeology Paradox," in *Encyclopedia of Earth*, ed. Cutler J. Cleveland (Washington, DC: Environmental Information Coalition, National Council for Science and the Environment), first published in *Encyclopedia of Earth*, July 14, 2012 (accessed September 1, 2012), http://www.eoearth.org/article/ Labrador_Innu_land_claims_and_the_indigenous_archaeology_paradox.

49. Colin Samson, "A Colonial Double-Bind: Social and Historical Contexts of Innu Mental Health," in *Healing Traditions: The Mental Health of Aboriginal Peoples in Canada*, ed. Laurence J. Kirmeyer and Gail Guthrie Valaskakis (Vancouver: University of British Columbia Press, 2009), 128–29. Samson, who had been with the Innu since 1994, observed that "by resorting to medical and pan-Indian healing techniques, the Innu villages . . . gear up for . . . a mass institutionalization of the problems." He observed how these medical and pan-Indian healing techniques were funded, while those that sought to preserve the "closely entwined structures of Innu medicine and spirituality" were not.

50. Lane et al., "Mapping the Healing Journey."

51. Ibid., 39.

52. Gerald Taiaiake Alfred, *Peace, Power, Righteousness: An Indigenous Manifesto* (Don Mills, ON: Oxford University Press, 1999).

53. Sharon H. Venne, "Treaty and Constitution in Canada," in *Critical Issues in Native North America* (Copenhagen: International Working Group for Indigenous Affairs, 1989), 96.

54. M. Annette Jaimes Guerrero, "'Patriarchal Colonialism' and Indigenism: Implications for Native Feminist Spirituality and Native Womanism," *Hypatia* 18, no. 2 (2003): 58–69.

55. Roger Maaka and Augie Fleras, "Contesting Indigenous Peoples Governance: The Politics of State-Determination vs. Self-Determining Autonomy," in *Aboriginal Self-Government in Canada: Current Trends and Issues*, ed. Yale D. Belanger (Saskatoon: Purich, 2008).

Chapter 6

1. Simon J. Ortiz, *Speaking for the Generations: Native Writers on Writing* (Tucson: University of Arizona Press, 1997).

2. Women of All Red Nations, *WARN Report II* (Sioux Falls, SD: WARN, 1979), 1.

3. Andrea Smith, "Better Dead than Pregnant: The Colonization of Native Women's Reproductive Health," in *Policing the National Body: Race, Gender and Criminalization*, ed. Jael Silliman and Anannya Battacharjee (Cambridge, MA: South End Press, 2002); Meg Devlin O'Sullivan, "'We Worry about Survival': American Indian Women, Sovereignty, and the Right to Bear and Raise Children in the 1970s" (PhD diss., University of North Carolina, 2007).

4. Jodi Kim, "An 'Orphan' with Two Mothers: Transnational and Transracial Adoption, the Cold War, and Contemporary Asian American Cultural Politics," *American Quarterly* 61, no. 4 (2009): 855–80.

5. Andrea Smith, *Conquest: Sexual Violence and American Indian Genocide* (Cambridge, MA: South End Press, 2005).

6. Women of All Red Nations. *WARN Report II*, 1.

7. Indigenous Women's Network, "About IWN" (accessed September 1, 2012), http://indigenouswomen.org/.

8. Jo-Anne Fiske, "'The Womb Is to the Nation as the Heart Is to the Body': Ethnopolitical Discourses of the Canadian Indigenous Women's Movement," *Studies in Political Economy* 51 (Fall 1996): 65.

9. "First Nations/Metis Human Rights Law: The History of NWAC's Position and Options for Future Action" (*NWAC Special Assembly, March 18–22*, Ottawa, 1988).

10. Lilianne Krosenbrink-Gelissen, *Sexual Equality as an Aboriginal Right: The Native Women's Association of Canada and the Constitutional Process on Aboriginal Matters 1982–1987*, Nijmegen Studies in Development and Cultural Change, vol. 7 (Saarbrücken: Verlag Breitenbach, 1991).

11. Jeannette Armstrong, "Land Speaking," in *Speaking for the Generations: Native Writers on Writing*, ed. Simon Ortiz (Tucson: University of Arizona Press, 1998), 176.

12. Fiske, "Womb Is to the Nation," 71.

13. Ibid., 71 72.

14. Ibid., 72.

15. Teresa Nahanee, "Dancing with a Gorilla: Aboriginal Women, Justice and the Charter," in *Aboriginal Peoples and the Justice System: Report of the National Round Table on Aboriginal Justice* (Ottawa: Royal Commission on Aboriginal Peoples, 1993), 372, quoted in Fiske, "Womb Is to the Nation," 76.

16. "Changing the Landscape: Ending Violence—Achieving Equality," in *The Final Report of the Canadian Panel on Violence against Women*, ed., Aboriginal Circle of the Canadian Panel on Violence against Women (Ottawa: Minister of Supply and Services Canada, 1993), 199, quoted in Fiske, "Womb Is to the Nation," 76.

17. Jo-Anne Fiske, "Constitutionalizing the Space to Be Aboriginal Women: The Indian Act and the Struggle for First Nation Citizenship," in *Aboriginal Self-Government in Canada*, ed. Yale D. Belanger (Saskatoon: Purich, 2008).

18. "Aboriginal Women, Self-Government and the Canadian Charter of Rights and Freedoms," in NWAC *Analysis in the Context of the 1991 "Canada Package" on Constitutional Reform* (Ottawa: Native Women's Association of Canada, 1991), 16.

19. James D. Wilets, "Conceptualizing Private Violence against Sexual Minorities as Gendered Violence: An International and Comparative Law Perspective," *Albany Law Review* 60 (1996): 989–1050.

20. Feminist activists sought redress from the patriarchal law that sanctioned violence in the domestic sphere. When domestic violence became criminalized, the patriarchal legal establishment switched from protecting the home as a male bastion of privilege to legislating "rights" to women's bodies in legislation like *Roe v. Wade*, where the United States inscribed a zone of moral contestation over their reproductive rights. See Lauren Berlant, "The Subject of True Feeling: Pain, Privacy, Politics," in *Cultural Pluralism, Identity Politics, and the Law*, ed. Austin Surat (Ann Arbor: University of Michigan Press, 2001), 68.

21. Fiske, "Womb Is to the Nation," 77–81.

22. Glen S. Coulthard, "Subjects of Empire: Indigenous Peoples and the 'Politics of Recognition' in Canada," *Contemporary Political Theory* 6, no. 4 (2007): 437–60.

23. Ibid., 451.

24. Gabrielle Slowey, *Navigating Neoliberalism: Self-Determination and the Mikisew Cree First Nation* (Vancouver: University of British Columbia Press, 2008), xiv.

25. Ibid., 15.

26. Gail Guthrie Valaskakis, "Telling Our Own Stories: The Role, Development, and Future of Aboriginal Communications," in *Aboriginal Education; Fulfilling the Promise*, ed. Marlene Brant Castellano, Lynn Davis, and Louise Lahache (Vancouver: University of British Columbia Press, 2000). See also Marlene Brant Castellano, "Heart of the Nations: Women's Contribution to Community Healing," in *Restoring the Balance: First Nations Women, Community, and Culture*, ed. Gail Guthrie Valaskakis, Madeline Dion Stout, and Eric Guimond (Winnipeg: University of Manitoba Press, 2009).

27. Kim Anderson, "Leading by Action: Female Chiefs and the Political Landscape," in *Restoring the Balance: First Nations Women, Community, and Culture*, ed. Gail Guthrie Valaskakis, Madeline Dion Stout, and Eric Guimond (Winnipeg: University of Manitoba Press, 2009), 99.

28. Ibid., 110.

29. Ibid., 115.

30. Canadian Feminist Alliance for International Action, "Canada's Failure to Act: Women's Inequality Deepens," submission to the UN Committee on the Elimination of

Discrimination against Women on the Occasion of the Committee's Review of Canada's 5th Report (2003), 41–42, quoted in ibid., 101.

31. Yale D. Belanger, "Future Prospects for Aboriginal Self-Government in Canada," in *Aboriginal Self-Government in Canada*, ed. Yale D. Belanger (Saskatoon: Purich, 2008).

32. Kiera L. Ladner, "Understanding the Impact of Self-Determination on Communities in Crisis," *Journal of Aboriginal Health* (November 2009): 89.

33. Ibid., 90.

34. Ibid.

35. Ibid., 94.

36. Ibid., 91–92.

37. Laurence Kirmeyer, Cori Simpson, and Margaret Cargo, "Healing Traditions: Culture, Community and Mental Health Promotion with Canadian Aboriginal Peoples," *Australasian Psychiatry* 11, suppl. (2003): S18. See also Michael J. Chandler and Christopher Lalonde, "Cultural Continuity as a Hedge against Suicide in Canada's First Nations," *Transcultural Psychiatry* 35, no. 2 (1998). It appears again in *Healing Traditions: The Mental Health of Aboriginal Peoples in Canada*, ed. Laurence J. Kirmeyer and Gail Guthrie Valaskakis (Vancouver: University of British Columbia Press, 2009).

38. Kirmeyer, Simpson, and Cargo, "Healing Traditions," S18.

39. Ladner, "Understanding the Impact," 97.

40. Ibid.

41. Ibid., 95.

42. Ibid., 95–96.

43. Jacinda Mack, "Nuxalk Perspectives on Sovereignty and Social Change" (master's thesis, York University, 2006), 2.

44. Ibid., 2.

45. Ibid.

46. Ibid., 5.

47. Ibid., 9.

48. Ibid., 11.

49. Ibid., 21.

50. Ibid., 37.

51. Jeannette Armstrong (Interviewee) and Hall, D. E. (Interviewer). (2007). *Native Perspectives on Sustainability: Jeannette Armstrong (Syilx)* [Interview transcript]. See chapter 1, note 75.

52. Michael Bopp and Phil Lane Jr., *The Nuxalk Nation Community Healing and Wellness Development Plan* (Lethbridge, AL: Four Worlds International, 2000).

53. Ibid., 2.

54. Ibid., 19.

55. Marketwire, "Nuxalk Nation Signs Reconciliation Protocol," December 2010.

Chapter 7

1. Dian Million, unpublished poem fragment from *traveling*.

2. Self-Determination Theory: An Approach to Human Motivation and Personality (accessed September 1, 2012), http://www.selfdeterminationtheory.org/.

3. Anthony D. Mancini, "Self-Determination Theory: A Framework for the Recovery Paradigm," *Advances in Psychiatric Treatment* 14, no. 5 (2008): 358, doi: 10.1192/apt. bp.107.004036.

4. HOSW, "Health Info: The Fifth Healing Our Spirit Worldwide (HOSW) Health, Healing and Self-Determination," *International Journal of Circumpolar Health* 64, no. 2 (2005): 194.

5. Sharon Parker, "Understanding Self-Determination: The Basics," in *First International Conference on the Right to Self-Determination* (Geneva, 2000) (accessed September 1, 2012), http://www.humanlaw.org/.

6. Self-Determination Theory website.

7. Ibid.

8. Nikolas Rose, *Inventing Our Selves: Psychology, Power, and Personhood* (Cambridge: Cambridge University Press, 1996). See also Nikolas Rose, *Powers of Freedom: Reframing Political Thought* (New York: Cambridge University Press, 1999).

9. Rose, *Powers of Freedom*, 4.

10. Ibid., 32.

11. Ann Laura Stoler, *Race and the Education of Desire: Foucault's History of Sexuality and the Colonial Order of Things* (Durham, NC: Duke University Press, 1995), quoted in Rose, *Powers of Freedom*, 39 f51.

12. Caroline L. Tait, "Disruptions in Nature, Disruptions in Society: Aboriginal Peoples of Canada and the 'Making' of Fetal Alcohol Syndrome," in *Healing Traditions: The Mental Health of Aboriginal Peoples in Canada*, ed. Laurence J. Kirmeyer and Gail Guthrie Valaskakis (Vancouver: University of British Columbia Press, 2009), 199.

13. Rose, *Inventing Our Selves*, 44.

14. Lauren Berlant, "Slow Death (Sovereignty, Obesity, Lateral Agency)," *Critical Inquiry* 33, no. 4 (2007): 765.

15. Ibid.

16. Rose, *Inventing Our Selves*, 17.

17. Ibid.

18. Eva Illouz, *Cold Intimacies: The Making of Emotional Capitalism* (Cambridge: Polity Press, 2007).

19. Eli Zaretsky, "Psychoanalysis and the Spirit of Capitalism," *Constellations* 15, no. 3 (2008).

20. Rose, *Inventing Our Selves*, 154. Many works emerged on therapeutic practices, or what Joseph Davis called the "psychic turn."

21. Ibid.

22. Ibid.

23. Thomas Lemke, *Biopolitics: An Advanced Introduction*, Biopolitics: Medicine, Technoscience, and Health in the 21st Century, ed. Monica J. Casper and Lisa Jean Moore. (New York: New York University Press, 2011), 99.

24. Alison Falby, "The Modern Confessional: Anglo-American Religious Groups and the Emergence of Lay Psychotherapy," *Journal of History of the Behavioral Sciences* 39, no. 3 (2003): 251.

25. Ibid., 264.

26. Elinor Ochs and Lisa Capps, "Narrating the Self," *Annual Review of Anthropology* 25 (1996): 19–43; Julie Gerhardt and Charles Stinson, "The Nature of Therapeutic Discourse: Accounts of the Self," *Journal of Narrative and Life History* 4, no. 3 (1994): 151–91; James A. Holstein and Jaber F. Gubrium, *The Self We Live By: Narrative Identity in a Postmodern World* (New York: Oxford University Press, 2000); and Dan P. McAdams, *The Redemptive Self* (New York: Oxford University Press, 2006).

27. Mariana Valverde, "Experience and Truth Telling in a Post-Humanist World: A Foucauldian Contribution to Feminist Ethical Reflections," in *Feminism and the Final Foucault,* ed. Dianna Taylor and Karen Vintges (Urbana: University of Illinois Press, 2004), 67. See Mariana Valverde, *Diseases of the Will: Alcohol and the Dilemmas of Freedom* (Cambridge: Cambridge University Press, 1998).

28. Don Coyhis and William L. White, "Alcohol Problems in Native America: Changing Paradigms and Clinical Practices," *Alcoholism Treatment Quarterly* 20, nos. 3/4 (2002); David Moore and Don Coyhis, "The Multicultural Wellbriety Peer Recovery Support Program: Two Decades of Community-Based Recovery," *Alcoholism Treatment Quarterly* 28, no. 3 (2010).

29. Moore and Coyhis, "Multicultural Wellbriety Peer Recovery."

30. Ibid., 275–76.

31. Eduardo Duran, Judith Firehammer, and John Gonzalez, "Liberation Psychology as the Path toward Healing Cultural Soul Wounds," *Journal of Counseling and Development* 86, no. 3 (2008).

32. Andrea Smith, *Native Americans and the Christian Right: The Gendered Politics of Unlikely Alliances* (Durham, NC: Duke University Press, 2008), 93.

33. Spero Manson, Janette Beals, Theresa O'Nell, Joan Piasecki, Donald Bechtold, Ellen Keane, and Monica Jones, "Wounded Spirits, Ailing Hearts: PTSD and Related Disorders among American Indians," in *Ethnocultural Aspects of Posttraumatic Stress Disorder,* ed. Anthony J. Marsella, Matthew J. Friedman, Ellen T. Gerrity, and Raymond M. Scurfield (Washington, DC: American Psychological Association, 1996).

34. Joseph P. Gone, "Encountering Professional Psychology: Re-Envisioning Mental Health Services for Native North America," in *Healing Traditions: The Mental Health of Aboriginal Peoples in Canada,* ed. Laurence J. Kirmeyer and Gail Guthrie Valaskakis (Vancouver: University of British Columbia Press, 2009).

35. Joseph P. Gone, "Introduction: Mental Health Discourse as Western Proselytization," *Ethos* 36, no. 3 (2008): 312.

36. Stephen Cornell and Joseph P. Kalt, "American Indian Self-Determination: The Political Economy of a Policy That Works," *Harvard Kennedy School Faculty Research Series* (2010), 29.

37. Yale D. Belanger, "Future Prospects for Aboriginal Self-Government in Canada," in *Aboriginal Self-Government in Canada,* ed. Yale D. Belanger (Saskatoon: Purich, 2008). See also Wayne Warry, *Ending Denial: Understanding Aboriginal Issues* (Peterborough, ON: Broadview Press, 2007).

38. Will Kymlicka, "Neoliberal Multiculturalism," keynote, Eminent Speakers at the Faculty of Arts Lectures, University of Ljubljana, Slovenia, video recorded March 2011 (accessed September 1, 2012), http://videolectures.net/ffeminent_kymlicka_neoliberal/.

39. Eva Mackey, *The House of Difference: Cultural Politics and National Identity in Canada* (Toronto: University of Toronto Press, 2002).

40. Aihwa Ong, "Neoliberalism as a Mobile Technology," *Transactions of the Institute of British Geographers* 32, no. 1 (2007).

41. Patricia Richards, "Of Indians and Terrorists: How the State and Local Elites Construct the Mapuche in Neoliberal Multicultural Chile," *Journal of Latin American Studies* 42, no. 1 (2010): 90.

42. Rauna Kuokkanen, "The Politics of Form and Alternative Autonomies: Indigenous Women, Subsistence Economies and the Gift Paradigm," in *Native American Indigenous Studies Conference*, ed. William D. Coleman, Globalization Working Papers (Minneapolis: Institute on Globalization and the Human Condition, 2007), 4.

43. Maria Battiste and Sakej Henderson, *Protecting Indigenous Knowledge and Heritage* (Saskatoon: Purie, 2000).

44. Julie Cruikshank, *The Social Life of Stories: Narrative and Knowledge in the Yukon Territory* (Lincoln: University of Nebraska Press, 1998).

45. Paul Nadasdy, "Politics of TEK: Power and the 'Integration' of Knowledge," *Arctic Anthropology* 36, nos. 1/2 (1999). Also see Paul Nadasdy, *Hunters and Bureaucrats: Power, Knowledge, and Aboriginal–State Relations in the Southwest Yukon* (Vancouver: University of British Columbia Press, 2003).

46. Stephanie Irlbacher-Fox, *Finding Dahshaa: Self-Government, Social Suffering, and Aboriginal Policy in Canada* (Vancouver: University of British Columbia Press, 2009).

47. Jodi Melamed, *Represent and Destroy: Rationalizing Violence in the New Racial Capitalism*, ed. Roderick A. Ferguson and Grace Kyungwon Hong, Difference Incorporated. (Minneapolis: University of Minnesota Press, 2011), 183.

48. Phyllis Ann Fast, *Northern Athabascan Survival: Women, Community, and the Future* (Lincoln: University of Nebraska Press, 2002), 230.

49. Ibid., 232.

50. Ibid., 258.

51. Tracy Friedel, "The More Things Change, the More They Stay the Same: The Challenge of Identity for Native Students in Canada," *Cultural and Pedagogical Inquiry* 1, no. 2 (2010): 24.

52. Gerald Taiaiake Alfred, *Wasáse: Indigenous Pathways of Action and Freedom* (Peterborough, ON: Broadview Press, 2005).

53. Pamela Amoss, *Coast Salish Spirit Dancing: The Survival of an Ancestral Religion* (Seattle: University of Washington Press, 1978).

54. Wayne P. Suttles, *The Economic Life of the Coast Salish of Haro and Rosario Straits: Coast Salish and Western Washington Indians* (New York: Garland, 1974). See also Wayne P. Suttles and Ralph Maud, *Coast Salish Essays* (Seattle: University of Washington Press, 1987).

55. Keith Thor Carlson, ed., *You Are Asked to Witness: The Sto:lo in Canada's Pacific Coast History* (Chilliwack, BC: Sto:lo Heritage Trust, 1997).

56. Vine Deloria, *Indians of the Pacific Northwest: From the Coming of the White Man to the Present Day* (New York: Doubleday, 1977).

57. "Cedar Project Hosts Event for Lummi Canoe Journey," *Whatcom Magazine*, 2011, 53.

58. James M. Fortier, "Pulling Together [Videorecording]," ed. James M. Fortier (Auburn: Muckleshoot Tribal Community, 2005).

59. George Clutesi, *Potlatch* (Sidney, BC: Gray's, 1969). See also Peter S. Webster and Kwayatsapalth, *As Far as I Know: Reminiscences of an Ahousat Elder* (Campbell River, BC: Campbell River Museum and Archives, 1983).

60. Frank Malloway, Heather Miles, and Tracey Joe, "Through the Eyes of Siyemches Te Yeqwyeqwi:Ws (Frank Malloway)," in *You Are Asked to Witness: The Sto:Lo in Canada's Pacific Coast History*, ed. Keith Thor Carlson (Chilliwack, BC: Sto:lo Heritage Trust, 1996).

61. *Oceanedge: The Journal of Applied Storytelling*, no. 3, "Tales of the Canoe Nation" (Spring 1995): 3.

62. "Our Way." 3rd Annual Coast Salish Gathering, Tulalip, Washington, 2008, 4.

63. Ibid.

64. Shelly Vendiola, "Preserving Our Shalangen: Promoting Non-Violence and Respect," *Indigenous Woman* (Fall 2003): 34.

65. Elise Krohn and Valerie Segrest, *Traditional Foods of Puget Sound Project* (Bellingham, WA: Northwest Indian College Cooperative Extension Office, 2010), 1.

66. Kuokkanen, " Politics of Form and Alternative Autonomies." See also Richard G. Newton and Madonna L. Moss, *Haa Atxaayi Haa Kusteeyix Sitee = Our Food Is Our Tlingit Way of Life: Excerpts from Oral Interviews* (Juneau, AK: US Department of Agriculture, Forest Service, Alaska Region, 2005); and Rauna Kuokkanen, "From Indigenous Economies to Market-Based Self-Governance: A Feminist Political Economy Analysis," *Canadian Journal of Political Science/Revue canadienne de science politique* 44, no. 2 (2011).

67. Nancy J. Turner, "Traditional Ecological Knowledge," in *The Rainforests of Home: Profile of a North American Bioregion*, ed. Peter K. Schoonmaker, Betinna Von Hagen, and Edward C. Wolf (Covelo, CA: Island Press, 1997), 275.

68. Charlotte Coté, *Spirits of Our Whaling Ancestors: Revitalizing Makah and Nuu-Chah-Nulth Traditions* (Seattle: University of Washington Press, 2010). This is an important first Native (Nuu-chah-nulth) account of the significance of returning to the whale.

69. Turner, "Traditional Ecological Knowledge," 277.

70. Michelle Daigle, "The Restoration of Traditional Food Systems: A Pathway toward the Regeneration of an Indigenous Future," in *Native American Students in Advanced Academia at the University of Washington Symposium*, Seattle, 2011.

71. Saul Vicente Vasquez, *Food Sovereignty and the Rights of Indigenous Peoples* (San Francisco: International Indian Treaty Council, 2008).

72. Ibid.

73. Ibid.

74. Melinda Cooper, *Life as Surplus: Biotechnology and Capitalism in the Neoliberal Era* (Seattle: University of Washington Press, 2010).

75. Lauren Berlant, *Cruel Optimism* (Durham, NC: Duke University Press, 2011).

76. Bernardo Alexander Attias, "To Each His Own Sexes?: Toward a Rhetorical Understanding of Molecular Revolution," in *Deleuze and Guattari: New Mappings in Politics, Philosophy, and Culture*, ed. Eleanor Kaufman and Kevin Jon Heller (Minneapolis: University of Minnesota Press, 1998).

77. Jane Bennett, *Vibrant Matter: A Political Ecology of Things* (Durham, NC: Duke University Press, 2010).

78. Kiera L. Ladner, "Understanding the Impact of Self-Determination on Communities in Crisis," *Journal of Aboriginal Health*, (November 2009): 89.

Selected Bibliography

Abadian, Sousan. "From Wasteland to Homeland: Trauma and the Renewal of Indigenous Peoples and Their Communities." PhD dissertation, Harvard University, 1999.

Aboriginal Affairs and Northern Development. "The Labrador Innu Comprehensive Healing Strategy." Labrador Innu Chronology of Events. Accessed September 1, 2012. http://www.aadnc-aandc.gc.ca/eng/1100100016951/1100100016952.

"Aboriginal Women, Self-Government and the Canadian Charter of Rights and Freedoms." In NWAC Analysis in the Context of the 1991 "Canada Package" on Constitutional Reform. Ottawa: Native Women's Association of Canada, 1991.

Adams, Howard. Prison of Grass: Canada from the Native Point of View. Trent Native Series, no. 1. Toronto: New Press, 1975.

Agamben, Giorgio. Remnants of Auschwitz: The Witness and the Archive. Translated by Daniel Heller-Roazen. New York: Zone Books, 2002.

Akiwenzie-Damm, Katerie, and Cheryl Sutherland. Residential School Update. Ottawa: First Nations Health Secretariat, Assembly of First Nations, 1998.

Akwesasne, ed. Basic Call to Consciousness. Rooseveltown: Akwesasne Notes Mohawk Nation, 1978.

Alexander, Jeffrey C. "On the Social Construction of Moral Universals: The 'Holocaust' from War Crime to Trauma Drama." European Journal of Social Theory 5, no. 1 (2002): 5–85.

Alfred, Gerald Taiaiake. Heeding the Voices of Our Ancestors: Kahnawake Mohawk Politics and the Rise of Native Nationalism. Toronto: Oxford University Press, 1995.

———. Peace, Power, Righteousness: An Indigenous Manifesto. 2nd ed. Don Mills, ON: Oxford University Press, 1999.

———. Wasáse: Indigenous Pathways of Action and Freedom. Peterborough, ON: Broadview Press, 2005.

Alioff, Maurie, and Susan Schouten Levine. "Interview: The Long Walk of Alanis Obomsawin." Cinema Canada (June 1987): 13.

Alkire, Sabina. "Human Development: Definitions, Critiques, and Related Concepts." In Oxford Poverty and Human Development Initiative Working Papers. Oxford: Oxford Department of International Development, 2010.

Altman, Jon, and Melinda Hinkson, eds. Coercive Reconciliation: Stabilise, Normalise, Exit Aboriginal Australia. Melbourne: Arena, 2007.

Amnesty International. *Canada: Stolen Sisters: A Human Rights Response to Discrimination and Violence against Indigenous Women in Canada,* October 4, 2004. Accessed November 29, 2012. http://www.unhcr.org/refworld/docid/42ae984b0.html.

———. *Maze of Injustice: The Failure to Protect Indigenous Women from Sexual Violence in the USA.* New York: Amnesty International USA, 2007.

Amoss, Pamela. *Coast Salish Spirit Dancing: The Survival of an Ancestral Religion.* Seattle: University of Washington Press, 1978.

Anaya, S. James. *Indigenous Peoples in International Law.* New York: Oxford University Press, 2004.

Anderson, Kim. "Leading by Action: Female Chiefs and the Political Landscape." In *Restoring the Balance: First Nations Women, Community, and Culture,* edited by Gail Guthrie Valaskakis, Madeline Dion Stout, and Eric Guimond, 99–124. Winnipeg: University of Manitoba Press, 2009.

Armstrong, Jeannette. "The Disempowerment of First North American Native Peoples and Empowerment through Their Writing." In *An Anthology of Native Canadian Writing in English,* edited by Daniel David Moses and Terry Goldie, 207–11. Oxford: University of Oxford Press, 1992.

———. "Land Speaking." In *Speaking for the Generations: Native Writers on Writing,* edited by Simon Ortiz, 179–94. Tucson: University of Arizona Press, 1998.

———. *Looking at the Words of Our People: First Nations Analysis of Literature.* Penticton, BC: Theytus Books, 1993.

———. *Slash.* Rev. ed. Penticton, BC: Theytus Books, 1988.

Armstrong, Jeannette, and D. E. Hall. *Native Perspectives on Sustainability: Jeannette Armstrong (Syilx)* 2007. [Interview transcript], 48:25. Accessed September 1, 2012, from the Native Perspectives on Sustainability Project website: http://www.nativeperspectives.net.

Ashley, David, and David Michael Orenstein. *Sociological Theory, Classical Statements.* Boston: Allyn and Bacon, 1990.

Assembly of First Nations. *Breaking the Silence: An Interpretive Study of Residential School Impact and Healing as Illustrated by the Stories of First Nations Individuals.* Ottawa: Assembly of First Nations, 1994.

———. *Royal Commission on Aboriginal Peoples at 10 Years: A Report Card.* Ottawa: Assembly of First Nations, 2006. Copy in possession of the author.

Attias, Bernardo Alexander. "To Each His Own Sexes?: Toward a Rhetorical Understanding of Molecular Revolution." In *Deleuze and Guattari: New Mappings in Politics, Philosophy, and Culture,* edited by Eleanor Kaufman and Kevin Jon Heller. Minneapolis: University of Minnesota Press, 1998.

Australian Human Rights and Equal Opportunity Commission. *Bringing Them Home: Report of the National Inquiry into the Separation of Aboriginal and Torres Strait Islander Children from Their Families.* Sydney: Human Rights and Equal Opportunity Commission, 1997.

Battiste, Maria, and Sakej Henderson. *Protecting Indigenous Knowledge and Heritage.* Saskatoon: Purie, 2000.

Bayefsky, Anne F. "Applying International Human Rights Law: Indigenous Women." *Canadian Yearbook of International Law* 20 (1982): 244–65.

Beattie, Melody. *Codependent No More: How to Stop Controlling Others and Start Caring for Yourself.* New York: Harper/Hazelden, 1987.

Behrendt, Larissa. "Consent in a (Neo)Colonial Society: Aboriginal Women as Sexual and Legal 'Other.'" *Australian Feminist Studies* 15, no. 33 (2000): 353–67.

Belanger, Yale D. "Future Prospects for Aboriginal Self-Government in Canada." In *Aboriginal Self-Government in Canada,* edited by Yale D. Belanger. Saskatoon: Purich, 2008.

Bennett, Jane. *Vibrant Matter: A Political Ecology of Things.* Durham, NC: Duke University Press, 2010.

Berlant, Lauren. *Cruel Optimism.* Durham, NC: Duke University Press, 2011.

———. "The Epistemology of State Emotion." In *Dissent in Dangerous Times,* edited by Austin Surat. Ann Arbor: University of Michigan Press, 2005.

———. "Slow Death (Sovereignty, Obesity, Lateral Agency)." *Critical Inquiry* 33, no. 4 (2007): 754–80.

———. "The Subject of True Feeling: Pain, Privacy, Politics." In *Cultural Pluralism, Identity Politics, and the Law,* edited by Austin Surat. Ann Arbor: University of Michigan Press, 2001.

Bierria, Alisa. "Pursuing a Radical Anti-Violence Agenda Inside/Outside a Non-Profit Structure." In *The Revolution Will Not Be Funded: Beyond the Non-Profit Industrial Complex,* edited by Incite! Women of Color Against Violence, 151–63. Cambridge, MA: South End Press, 2007.

Bird, Gloria. "Breaking the Silence: Writing As 'Witness.'" In *Speaking for the Generations: Native Writers on Writing,* edited by Simon J. Ortiz. Tucson: University of Arizona Press, 1998.

———. "Introduction, or the First Circle—Native Women's Voice." In *Writing the Circle: Native Women of Western Canada, an Anthology,* edited by Jeanne Martha Perreault and Sylvia Vance, xxx. Norman: University of Oklahoma Press, 1990.

Blank, Rebecca, and Maria Hanratty. "Responding to Need: A Comparison of Social Safety Nets in Canada and the United States." In *Small Differences That Matter: Labor Markets and Income Maintenance in Canada and the United States,* edited by David Card and Richard Freeman, 191–232. Chicago: University of Chicago Press, 1993.

Blauner, Robert. *Racial Oppression in the United States.* New York: Harper and Row, 1972.

Blocker, Jane. *Seeing Witness: Visuality and the Ethics of Testimony.* Minneapolis: University of Minnesota Press, 2009.

Bopp, Michael, and Phil Lane Jr. *The Nuxalk Nation Community Healing and Wellness Development Plan.* Lethbridge, Alberta: Four Worlds International, 2000.

Braroe, Niels Winther. *Indian and White: Self-Image and Interaction in a Canadian Plains Community.* Stanford, CA: Stanford University Press, 1975.

Brave Heart, Maria Yellow Horse, and Lemyra M. DeBruyn. "The American Indian Holocaust: Healing Historical Unresolved Grief." *American Indian and Alaska Native Mental Health Research Journal* 8, no. 2 (1998): 56–78.

Brave Heart-Jordan, Maria, and Lemyra DeBruyn. "So She May Walk in Balance: Integrating the Impact of Historical Trauma in the Treatment of Native American Indian Women." In *Racism in the Lives of Women: Testimony, Theory, and Guides to Antiracist Practice,* edited by Jeanne Adleman and Gloria M. Enguidanos-Clark, 345–68. New York: Haworth Press, 1995.

Breslau, Joshua. "Cultures of Trauma: Anthropological Views of Posttraumatic Stress Disorder in International Health." *Culture, Medicine and Psychiatry* 28, no. 2 (2004): 113–26.

Bumiller, Kristin. *In an Abusive State: How Neoliberalism Appropriated the Feminist Movement against Sexual Violence.* Durham, NC: Duke University Press, 2008.

Burgett, Bruce. "Sex, Panic, Nation." *American Literary History* 21, no. 1 (2009): 67–86.

Burstow, Bonnie. "Toward a Radical Understanding of Trauma and Trauma Work." *Violence Against Women* 9, no. 11 (2003): 1293–1317.

Camp, Jordan T. "'We Know This Place': Neoliberal Racial Regimes." *American Quarterly, In The Wake of Hurricane Katrina: New Paradigms and Social Visions* 61, no. 3 (2009): 693–717.

Campbell, Maria. *Halfbreed.* Toronto: McClelland and Stewart, 1973.

Canadian Feminist Alliance for International Action. "Canada's Failure to Act: Women's Inequality Deepens." UN Committee on the Elimination of Discrimination against Women on the Occasion of the Committee's Review of Canada's 5th Report, 2003.

Cardinal, Harold. *Unjust Society: The Tragedy of Canada's Indians.* Edmonton: M. G. Hurtig, 1969.

Carlson, Keith Thor, ed. *You Are Asked to Witness: The Sto:Lo in Canada's Pacific Coast History.* Chilliwack, BC: Sto:lo Heritage Trust, 1997.

Castellano, Marlene Brant. "A Healing Journey: Reclaiming Wellness." In *Final Report of the Aboriginal Healing Foundation.* Vol. 1, *A Healing Journey: Reclaiming Wellness.* Ottawa: Aboriginal Healing Foundation, 2006.

———. "Renewing the Relationship: A Perspective on the Impact of the Royal Commission on Aboriginal Peoples." In *Aboriginal Self-Government in Canada,* edited by John H. Hylton. Saskatoon: Purich, 1999.

Castells, Manuel. *The Power of Identity.* 3 vols. Vol. 2, *The Information Age: Economy, Society and Culture.* Oxford: Blackwell, 1997.

Chandler, Michael J., and Christopher Lalonde. "Cultural Continuity as a Hedge against Suicide in Canada's First Nations." *Transcultural Psychiatry* 35, no. 2 (1998): 191–219.

"Changing the Landscape: Ending Violence—Achieving Equality." In *The Final Report of the Canadian Panel on Violence against Women,* edited by Aboriginal Circle of the Canadian Panel on Violence against Women. Ottawa: Minister of Supply and Services Canada, 1993.

Chrisjohn, Roland D., and Sherry Woods. *The Circle Game: Shadows and Substance in the Indian Residential School Experience in Canada, a Report Submitted to the Royal Commission on Aboriginal Peoples.* Penticton, BC: Theytus Books, 1997.

Churchill, Ward, ed. *Marxism and Native Americans.* Boston: South End Press, 1983.

Clark, Michael T. "Wither the Nation-State?: The Subaltern and the Redeployment of Latin American Nationalism in the Era of Globalization." *Disposition* 19, no. 46 (1994): 27–44.

Clutesi, George. *Potlatch.* Sidney, BC: Gray's, 1969.

Cook-Lynn, Elizabeth. "American Indian Intellectualism and the New Indian Story." In *Natives and Academics: Researching and Writing about American Indians,* edited by Devon Mihesuah. Lincoln: University of Nebraska Press, 1998.

Cooper, Fredrick, and Randall Packard, eds. *International Development and the Social Sciences: Essays on the History and Politics of Knowledge*. Berkeley: University of California Press, 1997.

Cooper, Melinda. *Life as Surplus: Biotechnology and Capitalism in the Neoliberal Era*. Edited by Philip Thurtle and Robert Mitchell. Seattle: University of Washington Press, 2010.

Cornell, Stephen E. *Accountability, Legitimacy and the Foundations of Native Self-Governance*. Cambridge: Harvard Project on American Indian Economic Development, Malcolm Wiener Center for Social Policy, John F. Kennedy School of Government, Harvard University, 1998.

Cornell, Stephen, and Joseph P. Kalt. "American Indian Self-Determination: The Political Economy of a Policy That Works." *Harvard Kennedy School Faculty Research Series* 2010. Harvard Kennedy School, John F. Kennedy School of Government. Unpublished working paper.

———. "Pathways from Poverty: Economic Development and Institution Building on American Indian Reservations." *American Indian Culture and Research Journal* 14, no. 1 (1990): 89–125.

Coté, Charlotte. *Spirits of Our Whaling Ancestors: Revitalizing Makah and Nuu-Chah-Nulth Traditions*. Seattle: University of Washington Press, 2010.

Coulthard, Glen S. "Subjects of Empire: Indigenous Peoples and the 'Politics of Recognition' in Canada." *Contemporary Political Theory* 6, no. 4 (2007): 437–60.

Courtois, Christine A. *Healing the Incest Wound: Adult Survivors in Therapy*. New York: Norton, 1988.

Coyhis, Don, and William L. White. "Alcohol Problems in Native America: Changing Paradigms and Clinical Practices." *Alcoholism Treatment Quarterly* 20, nos. 3/4 (2002): 157–65.

Crossley, Nick. "Emotion and Communicative Action: Habermas, Linguistic Philosophy and Existentialism." In *Emotions in Social Life: Critical Themes and Contemporary Issues*, edited by Gillian Bendelow and Simon J. Williams. New York: Routledge, 1998.

Cruikshank, Julie. *The Social Life of Stories: Narrative and Knowledge in the Yukon Territory*. Lincoln: University of Nebraska Press, 1998.

Culleton, Beatrice. *In Search of April Raintree*. Winnipeg: Pemmican, 1983.

Daigle, Michelle. "The Restoration of Traditional Food Systems: A Pathway toward the Regeneration of an Indigenous Future." In *Native American Students in Advanced Academia at the University of Washington Symposium*. Seattle, 2011.

Danieli, Yael, ed. *International Handbook of Multigenerational Legacies of Trauma*. Plenum Series on Stress and Coping. New York: Plenum Press, 1998.

Davis, Joseph E. *Accounts of Innocence: Sexual Abuse, Trauma, and the Self*. Chicago: University of Chicago Press, 2005.

Deer, Sarah. "Decolonizing Rape Law: A Native Feminist Synthesis of Safety and Sovereignty." *Wicazo Sa Review* 24 (2009): 149–67.

———. "Sovereignty of the Soul: Exploring the Intersection of Rape Law Reform and Federal Indian Law." *Suffolk University Law Review* 38, no. 2 (2005): 455–66.

———. "Toward an Indigenous Jurisprudence of Rape." *Kansas Journal of Law and Public Policy* 121, no. 79 (2004): 121–54.

Deloria, Vine. *Indians of the Pacific Northwest: From the Coming of the White Man to the Present Day*. New York: Doubleday, 1977.

Deloria, Vine, and Clifford Lyttle. *The Nations Within: The Past and Future of American Indian Sovereignty*. New York: Pantheon Books, 1984.

Denetdale, Jennifer Nez. "Chairmen, Presidents, and Princesses: The Navajo Nation, Gender, and the Politics of Tradition." *Wicazo Sa Review* 21, no. 1 (2006): 9–28.

———. "Securing Navajo National Boundaries: War, Patriotism, Tradition and the Dine Marriage Act of 2005." *Wicazo Sa Review* 24, no. 2 (2009): 131–48.

Denis, Claude. *We Are Not You: First Nations and Canadian Modernity*. Peterborough, ON: Broadview Press, 1997.

Dennis, Philip A., Roxanne Dunbar-Ortiz, Bernard Nietschmann, Steadman Fagot Muller, and Jorge Jenkins Molieri. "The Miskito–Sandinista Conflict in Nicaragua in the 1980s." *Latin American Research Review* 28, no. 3 (1983): 214–34.

Drainville, Andre C. "The Fetishism of Global Civil Society: Global Governance, Transnational Urbanism and Sustainable Capitalism in the World Economy." In *Transnationalism from Below*, edited by Michael Peter Smith and Luis Eduardo Guarizo, 35–63. New Brunswick, NJ: Transaction, 1998.

Dunbar-Ortiz, Roxanne. "The Fourth World and Indigenism: Politics of Isolation and Alternatives." *Journal of Ethnic Studies* 12, no. 1 (1984): 79–105.

Duran, Eduardo. *Transforming the Soul Wound: A Theoretical/Clinical Approach to American Indian Psychology*. Meerut, India: Archana, 1990.

Duran, Eduardo, and Bonnie Duran. *Native American Postcolonial Psychology*. SUNY Series in Transpersonal and Humanistic Psychology. Albany: State University of New York Press, 1995.

Duran, Eduardo, Bonnie Duran, Maria Yellow Horse Brave Heart, and Susan Yellow Horse-Davis. "Healing the American Indian Soul Wound." In *Intergenerational Handbook of Multigenerational Legacies of Trauma*, edited by Yael Danieli, 341–53. New York: Plenum Press, 1998.

Duran, Eduardo, Judith Firehammer, and John Gonzalez. "Liberation Psychology as the Path toward Healing Cultural Soul Wounds." *Journal of Counseling and Development* 86, no. 3 (2008): 288–95.

Elias, Robert. *The Politics of Victimization: Victims, Victimology, and Human Rights*. New York: Oxford University Press, 1986.

Emberly, Julia V. *Defamiliarizing the Aboriginal: Cultural Practices and Decolonization in Canada*. Toronto: University of Toronto Press, 2007.

Eudaily, Sean Patrick. *The Present Politics of the Past: Indigenous Legal Activism and Resistance to (Neo)Liberal Governmentality*. Edited by Frank Wilmer. Indigenous Peoples and Politics. New York: Routledge, 2004.

Falby, Alison. "The Modern Confessional: Anglo-American Religious Groups and the Emergence of Lay Psychotherapy." *Journal of History of the Behavioral Sciences* 39, no. 3 (2003): 251–267.

Fanon, Frantz. *Black Skin, White Masks*. New York: Grove Press, 1967.

Fassin, Didier, and Mariella Pandolfi, eds. *Contemporary States of Emergency: The Politics of Military and Humanitarian Interventions*. New York: Zone Books, 2010.

Fassin, Didier, and Richard Rechtman. *The Empire of Trauma: An Inquiry into the Condition of Victimhood*. Princeton: Princeton University Press, 2009.

Fast, Phyllis Ann. *Northern Athabascan Survival: Women, Community, and the Future.* Lincoln: University of Nebraska Press, 2002.

Felman, Shoshana, and Dori Laub. *Testimony: Crises of Witnessing in Literature, Psychoanalysis, and History.* New York: Routledge, 1991.

"First Nations/Metis Human Rights Law: The History of NWAC's Position and Options for Future Action." In *NWAC Special Assembly, March 18–22.* Ottawa, 1988.

Fiske, Jo-Anne. "Constitutionalizing the Space to Be Aboriginal Women: The Indian Act and the Struggle for First Nation Citizenship." In *Aboriginal Self-Government in Canada,* edited by Yale D. Belanger. Saskatoon: Purich, 2008.

———. "Ordered Lives and Disordered Souls: Pathologizing Female Bodies of the Colonial Frontier." In *New Perspectives on Social Deviance,* edited by Lori Beaman, 234–45. Scarborough, ON: Prentice Hall Allyn and Bacon, 2000.

———. "'The Womb Is to the Nation as the Heart Is to the Body': Ethnopolitical Discourses of the Canadian Indigenous Women's Movement." *Studies in Political Economy* 51 (Fall 1996).

Fortier, James M. "Pulling Together." [Videorecording.] Edited by James M. Fortier. Auburn: Muckleshoot Tribal Community, 2005.

Foucault, Michel. *The History of Sexuality.* Vol. 1, *An Introduction.* New York: Random House, 1990.

Fournier, Suzanne, and Ernie Crey. *Stolen from Our Embrace: The Abduction of First Nations Children and the Restoration of Aboriginal Communities.* Vancouver: Douglas and McIntyre, 1997.

Four Worlds International. *Community Healing and Aboriginal Social Security Reform: A Study Prepared for the Assembly of First Nations–Aboriginal Social Security Reform Strategic Initiative.* Accessed September 1, 2012. http://www.4worlds.org/4w/ssr/INTRO105.html.

Fraser, Nancy. "Feminism, Capitalism and the Cunning of History." *New Left Review* 56 (March/April 2009): 97–117.

Friedberg, Lilian. "Dare to Compare: Americanizing the Holocaust." *American Indian Quarterly* 24, no. 3 (2000): 353–80.

Friedel, Tracy. "The More Things Change, the More They Stay the Same: The Challenge of Identity for Native Students in Canada." *Cultural and Pedagogical Inquiry* 1, no. 2 (2010): 22–45.

Furniss, Elizabeth. *The Burden of History: Colonialism and the Frontier Myth in a Rural Canadian Community.* Vancouver: University of British Columbia Press, 1999.

———. "A Sobriety Movement among the Shuswap Indians of Alkali Lake." Master's thesis, University of British Columbia, 1987.

Furniss, Elizabeth, and Cariboo Tribal Council. *Victims of Benevolence: The Dark Legacy of the Williams Lake Residential School.* Vancouver, BC: Arsenal Pulp Press, 1995.

Gagne, Marie-Anik. "The Role of Dependency and Colonialism in Generating Trauma in First Nations Citizens." In *International Handbook of Multigenerational Legacies of Trauma,* edited by Yael Danieli, 355–72. New York: Plenum Press, 1998.

Gathering Strength: Canada's Aboriginal Action Plan. Ottawa: Indian and Northern Affairs Canada, 1997.

Gerhardt, Julie, and Charles Stinson. "The Nature of Therapeutic Discourse: Accounts of the Self." *Journal of Narrative and Life History* 4, no. 3 (1994): 151–91.

Gone, Joseph P. "Encountering Professional Psychology: Re-Envisioning Mental Health Services for Native North America." In *Healing Traditions: The Mental Health of Aboriginal Peoples in Canada*, edited by Laurence J. Kirmeyer and Gail Guthrie Valaskakis. Vancouver: University of British Columbia Press, 2009.

———. "Introduction: Mental Health Discourse as Western Proselytization." *Ethos* 36, no. 3 (2008): 310–15.

Good, Byron J. "Mental Health Consequence of Displacement and Resettlement." *Economic and Political Weekly* 31, no. 24 (1996): 1504–8.

Gooderham, G. K. "Prospect." In *The Education of Indian Children in Canada: A Symposium Written by Members of Indian Affairs Education Division, with Comments by the Indian Peoples*, edited by L. G. P. Waller, 129. Toronto: Ryerson Press, 1965.

Graham, Jordan, and C. Michael Hogan. "Labrador Innu Land Claims and the Indigenous Archaeology Paradox." In *Encyclopedia of Earth*, edited by Cutler J. Cleveland. First published in *Encyclopedia of Earth*, July 14, 2012. Accessed September 1, 2012. http://www.eoearth.org/article/Labrador_Innu_land_claims_and_the_indigenous_archaeology_paradox.

Griffiths, Curt Taylor, J. Collin Yerbury, and Linda Weafer. "Canadian Natives: Victims of Socio-Structural Deprivation?" *Human Organization* 46, no. 3 (1987): 277–82.

Guerrero, M. Annette Jaimes. "'Patriarchal Colonialism' and Indigenism: Implications for Native Feminist Spirituality and Native Womanism." *Hypatia* 18, no. 2 (2003): 58–69.

Haig-Brown, Celia. *Resistance and Renewal: Surviving the Indian Residential School*. Vancouver: Tillacum Library, 1988.

Hanssen, Beatrice. *Critique of Violence: Between Poststructuralism and Critical Theory*. London: Routledge, 2000.

Harvard Project for American Indian Economic Development. "Overview." Accessed September 1, 2012. http://hpaied.org/.

Harvey, David. *A Brief History of Neoliberalism*. Oxford: Oxford University Press, 2005.

Hayner, Priscilla B. *Unspeakable Truths: Facing the Challenge of Truth Commissions*. New York: Routledge, 2001.

Helen-Hill, Barbara. *Shaking the Rattle, Healing the Trauma of Colonization*. Vancouver, BC: Theytus Books, 1995.

Herman, Judith. *Trauma and Recovery: The Aftermath of Violence—From Domestic Abuse to Political Terror*: Basic Books, 1992.

Hinkson, Melinda. "A 'National Emergency' in Australia: The Howard Government's Intervention in Northern Territory Aboriginal Affairs." *Indigenous Affairs*, no. 4 (2007): 38–44.

Hodgson, Maggie. *Impact of Residential Schools and Other Root Causes of Poor Mental Health (Suicide, Family Violence, Alcohol and Drug Abuse)*. Edmonton: Nechi Institute on Alcohol and Drug Education, 1990.

Holstein, James A., and Jaber F. Gubrium. *The Self We Live By: Narrative Identity in a Postmodern World*. New York: Oxford University Press, 2000.

Hooper, Charlotte. *Manly States: Masculinities, International Relations, and Gender Politics*. New York: Columbia University Press, 2001.

HOSW. "Health Info: The Fifth Healing Our Spirit Worldwide (HOSW) Health, Healing and Self-Determination." *International Journal of Circumpolar Health* 64, no. 2 (2005): 194.

Howard-Wagner, Deidre. "From Denial to Emergency." In *Contemporary States of Emergency: The Politics of Military and Humanitarian Interventions*, edited by Didier Fassin and Mariella Pandolfi. New York: Zone Books, 2010.

Hoy, Helen. *How Should I Read These? Native Women Writers in Canada*. Toronto: University of Toronto Press, 2001.

Ignatieff, Michael, and Amy Gutmann. *Human Rights as Politics and Idolatry*. Princeton, NJ: Princeton University Press, 2001.

Illouz, Eva. *Cold Intimacies: The Making of Emotional Capitalism*. Cambridge: Polity Press, 2007.

Incite! Women of Color Against Violence, ed. *The Revolution Will Not Be Funded: Beyond the Non-Profit Industrial Complex*. Cambridge, MA: South End Press, 2007.

Ing, N. Rosalyn. "Dealing with Shame and Unresolved Trauma: Residential School and Its Impact on the 2nd and 3rd Generation Adults." PhD diss., University of British Columbia, 2001.

Innu Nation. Accessed September 1, 2012. http://www.innu.ca/index.php?option=com_content&view=article&id=10&Itemid=7&lang=en.

Irlbacher-Fox, Stephanie. *Finding Dahshaa: Self-Government, Social Suffering, and Aboriginal Policy in Canada*. Vancouver: University of British Columbia Press, 2009.

Jackson, Robert H. *Quasi-States: Sovereignty, International Relations and the Third World*. Edited by Steve Smith. Cambridge Studies in International Relations. Cambridge: Cambridge University Press, 1990.

Jamieson, Kathleen. "Sex Discrimination and the Indian Act." In *Arduous Journey*, edited by J. Ponting. Toronto: McClelland and Stewart, 1986.

Jenness, Diamond. "Canada's Indians Yesterday. What of Today?" In *As Long as the Sun Shines and Water Flows*, edited by Ian L. Getty and Antoine S. Lussier, 159–63. Vancouver: University of British Columbia Press, 1983.

———. *The Indians of Canada*. 6th ed. Ottawa: National Museum of Canada, 1963.

Jilek, Wolfgang. *Indian Healing: Shamanic Ceremonialism in the Pacific Northwest Today*. Surrey, BC, Blaine, WA: Hancock House, 1982.

———. *Salish Indian Mental Health and Culture Change: Psychohygienic and Therapeutic Aspects of the Guardian Spirit Ceremonial*. Toronto: Holt, Rinehart and Winston of Canada, 1974.

Kelley, Robin D. G. *Freedom Dreams: The Black Radical Imagination*. Boston: Beacon Press, 2002.

Kim, Jodi. "An 'Orphan' with Two Mothers: Transnational and Transracial Adoption, the Cold War, and Contemporary Asian American Cultural Politics." *American Quarterly* 61, no. 4 (2009): 855–80.

King, A. Richard. *The School at Mopass: A Problem of Identity*. Edited by George and Louise Spindler. Case Studies in Education and Culture. New York: Holt, Rinehart and Winston, 1967.

Kirmeyer, Laurence J., Robert Lemelson, and Mark Barad, eds. *Understanding Trauma: Integrating Biological, Clinical, and Cultural Perspectives*. Cambridge and New York: Cambridge University Press, 2007.

Kirmeyer, Laurence, Cori Simpson, and Margaret Cargo. "Healing Traditions: Culture, Community and Mental Health Promotion with Canadian Aboriginal Peoples." *Australasian Psychiatry* 11, suppl. (2003): S15–S23.

Kirmeyer, Laurence J., Caroline L. Tait, and Cori Simpson. "The Mental Health of Aboriginal Peoples in Canada: Transformations of Identity and Community." In *Healing Traditions: The Mental Health of Aboriginal Peoples in Canada*, edited by Laurence J. Kirmeyer and Gail Guthrie Valaskakis. Vancouver: University of British Columbia Press, 2009.

Knockwood, Isabelle, and Gillian Thomas. *Out of the Depths: The Experiences of Mi'kmaw Children at the Indian Residential School at Shubenacadie, Nova Scotia.* 2nd ed. Lockeport, NS: Roseway, 1992.

Koshy, Susan. "From Cold War to Trade War: Neocolonialism and Human Rights." *Social Text* 58 (Spring 1999): 1–32.

Krohn, Elise, and Valerie Segrest. *Traditional Foods of Puget Sound Project.* Bellingham, WA: Northwest Indian College Cooperative Extension Office, 2010.

Kronk, Elizabeth Ann. "The Emerging Problem of Methamphetamines: A Threat Signaling the Need to Reform Criminal Jurisdiction in Indian Country." *North Dakota Law Review* 82, no. 4 (2006): 1249–71.

Krosenbrink-Gelissen, Lilianne E. *Sexual Equality as an Aboriginal Right: The Native Women's Association of Canada and the Constitutional Process on Aboriginal Matters 1982–1987.* Nijmegen Studies in Development and Cultural Change, vol. 7. Saarbrücken: Verlag Breitenbach, 1991.

Kuokkanen, Rauna. "From Indigenous Economies to Market-Based Self-Governance: A Feminist Political Economy Analysis." *Canadian Journal of Political Science/ Revue canadienne de science politique* 44, no. 2 (2011): 275–97.

———. "Globalization as Racialized, Sexualized Violence." *International Feminist Journal of Politics* 10, no. 2 (2008): 216–33.

———. "The Politics of Form and Alternative Autonomies: Indigenous Women, Subsistence Economies and the Gift Paradigm." In *Native American and Indigenous Studies Conference*, edited by William D. Coleman. Globalization Working Papers. Minneapolis: Institute on Globalization and the Human Condition, 2007.

Kymlicka, Will. "Neoliberal Multiculturalism." Keynote, Eminent Speakers at the Faculty of Arts Lectures, University of Ljubljana, Slovenia. Video recorded March 2011. Accessed September 1, 2012. http://videolectures.net/ffeminent_kymlicka_neoliberal/.

Ladner, Kiera L. "Understanding the Impact of Self-Determination on Communities in Crisis." *Journal of Aboriginal Health* (November 2009): 88–101.

Lambert, Craig A. "Trails of Tears, and Hope." *Harvard Magazine*, March/April 2008.

Lane Jr., Phil, Michael Bopp, Judie Bopp, and Julian Norris. *Mapping the Healing Journey: The Final Report of a First Nation Research Project on Healing in Canadian Aboriginal Communities.* Ottawa: Aboriginal Healing Foundation, 2002.

LaRocque, Emma. "Preface, or Here Are Our Voices—Who Will Hear?" In *Writing the Circle, Native Women of Western Canada*, edited by Jeanne Perreault and Sylvia Vance, x–xxx. Norman: University of Oklahoma Press, 1990.

Lavoie, John, John O'Neil, Jeff Reading, and Yvonne Allard. "Community Healing and Aboriginal Self-Government." In *Aboriginal Self-Government in Canada*, edited by Yale D. Belanger. Saskatoon: Purich, 2008.

Lawrence, Bonita. "Gender, Race, and the Regulation of Native Identity in Canada and the United States: An Overview." *Hypatia* 18, no. 2 (2003): 3–31.

Lee, Bobbi, with Don Barnett and Rick Sterling. *Indian Rebel: Struggles of a Native Canadian Woman, Life Histories from the Revolution.* Vancouver: Liberation Support Movement Information Centre, 1975.

Lemke, Thomas. *Biopolitics: An Advanced Introduction.* Biopolitics: Medicine, Technoscience, and Health in the 21st Century. Edited by Monica J. Casper and Lisa Jean Moore. New York: New York University Press, 2011.

Lucas, Phil. *For the Honour of All.* 57 minutes: Native American Public Broadcasting Consortium, 1985.

Lutz, Hartmut, ed. *Approaches: Essays in Native North American Studies and Literature.* Augsberg: Wibner, 2002.

Lutz, Hartmut, Jeannette Armstrong, Beth Cuthand, Maria Campbell, Jordan Wheeler, Lenore Keeshig-Tobias, Tomson Highway, Beatrice Mosionier, Thomas King, Greg Young-Ing, Ann Acco, Howard Adams, Daniel David Moses, Lee Maracle, Emma LaRocque, Ruby Slipperjack, Joy Asham Fedorick, Basil Johnston, and Rita Joe. *Contemporary Challenges: Conversations with Canadian Native Authors.* Saskatoon: Fifth House, 1991.

Maaka, Roger, and Augie Fleras. "Contesting Indigenous Peoples Governance: The Politics of State-Determination vs. Self-Determining Autonomy." In *Aboriginal Self-Government in Canada: Current Trends and Issues,* edited by Yale D. Belanger, 69–122. Saskatoon: Purich, 2008.

Machery, Pierre. *A Theory of Literary Production.* Translated by Geoffery Wall. London: Routledge and Kegan Paul, 1978.

Mack, Jacinda. "Nuxalk Perspectives on Sovereignty and Social Change." Master's thesis, York University, 2006.

Mackey, Eva. *The House of Difference: Cultural Politics and National Identity in Canada.* Toronto: University of Toronto Press, 2002.

Malloway, Frank, Heather Miles, and Tracey Joe. "Through the Eyes of Siyemches Te Yeqwyeqwi:Ws (Frank Malloway)." In *You Are Asked to Witness: The Sto:lo in Canada's Pacific Coast History,* edited by Keith Thor Carlson, 1–26. Chilliwack, BC: Sto:lo Heritage Trust, 1996.

Mancini, Anthony D. "Self-Determination Theory: A Framework for the Recovery Paradigm." *Advances in Psychiatric Treatment* 14, no. 5 (2008): 358–65.

Manson, Spero, Janette Beals, Theresa O'Nell, Joan Piasecki, Donald Bechtold, Ellen Keane, and Monica Jones. "Wounded Spirits, Ailing Hearts: PTSD and Related Disorders among American Indians." In *Ethnocultural Aspects of Posttraumatic Stress Disorder,* edited by Anthony J. Marsella, Matthew J. Friedman, Ellen T. Gerrity, and Raymond M. Scurfield, 255–83. Washington, DC: American Psychological Association, 1996.

Manuel, George, and Michael Posluns. *The Fourth World: An Indian Reality.* New York: Free Press, 1974.

Maracle, Lee. *Bobbi Lee: Indian Rebel.* Toronto: Women's Press, 1990.

Martens, Tony, Brenda Daily, and Maggie Hodgson. *The Spirit Weeps: Characteristics and Dynamics of Incest and Child Sexual Abuse with a Native Perspective.* Edmonton: Nechi Institute, 1988.

McAdams, Dan P. *The Redemptive Self.* New York: Oxford University Press, 2006.

Melamed, Jodi. *Represent and Destroy: Rationalizing Violence in the New Racial Capitalism.* Minneapolis: University of Minnesota Press, 2011.

Mellody, Pia. *Facing Codependence*. New York: HarperCollins, 1989.

Miller, Bruce G. *The Problem of Justice: Tradition and Law in the Coast Salish World.* Edited by Gerald M. Sider and Kirk Dombrowski. Lincoln: University of Nebraska Press, 2000.

Miller, Nancy K., and Jason Tougaw, eds. *Extremities: Trauma, Testimony, and Community*. Urbana: University of Ilinois Press, 2002.

Million, Dian. "Intense Dreaming: Theories, Narratives and Our Search for Home." *American Indian Quarterly* 35, no. 3 (2011): 314–33.

———. "Telling Secrets: Sex, Power and Narratives in Indian Residential School Histories." *Canadian Woman Studies/Les Cahiers de la Femme* 20, no. 2 (2000): 92–104.

Milloy, John Sheridan. *A National Crime: The Canadian Government and the Residential School System, 1879 to 1986*. Manitoba Studies in Native History, vol. 11. Winnipeg: University of Manitoba Press, 1999.

Moine, Louise. *My Life in a Residential School*. Saskatchewan: Provincial Chapter I.O.D.E. in cooperation with the Provincial Library of Saskatchewan, 1975.

Moon, Claire. "Healing Past Violence: Traumatic Assumptions and Therapeutic Interventions in War and Reconciliation." *Journal of Human Rights* 8, no. 1 (2009): 71–91.

Moore, David, and Don Coyhis. "The Multicultural Wellbriety Peer Recovery Support Program: Two Decades of Community-Based Recovery." *Alcoholism Treatment Quarterly* 28, no. 3 (2010): 273–92.

Morris, Glen T. "The International Status of Indigenous Nations within the United States." In *Critical Issues in Native North America*, edited by Ward Churchill, 1–14. Copenhagen: International Work Group for Indigenous Affairs, 1989.

Nadasdy, Paul. *Hunters and Bureaucrats: Power, Knowledge, and Aboriginal–State Relations in the Southwest Yukon*. Vancouver: University of British Columbia Press, 2003.

———. "Politics of TEK: Power and the 'Integration' of Knowledge." *Arctic Anthropology* 36, nos. 1/2 (1999): 1–18.

Nahanee, Teresa. "Dancing with a Gorilla: Aboriginal Women, Justice and the Charter." In *Aboriginal Peoples and the Justice System: Report of the National Round Table on Aboriginal Justice*, 359–82. Ottawa: Royal Commission on Aboriginal Peoples, 1993.

National Congress of American Indians. Resolution #MIC-06-008, "Resolution Requesting the Federal Government Adequately Fund Law Enforcement and Courts on Reservations" (June 2006). Accessed September 1, 2012. http://www.ncai.org/attachments/Resolution_SJQZvWynouItoZYDsHEtyZJlysYiCOKZUAiGKsZdLUPgdeixrrD_MIC-06-008_Law_Enforcement_Courts_Funding.pdf.

Newton, Richard G., and Madonna L. Moss. *Haa Atxaayi Haa Kusteeyix Sitee = Our Food Is Our Tlingit Way of Life: Excerpts from Oral Interviews*. Juneau, AK: US Department of Agriculture, Forest Service, Alaska Region, 2005.

Niezen, Ronald. *The Origins of Indigenism*. Berkeley and Los Angeles: University of California Press, 2003.

Nolan Jr., James L. *The Therapeutic State: Justifying Government at Century's End*. New York: New York University Press, 1998.

Ochs, Elinor, and Lisa Capps. "Narrating the Self." *Annual Review of Anthropology* 25 (1996): 19–43.

Olick, Jeffrey K., and Charles Demetriou. "From Theodicy to Ressentiment: Trauma and the Ages of Compensation." In *Memory, Trauma and World Politics: Reflections on the Relationship between Past and Present*, edited by Duncan Bell, 74–98. New York: Palgrave Macmillan, 2006.

O'Neil, John, Laurel Lemchuk-Favel, Yvon Allard, and Brian Postl. "Community Healing and Aboriginal Self-Government." In *Aboriginal Self-Government in Canada*, edited by John H. Hylton, 130–56. Saskatoon: Purich, 1999.

Ong, Aihwa. "Neoliberalism as a Mobile Technology." *Transactions of the Institute of British Geographers* 32, no. 1 (2007): 3–8.

Ortiz, Simon. *Speaking for the Generations: Native Writers on Writing*. Tucson: University of Arizona Press, 1997.

O'Sullivan, Meg Devlin. "'We Worry about Survival': American Indian Women, Sovereignty, and the Right to Bear and Raise Children in the 1970s." PhD diss., University of North Carolina, 2007.

"Ottawa Charter for Health Promotion." First International Conference on Health Promotion: The Move towards a New Public Health, November 17–21, Ottawa, 1986. http://www.who.int/healthpromotion/conferences/previous/ottawa/en/.

"Our Way." 3rd Annual Coast Salish Gathering, Tulalip, Washington, 2008.

Palmer, Andie Diane. *Maps of Experience: The Anchoring of Land to Story in Secwepemc Discourse*. Toronto: University of Toronto Press, 2005.

Parker, Sharon. "Understanding Self-Determination: The Basics." In First International Conference on the Right to Self-Determination. Geneva, 2000. Key Documents. Accessed September 1, 2012. http://www.humanlaw.org/.

Patterson, Sunni. "'We Know This Place.'" *American Quarterly, In The Wake of Hurricane Katrina: New Paradigms and Social Visions* 61, no. 3 (2009): 719–21.

Phelps, Teresa Godwin. *Shattered Voices: Language, Violence, and the Work of Truth Commissions*. Philadelphia: University of Pennsylvania Press, 2004.

Povinelli, Elizabeth A. *The Empire of Love: Toward a Theory of Intimacy, Genealogy, and Carnality*. Durham, NC: Duke University Press, 2006.

Probyn, Elspeth. "Writing Shame." In *The Affect Theory Reader*, edited by Melissa Gregg and Gregory J. Siegworth. Durham, NC: Duke University Press, 2010.

Pupavac, Vanessa. "Pathologizing Populations and Colonizing Minds: International Psychosocial Programs in Kosovo." *Alternatives* 27, no. 4 (2002): 489–511.

Ramos, Alcida Rita. "The Indian against the State." In *Indigenism: Ethnic Politics in Brazil*. Madison: University of Wisconsin Press, 1998.

Ranciere, Jacques. "Who Is the Subject of the Rights of Man?" *South Atlantic Quarterly* 103, nos. 2/3 (2004): 297–310.

Razack, Sherene H. "Gendered Racial Violence and Spatialized Justice: The Murder of Pamela George." *Canadian Journal of Law and Society* 15, no. 2 (2000): 91–130.

Re-evaluation Counseling Communities, ed. *Heritage*. Seattle: Rational Island Publishers, 1982.

The Report of the Royal Commission on Aboriginal Peoples. Ottawa: Royal Commission on Aboriginal Peoples, 1996.

Rice, Joanna. "Indigenous Rights and Truth Commissions." *Cultural Survival Quarterly* 35, no. 1 (2011). Accessed November 29, 2012. http://www.culturalsurvival.org/publications/cultural-survival-quarterly/none/indigenous-rights-and-truth-commissions.

Rice, John Steadman. *A Disease of One's Own: Psychotherapy, Addiction, and the Emergence of Co-Dependency*. New Brunswick, NJ: Transaction, 1998.

Richards, Patricia. "Of Indians and Terrorists: How the State and Local Elites Construct the Mapuche in Neoliberal Multicultural Chile." *Journal of Latin American Studies* 42, no. 1 (2010): 59–90.

Rifkin, Mark. *When Did Indians Become Straight?: Kinship, the History of Sexuality, and Native Sovereignty*. New York: Oxford University Press, 2011.

Rose, Nikolas. "Community, Citizenship, and the Third Way." *American Behavioral Scientist* 43, no. 9 (2000): 1395–411.

———. *Inventing Our Selves: Psychology, Power, and Personhood*. Cambridge: Cambridge University Press, 1996.

———. *Powers of Freedom: Reframing Political Thought*. New York: Cambridge University Press, 1999.

Ross, Luanna. *Inventing the Savage: The Social Construction of Native American Criminality*. Austin: University of Texas Press, 1998.

Ross, Rupert. *Returning to the Teachings: Exploring Aboriginal Justice*. Toronto: Penguin Canada, 2006.

Salzman, Michael B. "Cultural Trauma and Recovery: Perspectives from Terror Management Theory." *Trauma Violence and Abuse* 2, no. 2 (2001): 172–91.

Samson, Colin. "A Colonial Double-Bind: Social and Historical Contexts of Innu Mental Health." In *Healing Traditions: The Mental Health of Aboriginal Peoples in Canada*, edited by Laurence J. Kirmeyer and Gail Guthrie Valaskakis. Vancouver: University of British Columbia Press, 2009.

Samson, Colin, James Wilson, and Jonathan Mazower. *Canada's Tibet: The Killing of the Innu*. London: Survival International, 1999.

Sanders, Will. "Ideology, Evidence and Competing Principles in Australian Indigenous Affairs: From Brough to Rudd via Pearson and the NTER." *Australian Journal of Social Issues* 45, no. 3 (2010): 307–31.

Sangster, Joan. *Regulating Girls and Women: Sexuality, Family, and the Law in Ontario, 1920–1960*. Toronto: Oxford University Press, 2001.

———. "She Is Hostile to Our Ways: First Nations Girls Sentenced to the Ontario Training School for Girls, 1933–1960." *Law and History Review* 20, no. 1 (2002): 59–96.

Schaef, Anne Wilson. *When Society Becomes an Addict*. San Francisco: Harper and Row, 1987.

Schaffer, Kay, and Sidonie Smith. *Human Rights and Narrated Lives: The Ethics of Recognition*. New York: Palgrave Macmillan, 2004.

Scheff, Thomas J. "Socialization of Emotion: Pride and Shame as Causal Agents." In *Research Agendas in the Sociology of Emotions*, edited by Theodore D. Kemper, 281–303. Albany: State University of New York Press, 1990.

Self-Determination Theory: An Approach to Human Motivation and Personality. Accessed September 1, 2012. http://www.selfdeterminationtheory.org/.

Silman, Janet. *Enough Is Enough: Aboriginal Women Speak Out (as Told to Janet Silman)*. Toronto: Women's Press, 1987.

Simpson, Audra. "Commentary: The 'Problem' of Mental Health in Native North America: Liberalism, Multiculturalism, and the (Non)Efficacy of Tears." *Ethos* 36, no. 3 (2008): 376–79.

Slipperjack, Ruby. *Honour the Sun: Extracted and Revised from the Diary of the Owl.* Winnipeg: Pemmican, 1987.

Slowey, Gabrielle. *Navigating Neoliberalism: Self-Determination and the Mikisew Cree First Nation.* Vancouver: University of British Columbia Press, 2008.

Smith, Andrea. "Better Dead than Pregnant: The Colonization of Native Women's Reproductive Health." In *Policing the National Body: Race, Gender and Criminalization*, edited by Jael Silliman and Anannya Battacharjee. Cambridge, MA: South End Press, 2002.

——. *Conquest: Sexual Violence and American Indian Genocide.* Cambridge, MA: South End Press, 2005.

——. *Native Americans and the Christian Right, the Gendered Politics of Unlikely Alliances.* Durham, NC: Duke University Press, 2008.

Smith, Justine. "Indigenous Performance and Aporetic Texts." *Union Seminary Quarterly Review* 59, nos. 1/2 (2005): 114–24.

Stoler, Ann Laura. *Race and the Education of Desire: Foucault's History of Sexuality and the Colonial Order of Things.* Durham, NC: Duke University Press, 1995.

——. "Tense and Tender Ties: The Politics of Comparison in North American History and (Post) Colonial Studies." *Journal of American History* 88, no. 3 (2001): 829–65.

Stremlau, Rosemarie. "Rape Narratives on the Northern Paiute Frontier: Sara Winnemucca, Sexual Sovereignty, and Economic Autonomy, 1844–1891." In *Portraits of Women in the American West*, edited by Dee Garceau-Hagen: Routledge, 2005.

Stringer, Rebecca. "A Nightmare of the Neocolonial Kind: Politics of Suffering in Howard's Northern Territory Intervention." *Borderlands e-journal*, no. 2 (2007). http://www.borderlands.net.au/issues/vol6no2.html.

Suttles, Wayne P. *The Economic Life of the Coast Salish of Haro and Rosario Straits.* Vol. 1 of *Coast Salish and Western Washington Indians.* New York: Garland, 1974.

Suttles, Wayne P., and Ralph Maud. *Coast Salish Essays.* Seattle: University of Washington Press, 1987.

Tait, Caroline L. "Disruptions in Nature, Disruptions in Society: Aboriginal Peoples of Canada and the 'Making' of Fetal Alcohol Syndrome." In *Healing Traditions: The Mental Health of Aboriginal Peoples in Canada*, edited by Laurence J. Kirmeyer and Gail Guthrie Valaskakis. Vancouver: University of British Columbia Press, 2009.

Trask, Haunani-Kay. *From a Native Daughter: Colonialism and Sovereignty in Hawai'i.* Monroe, ME: Common Courage Press, 1993.

Trevithick, Scott. "Native Residential Schooling in Canada: A Review of the Literature." *Canadian Journal of Native Studies* 18, no. 1 (1998): 49–86.

Trouillot, Michel-Rolph. *Silencing the Past: Power and Production of History.* Boston: Beacon Press, 1995.

Tshikapisk Foundation. Accessed September 1, 2012. http://www.tshikapisk.ca/home/mission.htm.

Turner, Nancy J. "Traditional Ecological Knowledge." In *The Rainforests of Home: Profile of a North American Bioregion*, edited by Peter K. Schoonmaker, Betinna Von Hagen, and Edward C. Wolf. Covelo, CA: Island Press, 1997.

Valaskakis, Gail Guthrie. "Indian Country: Negotiating the Meaning of Land in Native America." In *Disciplinarity and Dissent in Cultural Studies*, edited by Cary Nelson and Dilip Parameshwar Gaonkar, 149–69. New York: Routledge, 1996.

———. "Telling Our Own Stories: The Role, Development, and Future of Aboriginal Communications." In *Aboriginal Education: Fulfilling the Promise*, edited by Marlene Brant Castellano, Lynn Davis, and Louise Lahache. Vancouver: University of British Columbia Press, 2000.

Valverde, Mariana. *Diseases of the Will: Alcohol and the Dilemmas of Freedom*. Cambridge: Cambridge University Press, 1998.

———. "Experience and Truth Telling in a Post-Humanist World: A Foucauldian Contribution to Feminist Ethical Reflections." In *Feminism and the Final Foucault*, edited by Dianna Taylor and Karen Vintges. Urbana: University of Illinois Press, 2004.

Vasquez, Saul Vicente. *Food Sovereignty and the Rights of Indigenous Peoples*. San Francisco: International Indian Treaty Council, 2008.

Vendiola, Shelly. "Preserving Our Shalangen: Promoting Non-Violence and Respect." *Indigenous Woman*, Fall 2003.

Venne, Sharon H. "Treaty and Constitution in Canada." In *Critical Issues in Native North America*. Copenhagen: International Working Group for Indigenous Affairs, 1989.

Vrasti, Wanda. "How to Use Affective Competencies in Late Capitalism." British International Studies Association Annual Conference, University of Leicester, December 2009. Accessed September 12, 2012. http://www.bisa.ac.uk/index.php?option=com_bisa&task=view_public_papers_author_char_search&char_search=V.

Warry, Wayne. *Ending Denial: Understanding Aboriginal Issues*. Peterborough, ON: Broadview Press, 2007.

Washinawatok, Ingrid. "International Emergence: Twenty-One Years at the United Nations." *Indigenous Woman* 4, no. 2 (2001): 12–15.

Watson, Irene. "In the Northern Territory Intervention: What Is Saved or Rescued and What Cost?" *cultural studies review* 15 (2009): 2.

Webster, Peter S., and Kwayatsapalth. *As Far as I Know: Reminiscences of an Ahousat Elder*. Campbell River, BC: Campbell River Museum and Archives, 1983.

White, Richard. "Using the Past: History and Native American Studies." In *Studying Native America*, edited by Russell Thornton, 217–43. Madison: University of Wisconsin Press, 1998.

White House. "Remarks by the President before Signing the Tribal Law and Order Act." July 29, 2010. Transcript. Accessed August 30, 2012. http://www.whitehouse.gov/photos-and-video/video/signing-tribal-law-and-order-act#transcript.

Whittier, Nancy. *The Politics of Child Sexual Abuse: Emotion, Social Movements, and the State*. New York: Oxford University Press, 2009.

Wild, Rex, and Pat Anderson. *Ampe Akelyernemane Meke Mekarle, "Little Children Are Sacred": Report of the Northern Territory Board of Inquiry into the Protection of Aboriginal Children from Sexual Abuse*. Northern Territory Government, Darwin, 2007. http://www.nt.gov.au/dcm/inquirysaac/pdf/bipacsa_final_report.pdf.

Wilets, James D. "Conceptualizing Private Violence against Sexual Minorities as Gendered Violence: An International and Comparative Law Perspective." *Albany Law Review* 60 (1996): 989–1050.

Williams, Randall. *The Divided World: Human Rights and Violence*. Minneapolis: University of Minnesota Press, 2010.

Wilson, Angela Cavender. "American Indian History or Non-Indian Perceptions of American Indian History?" In *Natives and Academics: Researching and Writing about American Indians,* edited by Devon A. Mihesuah. Lincoln: University of Nebraska Press, 1998.

Wolhuter, Lorraine, Neil Olley, and David Denham. *Victimology: Victimisation and Victims' Rights.* London: Routledge, 2008.

Women of All Red Nations. *WARN Report II.* Sioux Falls, SD: WARN, 1979.

Woody, Elizabeth. "In Memory of Crossing the Columbia." In *Dancing on the Rim of the World: An Anthology of Northwest Native American Writing,* edited by Andrea Lerner. Tucson: University of Arizona Press, 1990.

Zaretsky, Eli. "Psychoanalysis and the Spirit of Capitalism." *Constellations* 15, no. 3 (2008): 366–81.

Zentner, Henry. *Indian Identity Crisis; Inquiries into the Problems and Prospects of Societal Development among Native Peoples.* Calgary: Strayer, 1973.

Index

About the Author

Dian Million (Athabascan) is an associate professor of American Indian studies at the University of Washington, Seattle. Million has a PhD in ethnic studies from the University of California, Berkeley. As an active Northwest writer, Dian Million has published a variety of articles, essays, and poetry in numerous venues over the years. A representative example would include *Canadian Woman Studies/Les Cahiers de la femme: National Identity and Gender Politics, Social Justice,* and *Reinventing the Enemy's Language.*